BLEEDING OUT

BLEEDING OUT

The Devastating Consequences of
Urban Violence—and a Bold
New Plan for Peace in the Streets

THOMAS ABT

BASIC BOOKS
New York

Basic Books
Hachette Book Group
1290 Avenue of the Americas, New York, NY 10104
www.basicbooks.com

Printed in the United States of America
First Edition: June 2019

Published by Basic Books, an imprint of Perseus Books, LLC, a subsidiary of Hachette Book Group, Inc. The Basic Books name and logo is a trademark of the Hachette Book Group.

The Hachette Speakers Bureau provides a wide range of authors for speaking events. To find out more, go to www.hachettespeakersbureau.com or call (866) 376-6591.

The publisher is not responsible for websites (or their content) that are not owned by the publisher.

Print book interior design by Jeff Williams.

Library of Congress Cataloging-in-Publication Data Names: Abt, Thomas, author.

Title: Bleeding out: the devastating consequences of urban violence—and a bold new plan for peace in the streets / Thomas Abt.

Description: First edition. | New York: Basic Books, [2019] | Includes bibliographical references and index.

Identifiers: LCCN 2018055824| ISBN 9781541645721 (hardcover: alk. paper) | ISBN 9781541645714 (ebook)

Subjects: LCSH: Violence—United States. | Violent crimes—United States. | Victims of violent crimes—United States. | Urban policy—United States. | Community development—United States.

Classification: LCC HN90.V5 A28 2019 | DDC 303.60973—dc23

LC record available at https://lccn.loc.gov/2018055824

ISBNs: 978-1-5416-4572-1 (hardcover), 978-1-5416-4571-4 (ebook)

LSC-C

10 9 8 7 6 5 4 3 2 1

For my parents,
Clark and Wendy Abt,
whose passion for justice
has been my richest inheritance

CONTENTS

CHAPTER 1

BLEEDING OUT

IMAGINE THIS: YOU ARE A TRAUMA SURGEON WORKING THE MIDNIGHT shift in an urban emergency room in the United States of America. A young man, unconscious, lies before you on a gurney. He has been shot in the thigh and is bleeding profusely. Judging from the entry and exit wounds, as well as the amount of hemorrhaging, the bullet most likely sliced the femoral artery, one of the largest blood vessels in the body. Without assistance, this young man will die within minutes. As his doctor, what do you do? Or, more precisely, what do you do *first*?

The young man's clothes are old and dirty. He may be jobless, homeless, lacking a decent education. Do you start treatment by finding him a job, locating an apartment, or helping him get his GED?

The young man has also been involved in some sort of altercation and may be dangerous. Perhaps precautionary measures are in order. Before he wakes up, do you put him in restraints, alert hospital security, or call the police?

Of course not. Instead, you take the only sensible and humane course of action available at the time. First you stop the bleeding, because unless you stop the bleeding, nothing else matters.

In 2017, 17,284 people were murdered in the United States. That is more than forty-seven per day. Americans are killed at a rate roughly seven times higher than people in other high-income countries, driven by a gun homicide rate that is twenty-five times higher. As citizens, we do not bear this risk equally: the nation's number one victims of violence are disadvantaged and disenfranchised young African American and Latino men. For young Latino men, homicide is the second-leading cause of death. For young black men, it is not just the leading cause of death; homicide accounts for more deaths *than the nine other top causes combined.*[1]

Every murder causes immeasurable suffering. No statistic can capture a child's lost potential or a mother's grief, but when the collective costs of murder are estimated, they are staggering: anywhere from $173 billion to $332 billion in criminal justice and medical costs, lost wages and earnings, damaged and devalued property, and diminished quality of life. That's between $531 and $1,020 per American, paid out in higher taxes, higher insurance premiums, and lower property values. And that is just the price of homicide—the human and economic costs of all violent crime run even higher.[2]

Urban violence, also described as street, gang, youth, community, or gun violence, accounts for more violent deaths than any other category of crime. It is the violence that plagues the most disadvantaged communities in our cities. It involves, for the most part, young men killing or wounding other young men in tragic and brutal cycles of retribution. Disputes that were once decided with words or fists now result in gunfire that claims not only combatants but also bystanders who just happen to be nearby when one enemy spots another.

It has become fashionable in some circles to describe urban violence as an infectious disease, spreading from person to person like the flu. This comparison has been helpful in reframing urban violence as a matter of public health, but it lacks one thing: urgency. Some diseases require immediate action, but many do not. Urban violence is better understood as a grievous injury, a gushing wound that demands immediate attention in order to preserve life and limb.

A life-threatening injury is an acute emergency, while a disease can be a chronic condition that demands a less vigorous response.

In this book, I propose a series of lifesaving treatments to address urban violence, right now, without further delay. Urban violence is the most widely studied form of crime, and there is enough reliable research out there to provide a strong sense of how best to tackle the issue today. Murder on the streets of our cities is a deadly serious problem, but it is also a solvable one.

Recognizing that the fastest route between two points is a straight line, these treatments address urban violence by focusing attention and resources on the most dangerous people, places, and things—the factors driving the majority of the mayhem. An approach the experts call the Gun Violence Reduction Strategy reduces gun and gang violence by confronting would-be shooters with a double message that pairs offers of assistance with threats of punishment. Hot spots policing temporarily cools crime locations, getting guns off the streets and giving neighborhoods an opportunity to recover.

These efforts also balance punishment with prevention. Cognitive behavioral therapy helps high-risk adolescents manage their emotions, address conflicts constructively, and think carefully about the consequences of their actions. Investing in crime-prone places by removing blight and restoring services makes them less susceptible to violence.

Finally, just as treatment for injuries requires partnerships between patients and their health care providers, peace in the streets requires cooperation between communities and criminal justice authorities. A lasting peace cannot be achieved without improvements in the perceived fairness of criminal justice institutions, especially the police. The principles of procedural fairness, by which criminal justice officials learn to treat residents with respect, offer them opportunities to be heard, and become more transparent about what they do and why they do it, can rebuild confidence and renew partnerships while restoring public safety.

This book concludes with a concrete proposal that combines all these strategies into a single effort that can reduce homicide rates by over 50 percent in eight years—just two mayoral or presidential terms. In Chicago, this proposal would prevent more than fifteen hundred murders. In Baltimore, it would avoid almost eight hundred. Nationally, these efforts would save more than twelve thousand lives and avoid approximately $121 billion in social costs. Put these proposals into place and in a decade the US murder rate will resemble Canada's.

In short, this is a book about how to stop the bleeding. It offers a new paradigm for addressing urban violence in America, examining it as if it were a young man hemorrhaging on a hospital gurney. The metaphor of a patient passing through an emergency room is fitting, as urban violence is in fact a national emergency that demands our urgent attention.

BEFORE GOING FURTHER, it may be helpful to explain what I mean by *urban violence*. *Violence* here means physical force that results or could result in serious injury or death. This definition includes only the most concrete and potentially lethal forms of violence. This book measures urban violence primarily in terms of homicides, its most important and reliable indicator.

Urban means, literally, something relating to cities or towns. Violence can happen anywhere, but in 2017, 70 percent of all homicides in the US happened in cities with populations of 25,000 or more. In this book, urban also means something more: it refers to violence that generally occurs outside the home, on the streets or in other public spaces where people congregate.[3]

Urban violence is largely the province of young men. One of the most consistent findings in criminology is that age and lawbreaking are strongly related, and especially so for violence. The likelihood and frequency of violent offending rise in late adolescence, peak during the late teens to early twenties, and then begin a steady decline. Violence is also overwhelmingly perpetrated by men, who are also its primary victims. In 2017, 88 percent of homicide perpetrators were male, as were 79 percent of homicide victims.[4]

Urban violence is committed with hands and feet as well as bottles, bats, sticks, knives, and other deadly instruments, but when it comes to murder, firearms are by far the most frequently used. In 2017, 72 percent of all homicides were committed with a gun, typically a handgun, and in the most violent cities the rate can reach as high as 90 percent.[5]

Urban violence can occur in the course of other street crimes, especially robbery, but often it is sparked by arguments, conflicts, or "beefs" of some kind. These disputes often involve long-standing rivalries between groups known as gangs, cliques, sets, crews, and so on. In 2017, 64 percent of all homicides where a motive was identified were the result of disputes of some kind, and with stronger data the percentage would probably be higher. Many of these conflicts are connected to cycles of retaliatory violence that go back years, even generations. In these instances, today's perpetrator is likely to be tomorrow's victim, with the next shooting planned in the emergency room of the last one. For many who commit murder, it's all about payback.[6]

Race matters when it comes to urban violence. African Americans, particularly men, are disproportionately impacted by deadly violence: in 2017, homicide victimization rates for black men were 3.9 times higher than the national average and black people accounted for 52 percent of all known homicide victims, despite representing only 13 percent of the US population. As we will learn, high rates of violence in poor communities of color come not from deficiencies in culture or values but from long legacies of racial persecution that have resulted in concentrated poverty and disadvantage.[7]

I should also explain what I *don't* mean by "urban violence." For the purposes of this book, urban violence does not include nonlethal violence, such as slaps, pushes, or punches, that do not risk sending someone to the hospital or the morgue. Nor does it mean nonphysical verbal or emotional abuse; or nonphysical forms of injustice and oppression, such as economic violence; or violence that generally occurs in private locations such as homes or schools.

Urban violence, as I use the term, does not include sexual violence or violence between intimate partners and family members. It also excludes violence perpetrated by the state or by highly organized criminal groups. These kinds of violence, although they may involve serious injury or death and occur in a city in public, are important but not the focus here.

The justification for all these exclusions is simple: to address different kinds of violence, different approaches are required. There is no universal anti-violence strategy; what works in addressing one form of violence may not work with another. A key question for any antiviolence effort, for example, is deciding how many and what kind of partners should participate. The answer will vary widely depending on the kind of violence: preventing bullying in schools involves partnerships between educators and parents, while combating organized crime requires the coordination of traditional law enforcement institutions.[8]

WHY SHOULD WE as a society prioritize reducing violence? And why should we focus on urban violence in particular? The reasoning is simple but powerful: the most urgent and fundamental human need is to be secure, free from the dangers that might suddenly end our lives. We all need food, water, and air to survive, but we can live for roughly three weeks without food, three days without water, and three minutes without air, whereas violence can kill in a second.

Violence, or the threat of it, is ubiquitous. It is in us, around us, and has been with us since time began. In nature, plants are eaten by animals, which are preyed upon by other animals along the ecological food chain, and violent competition among animals is routine. We humans have only recently distanced ourselves from the natural world, and so, not surprisingly, our history and prehistory is filled with murder and mayhem. Many regions of the world remain plagued by civil war, sectarian strife, ethnic cleansing, terrorism, transnational organized crime, and other kinds of violent conflict. According to cognitive psychologist Steven Pinker, scientists have not discovered a single source for violent impulses in the brains of humans and other mammals. Instead, they have identified many, mirroring the many reasons why we resort to violence. Humans and animals use violence as a tool to achieve status and dominance, to deter predators, and to prey on others, among other motivations. Psychological research shows that we are at our most violent not as young adults but as unsocialized toddlers, when we fortunately lack the capacity to effectuate our often-murderous intentions.[9]

As observed by former crime reporter and writer Jill Leovy, "The safe take safety for granted. They assume that they are safe because safety is a state of nature, and that violence is an aberration." But the peace and tranquility enjoyed by many is a relatively recent development, painstakingly produced over centuries, even millennia, of institution- and system-building. Even this progress remains strikingly uneven and unequal, with the wealthy and privileged able to insulate themselves from violence while the poor and powerless remain in peril. According to Gary Haugen, a human rights lawyer and activist who has documented the devastating impact of everyday violence on the world's least fortunate, protecting the poor is the most effective anti-poverty measure available today. "If you are not safe," he argues, "nothing else matters."[10]

Murder is the most serious form of violence and the most direct threat to personal safety. It is the pinnacle of social injustice; it is simply the worst thing one person can do to another. This understanding of murder is shared across regional, national, cultural, and religious boundaries, and it is based on the near-universal recognition that a single homicide causes more human suffering on average than any other individual act of wrongdoing. Empirically, the social costs—for victims and perpetrators, law enforcement, the health care system, and society more generally—of homicide far exceed those of other crimes. One frequently cited study estimates the cost of a single murder to be 51 times higher than an armed robbery, 119 times higher than an aggravated assault, and an astounding 420 times higher than a burglary.[11]

Importantly, homicide is also the best-measured form of crime and violence. While other violent crimes may go unreported, virtually all

murders are known to the authorities because they produce an undeniable piece of physical evidence: a dead body. In low-income nations
with scant crime statistics, homicides are often the only category of
crime for which there is even semireliable information, and even in
the US, homicide is the only category of offense where we know the
numbers with absolute confidence. Homicide is also a useful indicator
of trends in violent crime generally, as other offenses tend to rise and
fall in unison with homicide over the medium and long terms.[12]

Here in the US, urban violence accounts for more homicides than
any other type of violence. Since October 2001, over four hundred people have died in domestic terrorist attacks and over five hundred have
died in mass shootings. During that same period, at least one hundred
thousand lost their lives to urban violence. In 2017, urban violence
accounted for approximately 88 percent of all murders, although this
figure should be taken with a large grain of salt given that the circumstances of more than 40 percent of murders are unknown.[13]

One might believe, given how crime and violence are often portrayed in the media, that murder rates have never been higher. This
is not the case. In 1964, homicide rates in the US began to climb
steadily, rising from a rate of 4.9 murders per one hundred thousand
residents to 9.8 murders in 1991. From there, rates dropped dramatically until 2000, then decreased modestly until 2014, reaching a floor
of 4.5 murders. After that, rates rose dramatically in 2015 and 2016,
then plateaued in 2017 at almost exactly the same levels as they were
in 1964. Violent crime and property crime rates have risen and fallen
roughly in tandem with homicide rates.[14]

Looking back, one might observe that the US experienced a
remarkable decline in violence and crime over the past twenty-five
years. Another equally valid observation is that after more than fifty
years we have made no progress whatsoever. This failure has cost
hundreds of thousands of lives, trillions of dollars, and immeasurable pain and suffering. The nation remains an ugly outlier among
wealthy countries, infamous for its bloody violence, as it has been for
decades.[15]

If homicide is simultaneously the most serious and best-measured form of violence, and urban violence is associated with more homicides than any other, then there is a strong case for urgently addressing this form of violence. By focusing on urban violence, we can save lives and keep families and communities intact while bringing the nation into parity with its wealthy peers. Providing public safety is the most fundamental priority for any society, and collectively we are failing to fully meet our obligations to our fellow citizens, especially for the least powerful and most persecuted among us.

THIS BOOK IS a work of forward-looking pragmatism. It offers concrete recommendations on what to do about urban violence now. It collects the most reliable evidence currently available and also draws on the real-world experiences of those who have faced violence firsthand. This book, in short, is both evidence- and community-informed. *Evidence-informed* means making recommendations that are informed by the best evidence and data currently available. *Community-informed* means giving voice to those most impacted by urban violence and meaningfully including them in the decision-making process for addressing it.

The recommendations in this book are primarily based on impact evaluations. Lots of them. Impact evaluations do what their name implies; they evaluate things to see whether they had an impact. They are designed to answer a simple question: "Did this program or policy reach its intended goals?" The evaluations in this book all concern programs and policies designed to reduce crime and, especially, violence. In this book, I ask a simple but powerful question: "When trying to reduce urban violence, what works?"[16]

Most of the impact evaluations in this book are drawn from systematic reviews—a relatively recent development in the social sciences. Originating in medicine, these reviews exhaustively gather and rigorously interpret the results of multiple evaluations. They set clear goals, use transparent methodologies, and focus only on the most reliable studies. Systematic reviews are now widely regarded as providing the strongest evidence of "what works" when evaluating programs and policies. In some areas, however, there are no systematic reviews. There may not even be impact evaluations. At times, then, I've had to rely on the best evidence available while offering cautions as to the confidence one can have when coming to conclusions.[17]

Even when plentiful, such evidence only goes so far. To truly understand urban violence, research must be blended with practice; book smarts must be blended with street smarts. In preparation for this book, I traveled across the country interviewing current and former shooters, gang members, mothers who had lost sons to violence, police officers, outreach workers, social service providers, and others. In Baltimore, Boston, Chicago, Los Angeles, and New York, among other places, I conducted dozens of face-to-face interviews. Some of these conversations were inspiring, others were sobering, and many were both. Here are a few examples.

Erik King is an educator, helping to keep youth engaged and successful at school. As a child, he learned the language of violence, enduring abuse, loss, isolation and poverty. As a young man, he spoke the language himself, becoming an enforcer for a number of New York City gangs. He was shot, stabbed, and beaten, but ultimately Erik turned away from violence because of the love and support of a few friends and family members who believed in him, even when he did not believe in himself.

Like his father before him, Deputy Chief Phillip Tingirides always wanted to be a cop. Once he joined the Los Angeles Police Department, he saw that some officers treated people with respect while others looked for conflict. He decided to emulate the officers who forged strong connections with the neighborhoods they served. "If you have the trust of the community, they'll help you, but not if they think you're only out to lock them up." Tingirides now leads one of the most successful neighborhood-policing initiatives in the nation.

Few meeting Eddie Bocanegra, an executive at a large nonprofit in Chicago, would believe that he served fourteen years in prison for first-degree murder. Since then, he has spent his life in service, pioneering a number of community-based programs to build resiliency among those impacted by violence. Eddie now leads READI Chicago, an ambitious initiative to provide jobs, skills, and treatment for those at the very highest risk for violent offending and victimization, leveraging his years as a gang member and inmate to help others find safer and better futures.

These accounts, and others like them, bring home the humanity of those impacted most by violence. Too often, Americans believe that violence is a problem that "other" people face. Those caught up in the cycle of violence are simply different from the rest of us, the thinking goes—and of course race fundamentally shapes such thinking. One of the goals of this book is to help those of us who are safe to realize that we are not so different from those who live their lives under the constant threat of danger. Real stories, from real people who have experienced or witnessed violence up close and personal, help to bring this point home.

Some might believe that the academic and community perspectives are too different to be reconciled, but that has not been my experience. Over the years, I have constantly compared what I learn from researchers with what I hear and see in neighborhoods. Perhaps surprisingly to some, social scientists and the street are largely in agreement on urban violence, one reinforcing the another as they see the same phenomenon through different lenses, with each perspective being necessary but not sufficient for a full understanding of the issue.

This book also draws upon my own background and experiences. For more than twenty years, I have worked as an educator, prosecutor, policy maker, and now researcher focused on urban violence. I have worked cases, pushed programs, looked at the numbers, and read studies. While I was teaching high school in Washington, DC, one of my favorite students was murdered. As an assistant district attorney working in New York City, I prosecuted criminals and comforted victims. While working for President Barack Obama and New

York governor Andrew Cuomo, I advocated for policies to address these issues. Now, at the Harvard Kennedy School of Government, I mix research with real-world experience in order to better understand what can be done about crime and violence.

LIKE A PATIENT in an emergency room, this book begins with triage, proceeds to diagnosis, continues with treatment, then ends with prognosis. Triage ensures that we treat the most urgent injuries and illnesses first. A diagnosis is necessary to determine the origin of a patient's symptoms. Treatment describes the care that must be provided. Finally, a prognosis forecasts the patient's future progress.

Chapter 2, "Triage," describes the tremendous toll urban violence takes on individuals, communities, and the nation, illustrating the centrality of violence and the fear of violence to urban life. It also documents society's collective failure to prioritize urban violence, arguing that decision-makers, like doctors in the ER, must urgently attend to the enormous harm it causes.

Chapters 3, 4, and 5—which together form part 1, "Diagnosis"— examine urban violence in America. Chapter 3 explores a fundamental finding related to urban violence: that crime and, especially, violence are "sticky," meaning that they tend to cluster around small numbers of dangerous people, places, and behaviors. Chapter 4 examines a second fundamental finding: that a balance of punishment and prevention works far better to reduce urban violence than either approach in isolation. Chapter 5 investigates the ongoing crisis of confidence in criminal justice to uncover a third fundamental finding: that in order to promote safety, we must build legitimacy—and vice versa.

Chapters 6, 7, and 8—which form part 2, "Treatment"—are about the policies proven to actually reduce urban violence. Chapter 6 examines people-based strategies that deter dangerous offenders and prevent young people from becoming dangerous in the first place. Chapter 7 describes place-based strategies to lower violent crime in the locations where it happens the most. Chapter 8 identifies behaviors that facilitate and aggravate violence—gun carrying, gang-banging, and violent drug dealing—and identifies concrete strategies to address them.

Chapters 9, 10, and 11—which form part 3, "Prognosis"—collectively offer a positive vision for a safer and more peaceful urban America. Chapter 9 explores how to change the national narrative around urban violence to better promote smart policies and successful strategies. Chapter 10 provides a series of inspiring stories from real people about how they struggled, survived, and ultimately succeeded, despite being deeply impacted by the violence surrounding them. Chapter 11 culminates with two concrete plans—one local and one national—to reduce homicide rates by over 50 percent over eight years. The first plan is for a single locality; the second includes the forty most violent cities in the country.

THIS IS NOT a book about where we end up; it is about where we begin, and on that it does not equivocate: we must start with violence itself. High rates of violent crime are the structural linchpin of urban poverty, trapping poor people in neighborhoods of concentrated disadvantage. Violence is not simply a manifestation of poverty; it is a force that *perpetuates* poverty as well. Poverty might precede violence, but reducing poverty requires working backward, beginning with the violence we experience today. Similarly, while high rates of gun ownership—more than one for every adult American—have an undeniable impact on deadly violence in our cities, we need not wait until the national debate on gun control is resolved to act. By beginning with the guns in the hands of the most dangerous people, in the most dangerous places, we can make an immediate difference.

To get started, we must stop seeing urban violence as an argument to be won and instead look at it as a problem to be solved. On the right, racist blame-shifting and fearmongering must be rejected. On the left, race-based mistrust of law enforcement must be addressed. A diverse new political constituency must be created to demand practical solutions to the pressing challenge of urban violence. This movement should bring together those who have suffered from violence with those who wish to help them. Fortunately, this group does not need to be large; it just needs to be loud.

If we can stop the bleeding, redemption and recovery are possible. The proposals in this book are modest in scope but potentially transformative in impact. With violence under control, we could unleash the potential of millions of people while saving billions of dollars. We could also build bridges over the divides that separate cops from communities, the privileged from the poor, and whites from their fellow African American and Latino citizens. Anti-violence efforts are not a substitute for broader and deeper efforts to remedy economic and social injustice—they are, rather, an essential aspect of them.

This book talks a lot about social science, but it was not written for my colleagues in academia. It was written for you, the concerned reader, because without you, little of consequence will be accomplished. I spent almost a decade in government lobbying for many of the strategies set out in this book, with some successes but also a few failures and frustrations. At times my recommendations have made sense but lacked public recognition and support. This book is, in essence, an effort to cut out the middleman—if I can convince you that there are solutions available to radically reduce the problem of urban violence, my hope is that policy makers and politicians will fall in line when you demand action. As you read, I will challenge you to reexamine how you think and feel about violence, crime, urban policy, and maybe even race and politics. You may be persuaded by the science or by the stories, but one way or another, my hope is that you will come to the same conclusion: more can and should be done to stop the bleeding and save lives.

CHAPTER 2

TRIAGE

I'VE KNOWN KIM ODOM FOR YEARS. SHE IS A COFOUNDER OF OPERA-tion LIPSTICK, a first-of-its-kind effort in Boston that works to prevent firearms trafficking by helping women refuse to buy or store guns for the men in their lives. She was also a member of a Boston delegation that went to Washington in 2011 to participate in the National Forum on Youth Violence Prevention—an effort I helped to organize. When Kim speaks, her voice carries an undeniable authority amplified by her natural charisma and charm. Warmth and goodness seem to emanate naturally from her and her husband, Ronald, both of whom are pastors. When she talks about violence, however, people listen extra closely, because she speaks from her own broken heart.[1]

Kim's son, Steven Odom, was murdered on October 4, 2007. He was thirteen years old. Steven was an innocent bystander—he and his friends were walking home from a basketball game when they were mistakenly targeted by gang members. Shots rang out. Steven fell.

When Kim and I sat down to talk, it had been almost exactly ten years since the murder. Kim had told Steven's story before, but she still recounted it in fits and starts. Her voice cracked, her eyes watered, she took deep breaths. She broke down and cried, recovered, then cried again. "It's so hard to talk about Steven, but his life mattered, and if I don't talk about him, who will? In a sense, he left us his voice to carry."

Kim remembered the little things about that terrible evening. "I heard four shots—they sounded like firecrackers. I looked out the window and saw a basketball rolling down the street—it came to rest at the tires of our car." She went to investigate and saw someone lying in the street. "As I got closer, I could see his clothes. I kept saying, 'I think it's Steven.'" As she got closer, step by step, she witnessed what no parent should ever see: her beautiful son, lying in the street, shot in the head.

Kim's mind went blank. Later, in the hospital, a nurse had the nerve to comment that she seemed calm. "I'm numb," she replied. For weeks after Steven's death, Kim couldn't eat or sleep. She could barely even get out of bed. Not only was she numb, she was immobilized with grief.

Kim struggled to maintain her faith. "God, like this?" she asked. "I know tragedy happens, but Steven murdered?" The Odoms had constantly quoted scripture: "No evil shall befall you, nor shall any plague come near your dwelling." Now she was questioning those sacred words. The night before the shooting, she and Ronald had placed Steven and their other children inside a prayer circle, invoking the Lord's protection. "The plague came and now my son is gone—what do I do with that?"

"I took that scripture literal," Kim told me. "Now, my interpretation has changed. It's not that I've given up on my faith—I still believe and trust in God—but at the same time it's hard."

Ten days after the murder, the young man suspected of killing Steven was murdered himself. He was eighteen. Another young man who was with the alleged killer at the time was shot and paralyzed a few weeks later. He was twenty and will spend the rest of his life in a wheelchair. Finally, the boy who provided the gun was arrested, prosecuted, and sentenced to six to eight years in prison. He was sixteen.

People asked Kim whether she was happy with what happened to the young men involved in the death of her son. Kim was shocked, almost offended by these questions. "Happy? We're not happy. We're heavy. My husband and I are preachers, we preach and teach forgiveness. We feel heavy because now there are four families that are suffering the pain from this vicious cycle of violence."

Before his death, Steven had witnessed what violence was doing to Dorchester, the neighborhood in Boston where he and his family lived. Exactly one year before the shooting, Steven wrote in his school journal about how gangs and drugs were impacting his community. "It's a shame that somebody gets shot and killed every day," he wrote. "That's why we seriously need peace." The coincidence of the timing haunts Kim to this day.

The Odoms' loss cannot be quantified. Every death and injury associated with urban violence is a distinct tragedy with unique circumstances that causes indescribable suffering, but the collective costs of violence to neighborhoods like Dorchester can be measured. When those costs are tallied and then multiplied across all the Dorchesters in the United States, they become enormous. To save the Stevens of the future, we must address the devastating violence that threatens them and their communities.

IN HOSPITAL EMERGENCY rooms, triage is a necessity. Incoming patients' vital signs—blood pressure, heart rate, respiratory rate, oxygen levels, body temperature—are assessed in order to answer a simple but crucial question: Is this patient about to die? Patients with life-threatening injuries or illnesses are treated immediately, while others wait their turn. Hemorrhage, or bleeding out, is the most frequent cause of preventable postinjury death in the United States.[2]

In medicine, the necessity of this process is apparent; fail to prioritize and patients perish needlessly. The underlying logic is based on a simple but powerful rule: one cannot help everyone with everything, so first do the most important things for those most in need. By using their limited resources efficiently, hospitals help as much and save as many as they can.

Doctors and nurses triage violent injuries, but as a society we fail to do the same for violence more generally. Shootings, stabbings, and beatings claim thousands of lives each year yet receive only lip service

from politicians. Outside the ER, the urgency of these injuries evapo-
rates and accountability is lost. Leave one young man to bleed out on
a hospital gurney and heads will roll. Neglect thousands of young men
as they die in their neighborhoods and you're on course for reelection.

Controlling deadly violence is the most underappreciated aspect
of urban governance. The costs of violence are enormous, yet the issue
is an afterthought in many policy circles. This must change. We must
triage more effectively.

This chapter makes the provocative claim that the first thing that
must be done to help the urban poor is also the most obvious: we must
keep them safe from lethal violence. We must start by stopping the
bleeding.

Concentrated Poverty Causes Violence

Urban poverty passes from generation to generation. Poor parents
struggle to give their children the opportunities they lacked. Needing
support themselves, they find it harder to offer support. Sadly, hardship for poor parents usually results in hardship for their kids.

Just like people, poor neighborhoods tend to stay poor. In the
most disadvantaged urban neighborhoods, housing is highly unsta-
ble, marked periodically by disruptive evictions. Schools in these
neighborhoods are often described as "dropout factories," with siz-
able proportions of the student body failing to graduate. Waste sites,
landfills, incinerators, and other environmental hazards dot the land-
scape. Access to jobs, transportation, and other services is severely
constricted.

Individually, each of these challenges is daunting. Collectively, they
are overwhelming. Concentrated poverty puts individuals, families,
and communities under intense and unrelenting pressure. When it
persists over long periods, it leads to criminality and violence. No one
kind of deprivation is responsible; instead, it is multiple deprivations,
all operating at the same time, all fixed on the same people living in

the same place, that eventually result in high levels of victimization and crime.

Outsiders often ask, Why would anyone stay in such desperate circumstances? Why don't people leave, escape, move to better neighborhoods to make a new start? The short answer is that they stay because they have little choice.

It is impossible to examine concentrated urban poverty without acknowledging America's shameful legacy of racial segregation. For most of the last century, African Americans were deliberately excluded from desirable neighborhoods via redlining, blockbusting, restrictive covenants, and other forms of public and private discrimination. This persecution left black people with nowhere to go but areas with inferior housing and schools, inadequate public transportation, and insufficient access to capital. This discrimination spanned generations, creating long legacies of handicaps, hindrances, obstacles, and impediments, all designed to keep black people locked into the least desirable locations and separate from white society.[3]

As industries and businesses left cities in the 1960s, '70s, and '80s, African Americans and other minorities concentrated in urban communities were particularly vulnerable to job losses. At the same time, the end of outright racial segregation allowed middle-class whites and minorities to migrate out of poor, racially mixed neighborhoods. Both forces served to further concentrate poverty among poor people of color, further magnifying its impact.[4]

"It is the cumulative effect of living in concentrated disadvantage, over generations, that is particularly severe," wrote sociologist Patrick Sharkey in his aptly titled book *Stuck in Place*. Sharkey showed that 70 percent of African Americans living in the nation's poorest neighborhoods today are from families who lived in those same communities in the 1960s. "The American ghetto appears to be inherited," he concluded. Racial persecution combined with other forces to trap generations of black people in conditions of concentrated poverty.[5]

As a consequence of discrimination, deindustrialization, and out-migration, poor African Americans live in neighborhoods far more segregated and disadvantaged than those occupied by similarly situated whites. In fact, disadvantaged white neighborhoods fare better than average black ones in almost all US cities. There is simply no large American city where black and white people live in "ecological equality."[6]

Not surprisingly, many of America's most violent cities are also its most segregated, with long histories of racial strife. Detroit, perennially among the nation's "murder capitals," has had federal troops called in not once but twice to restore calm after race riots. Baltimore was a national leader in racial discrimination, legislating one of the first residential segregation ordinances in the nation. Chicago remains one of the most segregated large cities and led the country in the use of racially restrictive covenants in the 1940s. Latinos have suffered similarly to African Africans in terms of racial segregation, with similar results, although the levels of segregation and poverty have been generally less pronounced.[7]

While segregation is associated with high rates of violence, it does not cause violence directly. Instead, segregation produces communities of concentrated poverty and disadvantage, and it is in these conditions of concentrated disadvantage that violence thrives.[8] As the National Academy of Sciences, the nation's preeminent scientific authority, has observed, "For reasons of social disadvantage, neighborhood residence, and limited life chances that disproportionately affect them, black people relative to whites have been more involved in violent crime and are more frequently arrested for such crimes."[9]

Racial disparities in crime and punishment are real, but they have been produced in large part by a sustained campaign of persecution by whites against disempowered racial minorities, particularly African Americans. Officially, that effort has ended; overt racial discrimination has been prohibited by law for decades. Nevertheless, the brutal legacy of that campaign—racism, segregation, concentrated poverty, and violence—remains.

Violence Perpetuates Concentrated Poverty

Across America's cities, murderous violence ravages poor communities of color. Every single means of bettering oneself and one's community is hampered by high rates of homicide, if not blocked altogether. School attendance suffers when children are afraid to walk to school. Physical and mental health is impaired by the trauma of experiencing or witnessing violent events. Commercial and financial activity is strangled by the presence of violent crime.

Urban violence is a cycle operating within the cycle of concentrated poverty. In distressed neighborhoods, violence begets violence. An insult leads to a beating, then to a shooting, and on to a killing. Far too often, this tit-for-tat sequence is allowed to escalate, creating a feedback loop of destruction. Feuds between individuals, groups, or even neighborhoods can go on for generations, reminiscent of the Hatfields and McCoys, with participants often unaware of how or why the conflict began.

The cycle of violence perpetuates not only itself but poverty as well. Violence is among the strongest social forces keeping poor people poor. In a systematic review of thirty-four studies, researchers found that violent crime, especially murder, is highly correlated with poverty. If inadequate education, employment, housing, and health are threads in the knot of concentrated poverty, then violence is the hand pulling them tight, making them impossible to tease apart.[10]

Violence creates fear, and this fear is toxic to already-struggling people and places. When someone is murdered, everyone in the neighborhood knows. People talk and worry they might be next. Outside the neighborhood, others talk as well, and over time a neighborhood becomes associated with violence. At its worst, violence stains the reputation of entire cities, earning them morbid nicknames like "Bodymore" and "Chiraq."

Living in fear takes a terrible toll. In many poor urban neighborhoods, adults turn to risky behaviors such as substance abuse, unprotected sex, and aggression to cope with the anger, frustration, and anxiety caused by chronic exposure to violence. As they grow older, a lifetime of living with stress catches up to them, elevating their risk for serious illnesses, including cancer, lung disease, and heart disease. In a study of African American women living on Chicago's South Side, just over half reported experiencing a serious traumatic event (such as witnessing the murder of a friend or relative), and just under a third of the participants had been diagnosed with post-traumatic stress disorder (PTSD).[11]

Tragically, it may be children who suffer most from the fear and anxiety caused by exposure to violence. In 2015, a series of landmark studies were released on income mobility in the United States. Among other findings, economists Raj Chetty and Nathaniel Hendren observed that poor kids growing up in violent neighborhoods were less likely to move up the economic ladder than those who lived in equally poor but less dangerous settings. As Chetty and Hendren noted, "Counties that produce better outcomes for children in low-income families tend to have . . . lower rates of violent crime."[12]

Two years later Patrick Sharkey built upon Chetty and Hendren's findings, taking them a step further. Using sophisticated statistical analysis, Sharkey and a colleague were able to uncover an if-then connection between violence and economic mobility and concluded that exposure to violence was a "central mechanism" for limiting children's chances to improve their lives as adults. Simply put, violence hurts the upward mobility of poor kids, trapping them in poverty. Sharkey showed that exposure to violence compromised children's ability to function and learn in school, causing them to fall behind academically and damaging their long-term prospects for earning more income. Exposure to violence did not make kids any less smart, but it occupied their minds, making it harder for them to focus and concentrate. Other studies indicate that more than half of urban youths exposed to violence suffer from some form of PTSD.[13]

Fear also leads to avoidance. People naturally want to escape danger in order to stay safe. When residents, workers, customers, and tourists avoid a block, neighborhood, or city, the civic and commercial life of those locations drains away. People relocate, refuse to visit, and decline to invest in places they believe are dangerous.

Avoidance devastates local businesses, strangling their economic prospects. In Washington, DC, each homicide has been estimated to cost the city two retail or service businesses. Avoidance also destroys residential and commercial property values. In Oakland, each murder cost the city an estimated $24,600 in average home value in the next year. Across five cities, every homicide lowered nearby property values by 1.5 percent in the following year.[14]

Depopulation is also a massive challenge for cities suffering from historically high rates of crime and violence. Of the seven cities infamously known as "murder capitals" over the last thirty years—Birmingham, Alabama; Detroit, Michigan; Flint, Michigan; New Orleans, Louisiana; Richmond, Virginia; St. Louis, Missouri; and Washington, DC—five experienced significant losses in population, and in the two cities where population increased or stayed level—Richmond and Washington, DC—rates of violence declined in recent years.[15]

All of these factors lead to lower tax revenues, which results in fewer public services, particularly for poor residents and communities. Urban violence thus triggers a brutal process of private and public dis-investment, deepening and hardening the conditions that created it.

While the poor suffer most, everyone pays a price for high rates of homicide. Three credible, peer-reviewed, and frequently cited studies estimate the cost of a single murder to be, respectively, $10 million, $13.5 million, and $19.2 million. These estimates include direct costs such as lost labor and property damage, as well as medical and justice system costs. They also capture indirect costs such as diminished quality of life and the avoidance behaviors previously described. In total, the annual price tag for homicide alone, not including any other violent crime, ranges from $173 billion to $332 billion—between $531 and $1,020 per American.[16]

These costs are passed on to us, the general public, in a number of ways. Most obviously, we pay them via taxes. Every year, approximately $284 billion in American taxpayer dollars are spent on federal, state, and local criminal justice systems. We also pay via elevated insurance rates: for example, many of those treated for gunshots, stab wounds, and other traumatic injuries are uninsured, resulting in higher medical and disability premiums for others. Finally, as we've seen, violence has a massively negative impact on economic activity as well as residential and commercial property values.[17]

One can quibble with the exact amounts of these estimates, but the point is not to put forward precise figures but instead to illustrate that the damage caused by urban violence is real, its scope is massive, and it plays a key role in perpetuating urban poverty.

To Address Concentrated Poverty, Put Violence First

Since high rates of violence are caused by concentrated poverty, it is understandable that some—especially those on the political left— believe that the best way to curb such crime is by attending to "root causes." Less poverty will lead to less violence, they quite reasonably believe.

When one makes a static comparison—looking at just one point in time—there are clear correlations between crime, violence, and poverty. Rich countries, on average, have less crime and violence than poor countries, and the same is true for rich and poor neighborhoods. These comparisons reinforce the intuitive notion that those who have more commit less crime and vice versa. However, when these comparisons become dynamic—that is, when we measure change over time—these associations break down. More specifically, when income, wealth, or inequality changes incrementally, researchers do not always find corresponding changes in crime or violence. Correlation, in this case, is not the same as causation. Looking back over the twentieth century in the United States, one can see that changes in prosperity, inequality, and criminality have been largely unrelated: the murder rate declined during the Great Depression, rose during the booming 1960s, and stayed near historic lows during the Great Recession, which began in late 2007.[18]

Furthermore, root causes do not explain why crime and especially violence concentrate among small numbers of places and people. Many are poor, a few are criminals, and fewer still are killers. While most murderers may be poor, the overwhelming majority of the poor are not murderers. As criminologist David Kennedy has observed, "If single-parent families or poverty . . . were the main drivers of gun violence, that should result in vastly more violence than there is."[19]

Last and perhaps most importantly, addressing root causes cannot and will not stop the bleeding. Ending poverty, inequality, and even racism are all important long-term goals, but they are not concrete plans for anti-violence action. Meaningful progress on fundamental socioeconomic conditions will take generations to achieve. People living with the reality of urban violence need relief right now.

Focusing on violence will not only save lives, but it is, again, the necessary first step on the path to those larger goals. Urban violence acts as a linchpin for urban poverty, locking the conditions of concentrated poverty into place and undermining efforts to achieve broader social and economic progress. Teachers cannot teach and schools cannot educate when surrounded by violence. Doctors and hospitals cannot treat whole neighborhoods suffering from trauma-induced anxiety and depression. Businesses will not stay or hire in areas where murder is commonplace. Some measure of security must be provided before the broader and deeper process of recovery can begin. Communities confronting high rates of violence must start where they are, with the violence that is right in front of them. The surest path to prosperity begins with peace.

Some are squeamish about violence, preferring to approach such a dark, difficult, and sensitive subject indirectly. But as we will see, indirect measures are generally inadequate to deal with highly concentrated social phenomena like urban violence.

Anti-violence efforts should not replace broader socioeconomic agendas to improve the welfare of the most disadvantaged in our nation's cities. In fact, evidence- and community-informed anti-violence strategies are essential elements of such agendas and should be thought of as short- and medium-term bridges to longer-term solutions.

To put it another way, I am not suggesting that working to end violence is the only thing we should do in order to alleviate urban poverty. I am not even arguing that it is the most important thing. What I am saying is that, in cities suffering from high rates of violence, efforts to address such poverty should begin with controlling violence. Violence should be dealt with first, not last, simply as a matter of sequence.

Consider what reducing violence in our cities could mean for their ability to offer aid to the poor. Lowering homicides by just 25 percent could create billions of dollars in housing value. In Boston, a 25 percent drop in the homicide rate would create $11 billion in value. In Philadelphia, $8 billion. In Seattle, Dallas, and Chicago, housing values would grow by $7 billion, $6 billion, and $6 billion respectively. Lowering lethal violence can produce a massive "peace dividend" in tax revenues that cities could spend to benefit their most disadvantaged residents. In Chicago, a 25 percent reduction in homicide could allow the city to bolster spending on community services by up to 66 percent. In Philadelphia, a similar reduction would enable city leaders to double spending on homeless and housing assistance.[20]

According to Sharkey, "Violence is the fundamental challenge of cities. City life just doesn't work when public spaces are violent." Any urban revival depends on a modicum of public security—ask any mayor and they will agree. Improvements in public safety can unlock the social and economic potential of millions of urban residents living in thousands of neighborhoods in hundreds of cities across the country.[21]

In the United States, nearly thirty-eight million people live in census tracts where more than 30 percent of residents live below the poverty line. Almost one in three African Americans live in such areas. High rates of shootings and killings hold these people hostage, keeping them in a permanent state of distress. Promoting peace in these communities can have enormously positive consequences, not just for community residents, but also for the country at large.[22]

A national urban renaissance is currently under way, and it is largely the result of massive decreases in urban violence. That said, the work remains unfinished. Since 1991, the height of the nation's most recent crime wave, homicide rates have fallen in New York City by 86 percent and in Los Angeles by 73 percent. But peace has not reached every city—murder rates increased in Indianapolis, Pittsburgh, Phoenix, and Baltimore by 64, 53, 23, and 13 percent respectively over the same period.[23]

Moreover, reducing urban violence is not just a means of achieving broader social and economic justice. Rather, it is a fundamental measure of such justice in and of itself. Racial disparities in violent victimization are just as important as other race-based differences in criminal justice and beyond. Curbing street violence could very well be the first step toward a new pro-urban, anti-poverty agenda. How we address urban violence could be a model for other social interventions and assistance, potentially transforming the public debate over how government can best serve its most disadvantaged and disenfranchised citizens.

Like ER surgeons, we must triage. If the patient is hemorrhaging, we must prevent them from bleeding out. By addressing violence in our cities first rather than last, we can both save lives and start the process of dismantling urban poverty. We can make it easier for the neediest among us to get a solid education, hold a steady job, and to stay in good health—in short, to live a decent life, with less hurt and fear and more opportunity.

THINK OF STEVEN Odom. Imagine him growing up, graduating from school, getting a job, having a family of his own. Imagine Kim Odom's joy and pride in attending his graduation, watching his wedding, holding her grandchildren for the first time. Now imagine this thousands of times over. Addressing urban violence is ultimately not about eliminating death and sorrow; it is about preserving life and joy.

In the next chapter, we will move from triage to diagnosis, examining how urban violence concentrates among the small numbers of people, places, and behaviors that disproportionately drive the problem. This means that not only should we start with violence, but we should begin where, and with whom, it is most dire.

PART I

DIAGNOSIS

CHAPTER 3

STICKY SITUATIONS

ON OCTOBER 23, 2016, DANIEL RICE KILLED KEVIN THOMAS. IT HAP-pened early on a Sunday morning in the South Bronx outside the Mott Haven Houses. As Rice and his brother approached, Thomas stood up—he had been expecting trouble from the Rice brothers, as he had recently broken their uncle's jaw during an argument.[1]

Rice's brother went first, punching Thomas in the face. Thomas, unfazed, took off his jacket, presumably preparing to fight back, but Rice pulled out a .45-caliber gun and fired: once, twice, ten times. Thomas fell forward onto his stomach, blood flowing from his body, arms, and legs. Rice and his brother left the scene undisturbed and unconcerned, knowing that no one would "snitch" for fear they might be next.

In and around the Mott Haven Houses, the threat of violence was omnipresent. The houses had some of the highest rates of gun violence in New York City. What's more, neither Rice nor Thomas was a stranger to violence. Both had been shot before, both had long criminal records with multiple convictions for violence and weapons offenses, and both had fearsome reputations. "[Rice] knows no one is ratting him out because they are scared of him," said a police investigator. As for Thomas, "he was a never-backdown type of person," according to his sister. "I don't feel like anybody really liked him. They feared him. That was the problem."

After the shooting, Thomas's mother looked out her window. From there, Rosa Martinez could see the precise spot where her son had perished. "Every little fight, they take out a gun," she said. "You lose a life for nothing."

BEFORE AN INJURY can be treated, it must be diagnosed. In the ER, lab tests, imaging studies, and other diagnostic procedures are conducted to learn what has happened to the patient. Similarly, before treating urban violence, we must first understand it.

Thomas's death, while unnecessary and tragic, was not entirely unexpected. The people and places involved had long histories of violence. Much of the killing in our society is equally predictable and preventable, and yet it persists.

This chapter explores a fundamental finding related to urban violence: crime and violence are "sticky," meaning that they tend to cluster around small numbers of dangerous people, places, and things. That finding yields a fundamental principle on how best to address urban violence: to reduce violence, focus on where it concentrates.

People, Places, and Things

Murder in the United States rarely happens at random. Homicides occur in predictable places, driven by identifiable people, and triggered by well-understood behaviors. Target these patterns and you can stop much of the killing. Focused strategies don't address 100 percent of the problem—nothing could—but they offer a highly viable alternative to the ineffectual and expensive status quo.

To appreciate the sticky nature of urban violence, we must understand it in context. As we've seen, poverty concentrates in certain communities. Within those communities, crime concentrates further still. Violence, particularly the potentially lethal violence that is the subject of this book, concentrates most of all, creating three concentric circles of disadvantage and dysfunction, with violence at the center.

Inside America's distressed neighborhoods, shootings and killings cluster in and around small groups of people, places, and things. Two leading criminologists, Lawrence Sherman and David Weisburd, have separately summarized the social science on the matter. Sherman observed that virtually every analysis of crime has found that it concentrates into small groups he described as "the power few." Weisburd argued that the concentration of crime is a "general proposition of universal validity," akin to the laws of gravity or buoyancy. Another set of researchers observed that crime concentration has been documented so frequently that the finding is "nearly axiomatic."[2]

While crime concentrates, violence concentrates further still. In 2015, half of the nation's gun homicides were clustered in just 127 cities and towns. More than a quarter of them happened in approximately 1,200 neighborhoods that contained just 1.5 percent of the US population. Taken together, these communities would fit into an area measuring just forty-two miles wide and long.[3]

Even these statistics overgeneralize. In Oakland, 60 percent of murders occur within a social network of approximately one to two thousand high-risk individuals—about 0.3 percent of the city's population. In New Orleans, a network of six hundred to seven hundred people, less than 1 percent of the city's population, accounts for more than 50 percent of its lethal encounters. In Chicago, 70 percent of nonfatal shootings and 46 percent of fatal ones happen inside a network containing just 6 percent of the city's residents.[4]

Even among the criminal groups known as gangs, cliques, or crews, mayhem is not distributed evenly among members. Most so-called gangs in the United States (with notable exceptions), are small and relatively disorganized, typically involving only twenty-five to thirty members. In my experience, in an average-sized group, generally only two or three members will reliably pick up a firearm and use it when there is a conflict. "Out of a whole gang, maybe five percent commit the real serious crimes like murder and kidnapping," pastor Raymond Solórzano, a former gang worker and also former gang member, told me. These individuals are often described by criminologists as "hot people," "impact offenders," or simply "shooters."[5]

These shooters are overwhelmingly male and young, typically less than twenty-five years old. Despite their youth, they have extensive juvenile and criminal histories, often including convictions for violent and weapons offenses. They tend to associate with others in pursuit of companionship and mutual protection—they shoot for others, not just themselves. Many of them have substance abuse problems, most frequently with alcohol.

Shooters are not just perpetrators; they are overwhelmingly the victims of violence as well. "You meet these kids who have been through some real shit," said former gang member and current educator Erik King. "Foster care, molestation, beatings. They have this empty look behind their eyes, and you can tell they're willing to do anything." With these young men, past is prologue.

Violence does not just cluster among people; it concentrates among places as well. In Boston, 70 percent of all shootings over a three-decade period were concentrated in areas covering approximately 5 percent of the city. In most cities, 4 percent of city blocks account for approximately 50 percent of crime. The areas where crime and violence cluster are known by criminologists as "hot spots," "microplaces," or "microlocations." As these names suggest, these areas are small, a few city blocks in size at most.[6]

Indeed, they are often much smaller than even that. A hot spot might be a street corner where gang members are known to congregate or pass by, a drug house where narcotics are sold, or a bar where fights and conflicts frequently occur. Law-abiding residents recognize these places and do their best to avoid them. Lawbreaking ones are attracted to such places, creating a crude self-selection process.

Civil libertarians often voice concerns about risk assessment, predictive policing, and the prospect of a criminal justice system driven by Big Brother, *Minority Report*-style technologies. These fears are understandable but, in the context of violence reduction, largely misplaced. Here is why.

To identify the people most likely to commit crimes of violence, the law enforcement strategies that are set out in this book rely almost exclusively on three factors: age, gender, and criminal history. It is a fact that young people commit the vast majority of violent crime and that violent individuals "age out" of such crime as they grow older. It is also a fact that violence is overwhelmingly perpetrated by men. Finally, a person's criminal and juvenile background is the only information demonstrated to have any predictive validity when it comes to whether the person will commit crimes, violent or otherwise, in the future. When considering who, where, and what to prioritize, the law enforcement strategies in this book rely on these three factors, and these factors only.[7]

Moreover, these tools are simply more rigorous ways of confirming what those closest to crime and violence already know all too well. To local residents and police, violence is no great mystery—dangerous people and places have formidable reputations that precede them. Everyone in the neighborhood knows not to hang around X person or go to Y location after dark, because both are likely to get one into deadly trouble. That said, when knowledge and memory is supplemented by rigorous data, it is more accurate and less biased than human observation and experience alone.

For children and youth without criminal or juvenile records, the preventative strategies in this book use other indicators to predict who might become a shooter someday, and, not surprisingly, these tools are less accurate. Nevertheless, these tools outperform human judgment in identifying which kids are most at risk for future violence. For those worried about stigmatizing or criminalizing youth based on bad data, keep this in mind: these tools are used only to decide who gets additional support, service, and treatment. Being identified as potentially violent in this context means more attention and more assistance, not more punishment.[8]

At their worst, some risk assessment tools conflate risk and need, allowing factors such as family, education, and employment to influence their results, which can result in racially biased outcomes. Those tools should be rejected and the strategies in this book do not use them. Risk assessment performs an incredibly important function in the criminal justice system by narrowing its scope and discretion, but it is essential to get it right. Rather than jettisoning risk-assessment instruments entirely, the best thing to do is to insist on transparency so the public can see precisely how these tools work and whether they are comfortable with them.[9]

Guns, gangs, and drugs complete the trifecta of deadly concentration. As will be explained later, it is better to understand these not as things but instead as behaviors. Along with "hot people" and "hot spots," a few "hot habits" are strongly associated with serious violence. The first is carrying illegal firearms. It is important to emphasize two qualifications here: it matters that the weapon is illegal and that it is carried in public. The vast majority of deadly urban violence is perpetrated by felons with no legal right to own or carry firearms. In addition, such violence overwhelmingly occurs out on the street, not in private or behind closed doors. Unlawfully and publicly possessing a firearm is a key proximate cause of lethal violence. Another risky habit is hanging out with people who are involved in violence. It turns out that the Greek storyteller Aesop was correct when he stated that a man can be known by the company he keeps. Your mother was right, too: birds of a feather do indeed flock together. For those who trust neither fables nor proverbs, sociologist Andrew Papachristos has demonstrated that one's risk for becoming involved in violence, as either a perpetrator or a victim, depends heavily on one's social network—whom one associates with. Not surprisingly, researchers discover these networks by looking at the concrete connections between people as revealed by their criminal histories—that is, who they were with when stopped by the police, when arrested, and when convicted of crimes.

In one study, Papachristos and colleagues recorded all instances of gun violence in Chicago over an eight-year period and looked at the social networks of the individuals involved. Of the more than eleven thousand documented shootings, 63 percent would have been predicted based on the victims' networks. The closer you are to someone engaged in violence, the more likely you are to become involved yourself. Gangs, crews, and cliques bring young men at elevated risk for violence into close proximity with others like them, magnifying the danger both individually and collectively. Papachristos's work has been repeated in numerous jurisdictions, each time with similar results.[10]

The third and final risky behavior is violent competition among drug dealers, as well as substance abuse among those with a proclivity for violence. You may be surprised to learn that liquor is more closely connected to homicide than illegal drugs, but the easy availability of alcohol, combined with its well-understood ability to lower inhibitions, allows it to play a larger role. At the peak of the crack cocaine epidemic in the late 1980s and early 1990s, much of America's urban violence was driven by drug rivalries among dealers, but today this happens less frequently. Now, more often than not, homicides happen after fights, disputes, and arguments with no immediate connection to criminal activity. In this context, alcohol, like guns, becomes a key facilitator in escalating arguments from uncomfortable confrontations to deadly conflicts.

Concentrations in crime and violence operate along what is known in statistics as a power law distribution. Created over a century ago by the economist Vilfredo Pareto to describe wealth and earnings in Italy, a power law describes a relationship between two variables in which a large share of one is generated by a small fraction of the other. The most famous example of this is Pareto's "80/20 rule," which states that 80 percent of outputs are generated by 20 percent of inputs. As described by Lawrence Sherman, when a power law relationship exists, a large number of "this" is produced by a small number of "that."[11]

On a graph, the power law distribution looks like a hockey stick, with a few of "that" at the blade end of the stick. Now compare this to the more familiar bell-shaped curve of a normal distribution, where values clump together at the middle of the distribution. Height follows a normal distribution, for example. American men are, on average, about five feet nine inches tall, and American women average five feet four inches. If height followed a power law distribution instead, there would be a few giants and lots and lots of short people (or vice versa). The same is true of highway driving speeds: most drivers operate at or about the speed limit. A highway with cars speeding along a power law distribution would be a dangerous place indeed.

Sherman's "power few" contribute disproportionately to violence. Many homicides happen when risky people are present in risky places while engaging in risky behaviors. Consider a typical scene that plays out in jurisdictions all across the country. It's Friday night at a local nightclub that for years has been the site of bloody altercations, including beatings, stabbings, and shootings. The nightclub is located near, but not necessarily in, several poor, gang-ridden neighborhoods. The hour is late, the music loud, and the bar crowded. Liquor flows freely. The club has hired security guards to keep guns and drugs off the premises, but their efforts are spotty and they view what goes on outside their establishment—even if it happens on their doorstep—as someone else's problem.

Two groups of young men—cliques, crews, or gangs, depending on your preferred nomenclature—are inside the club. Let's give them names: the 13th Street Boyz (13th Street) and the Killa Kartel (KK). Both 13th Street and KK are feeling strong, confident, and aggressive, not just because of the drinks they've ingested but also because each group is anchored by the presence of a member known to "handle his business" with a "heater." In short, these two are shooters.

True to their reputations, both shooters are carrying that night. The one from 13th Street has a Glock 19 tucked inside his waistband; a girlfriend snuck it past security and slipped it to him. The shooter from KK has a Smith & Wesson 9mm stashed outside in the glove compartment of a friend's car. Both have criminal histories preventing them from legally owning these weapons, but they have them just the same.

The members of 13th Street and KK are not strangers to one another. In fact, they have a long history of "beefs" and have exchanged words, blows, and even shots periodically over the years. At some point, two members of the rival groups bump shoulders in the crowded club, and one of the more inebriated members of 13th Street "pops off," insulting one of the young men from KK. The groups trade insults and threats, then face off. When they do, the shooter from 13th Street raises his shirt to reveal his Glock, signaling that he will start shooting if his rivals press further.

KK sulks off, momentarily deterred, but they promise retaliation. True to their word, after the club closes and as partygoers are leaving, KK's shooter retrieves his Smith & Wesson, finds his foes, and starts firing. Bullets fly as the crowd outside the club stampedes, then scatters. From this day forward, the dormant rivalry between 13th Street and KK is revived, the cycle of violent retaliation is reactivated, and in the weeks and months ahead the authorities will struggle mightily to contain the fallout from the groups' deadly tit-for-tat.

This tragedy occurs at the intersection of problem people, places, and behaviors. Every element of the scene matters: the setting, the protagonists, the antagonists, and of course the plot. These include (1) a dangerous location, (2) dangerous groups, with a couple of especially dangerous individuals, (3) illegal firearms, and (4) excessive alcohol. Each is a risk factor for violence, increasing the possibility of violence until an invisible tipping point is reached and then passed.

A recent addition to such scenes is the advent of what some call "cyberbanging," where social media platforms like Twitter, Facebook, and YouTube are used by gangs to insult, challenge, and threaten rivals. Conflicts online can quickly translate into violence on the street. To illustrate, consider another scenario involving 13th Street and KK.[12]

Like others their age, the young men of 13th Street and KK are avid consumers of social media, and members of the two groups regularly taunt each other online. The public and permanent nature of these threats and insults makes them particularly hard to ignore, but virtual disputes can remain online indefinitely until a particularly incendiary tweet or post provokes actual violence. One afternoon, members of 13th Street begin posting photos of the group posing directly outside several buildings where KK members are known to live. In the photos, they flash gang and gun signs, "dissing" the KK on their own "turf." KK members see these posts, recognize their own houses and neighborhood, and race to catch the offending 13th Street members. If they succeed, there will be violent confrontation. If they fail, it is almost certain that KK will retaliate, venturing into 13th Street territory to pose and post their own provocative photos. Eventually, the two groups will meet in the streets, with potentially deadly consequences.

The key to understanding these scenarios is to recognize their common elements. Violence does not typically happen just anywhere, at any time, to anyone. Its risk is not spread evenly throughout a neighborhood, nor is everyone living in a neighborhood in equal danger. A fearsome group may have only a few shooters—those most likely to kill or be killed. Guns and alcohol are ubiquitous but are most deadly in the wrong hands at the wrong time. Though most criminologists and crime-fighters understand this reality, the general public does not. Our general ignorance about how urban violence works is one of the main obstacles to curbing it.

The First Fundamental: Focus

Once we realize that a few people, places, and things disproportionately contribute to violent outcomes, we can start to envision effective solutions. When violence is predictable, it is preventable.

The nature of a solution, generally speaking, should match the nature of the problem. If violence is sticky, then we need sticky solutions. Given the concentrated nature of urban violence, as well as the relative scarcity of resources to address the problem, we must design a focused response. Being focused means targeting what matters most when it comes to urban violence. It also means avoiding sweeping generalizations in favor of careful analysis, as well as resisting simplistic solutions that sound solid in theory but do not work out in practice.

Across the policy spectrum, rigorous impact evaluations indicate that focused anti-crime strategies are the ones that are most likely to be successful. In criminal justice, this is true of policing, gang reduction, youth violence prevention, and adult and juvenile recidivism reduction strategies, among others. In public health, a systematic review of youth violence interventions found that effectiveness improved as interventions became more specific, with prevention programs targeting medium- and high-risk populations outperforming those focusing on low-risk or general populations. According to our most rigorous evidence, focus works.[13]

At the same time, focus is feasible, both as a matter of law and budgets. Focused interventions rarely require changes in legislation; they work with the laws on the books today. Furthermore, because they target a small number of key factors, they require relatively modest resources. Providing every poor child with anti-violence programming would be enormously expensive, but providing it only for those who demonstrate a real risk for future offending is affordable. While policy makers may lack the capacity to be everywhere or work with everyone, they have enough resources to work with whom and where it matters most.

Properly done, focused strategies can enhance the perceived legitimacy or rightfulness of anti-violence efforts. Indiscriminate and overly punitive approaches to violence reduction have collateral costs that create community resistance, and understandably so. Residents for the most part tolerate, even encourage, aggressive law enforcement tactics when they are used against the most dangerous offenders, but they protest when such tactics are applied to all young men, regardless of their propensity for violence.

Overbroad strategies can also stigmatize the law-abiding residents of high-crime neighborhoods. Community members will rightfully object to inaccurate and unfair overgeneralizations that vilify entire groups or neighborhoods as violent. The principle of focus recognizes that, even in the most dangerous areas, the peaceful are many and the violent are few. This is essential to building and maintaining community support.

One potential concern with the principle of focus is the issue of displacement. What if focused efforts simply shift violence from one area to another without eliminating or reducing it? Targeted strategies will fail if crime simply moves down the block or around the corner. This phenomenon is often described as the "balloon effect," because squeezing on one part of a balloon causes another part to expand.

Fortunately, a robust body of evidence establishes that when hot people and places are targeted, displacement is generally minimal. When anti-crime efforts are focused, neighboring areas actually tend to benefit—a case of NIMBY-ism ("not in my backyard") in reverse. Urban violence is not entirely concentrated, of course, and while displacement is usually nominal, there can be some. There are natural limits to the strategies articulated in this book, but they nevertheless represent our best hope for saving lives in urban America. To be effective, we must be selective. We must be focused.[14]

HOW SHOULD THE fundamental principle of focus be put into practice? Criminologist Mark Kleiman has proposed a strategy he describes as "dynamic concentration." To deter crime most efficiently, law enforcement should concentrate resources, communicate clearly with potential offenders about the consequences of their actions, and use sanctions that are swift, certain, and fair—but not necessarily severe.[15]

As Kleiman observes, it is costlier to reduce crime than it is to keep it down once reduced. "[Activity that is] inadequate to suppress a riot is ample once the riot is under control," Kleiman reasons. "The challenge is to find, even temporarily, enough additional capacity to do the job."[16]

Kleiman proposes focusing law enforcement resources temporarily in order to deter criminal offending. "Start somewhere: with a geographic region, a set of offenses, or a set of offenders. Borrow existing capacity from other areas, offenses, or offenders to concentrate on the chosen target." Once a low-crime equilibrium is achieved, resources can be redeployed elsewhere. Step by step, target by target, goal by goal, safety can be increased incrementally without large increases in capacity or resources.[17]

There are limitations to this strategy, however. First, it works only if crime is concentrated and remains so; it doesn't work when it can be easily displaced. Second, it works only if, once targets become safe, they cannot easily revert back into trouble. We should also be mindful that dynamic concentration assumes that the targets have limited or no ability to coordinate or move their operations in order to frustrate the strategy. It works best on relatively disorganized criminal behavior; highly organized crime is not as amenable to this strategy.

That said, many of the nation's strongest anti-crime, anti-violence strategies apply elements of dynamic concentration effectively. Focused deterrence strategies, for instance, target high-risk offenders and offending groups. Hot spots policing deploys additional police patrols to those high-crime microlocations. Both approaches have been evaluated numerous times and generally achieve positive results.

THE DEADLIEST MURDER and mayhem sticks in and around discrete people, places, and things. These constellations of risk are surprisingly stable and durable over time. While the nation has become more peaceable in recent years, certain communities remain mired in unrelenting civil conflict, at war with themselves, with neighbor pitted against neighbor.

To cool these conflicts, we must take our communities back, not all at once but person by person, block by block. To change the nation, we must first transform our most dangerous and disadvantaged neighborhoods. And to do that, we must focus on the violent few, in places like the Mott Haven Houses, with people like Daniel Rice and Kevin Thomas.

CHAPTER 4

CARROT AND STICK

FOCUS IS A FUNDAMENTAL PRINCIPLE FOR COMBATING URBAN VIO-
lence. Another is balance, the notion that balancing prevention and
punishment works far better than either approach in isolation. In hot
spots and for hot people, we need a range of incentives that promote
positive associations and activities while deterring violence—there
must be both carrot and stick.

Both "Tough" and "Soft"

In his book *Uneasy Peace,* Patrick Sharkey empirically examined
the contribution that "community nonprofits" made in reducing crime
from 1990 to 2012. His findings were stunning: for a city with one
hundred thousand people, each new nonprofit led to a 1 percent
drop in the city's murder and violent crime rates. Sharkey concluded
that community organizations played a substantial role in explaining
the historic decline in violence across the United States. This is an
extremely important finding, as increases in incarceration also reduced
crime during the same period but came with significant collateral costs
for poor communities of color. Sharkey's work shows us that there

are tools available in the anti-violence toolbox that do less damage to communities than traditional "tough on crime" strategies.[1]

This is not to say that law enforcement strategies do not work—they can—but the point is that neither "tough" nor "soft" approaches to crime have a monopoly on effectiveness. In fact, no city that has been successful in reducing urban violence can credibly attribute all of its success to a single tough or soft approach—it is always some combination of both. Punishment by itself has not worked. Neither has prevention.

There is an important caveat, however. Consistent with the fundamental of focus, strategies that directly target violence, not surprisingly, have the largest effects. Many early-prevention programs measure their results in terms of fewer behavior problems and aggressive incidents. Some measure crime and delinquency more concretely, looking at arrests or referrals to juvenile court. A few even distinguish between violent and nonviolent arrests, but none measure urban violence as consistently or directly as enforcement-oriented efforts such as hot spots policing.

There are at least two reasons for this. First, prevention programs are not intended solely to prevent violence, and evaluators cannot track everything, so they choose more general measures. Second, to examine criminal justice outcomes, evaluators of prevention programs must follow young program participants all the way into adulthood—something that is prohibitively expensive for many of them to do.

In addition, results of direct efforts are typically measured geographically, while indirect efforts are often measured individually. This is important because geographic efforts impact more people, and with individual approaches, there is always the question of whether the right individuals were selected.

In other words, one must make certain assumptions in order to believe that prevention programs will significantly impact violence in a neighborhood or city. There are good reasons to believe that it does: there have been studies showing that individuals who engage in significant amounts of crime and violence over their lifetimes begin by behaving antisocially in childhood. That said, based on the evidence available to us today, believing that helping certain individuals as children will lead to less violence in neighborhoods as a whole requires a leap of faith, albeit a short one.[2]

The Second Fundamental: Balance

The second fundamental of effective anti-violence efforts is balance, that is, maintaining a roughly equal emphasis between prevention and punishment. With people, balance means two things: First, it means recognizing that people respond to both positive and negative incentives. To fully motivate them to move away from crime and violence, both rewards and punishments must be used. Second, it means working with potentially violent kids and youth in order to help them avoid arrest and incarceration as adults.

With places, balance means investing in violent hot spots to permanently alter their violent nature, as well as temporarily increasing targeted policing efforts. With behaviors, it means limiting aggressive law enforcement to only the most dangerous behaviors, such as the illegal carrying of firearms. Overenforcement might lead to more arrests and more time in jail and prison, but it will not necessarily result in less violence. In fact, recklessly aggressive policing and prosecution may actually increase violence.[3]

With dangerous people, in problem places, and around risky behaviors, there should be a range of incentives that push away from violence while pulling toward peace. This may seem obvious, but it doesn't often occur in practice. In fact, many cities overrely on enforcement. This is a missed opportunity, as balancing sanctions with rewards is a proven means of changing behavior. Recent research on rehabilitation confirms that the use of positive incentives is at least as important as punishment when it comes to reducing recidivism. While we may be most concerned with negative, antisocial activities like violence, ultimately the goal is the development of positive, pro-social habits and behaviors. Future and former offenders must learn what to do as well as what not to do. It is good to break a bad habit, but it is better to replace it with a good one.[4]

Balanced approaches combine a healthy mix of immediacy and sustainability, reactivity and proactivity. Crime prevention requires identifying risky people, places, and behaviors early on, then addressing those risks before they lead to crime and violence. By definition, these approaches focus on future offenses, not those happening right now. Working with at-risk children and youth before they become involved in violence is important, but by definition, it will do nothing to reduce the violence being perpetrated by young men and adults currently caught up in the cycle of deadly aggression. Enforcement-oriented strategies are necessary to address the crime and violence that is happening right now or has just happened.

On the other hand, law enforcement surges are not sustainable over time. They cost too much, but more importantly, they can result in mass arrests and incarceration that decimate poor communities of color. Such approaches also do little to head off potential future perpetrators from offending because they fail to address the deeper causes of violence. Prevention strategies are more cost-effective than enforcement-oriented strategies that address crime only after it has been committed. For this reason, enforcement can be used to create anti-violence momentum, but prevention strategies should be used to sustain initial success. "Look, I believe in policing, but for prevention and social change we need strategies outside of law enforcement," Lieutenant Jose Lopez from the Chicago Police Department told me. "Kids at a young age need programs before they get drawn into a life of violence."[5]

Balanced approaches are also usually perceived as more legitimate than one-or-the-other strategies. Punishment-oriented approaches appeal to those who trust authority and demand accountability for criminal acts. Prevention-oriented ones appeal to those who are suspicious of authority and believe criminality is created by root causes. To bring a whole community together, both approaches are necessary.

Prevention can also build moral authority for punishment. In poor African American and Latino communities, many residents understandably see their young men as massively undersupported and overpunished. This leads them to reject any additional law enforcement efforts as unfair and illegitimate. Jury nullification, in which jurors ignore evidence of guilt due to a belief that the entire criminal justice system is unjust, is one example of this. Providing potential offenders with support and assistance makes them more morally accountable in the eyes of the community if their violent behavior persists. When residents see that help was offered first and that punishment was employed only as a last resort, they are more likely to support law enforcement efforts to protect the community from persistent perpetrators.

This raises an important political and practical question. Both within poor urban communities and beyond them, many doubt that the principles of balance and focus can be employed simultaneously. These skeptics believe that focusing attention and resources on high-risk places and people will always lead to an unbalanced, enforcement-oriented, overly punitive strategy—the kind of strategy that threatens to tear communities further apart.

Fortunately, we have strong evidence that says otherwise. In fact, the fundamental principles of focus and balance complement one another, as demonstrated in two recent pieces of scholarship by David Weisburd. Weisburd, along with fellow criminologist Cody Telep, conducted a systematic review of all policing strategies and came to three fundamental conclusions. First, policing is most effective when focused on high-activity places and people. Second, proactive problem-solving should be emphasized—in other words, law enforcement should move beyond reactive approaches to address underlying crime conditions. Third, relying on arrests and incarceration alone should be avoided. While arrests are an important tool, police have been found to be more effective when they also employ nonenforcement strategies supported by partners outside of the criminal justice system.[6]

In another study, Weisburd and several colleagues found that both
punishment and prevention strategies can be more effective and less
costly if they focus on the "micro level" instead of on larger communities or neighborhoods. Examining Seattle's approximately twenty-
four thousand city blocks over a sixteen-year period, Weisburd found
that just 1 percent of city blocks accounted for 23 percent of all crime
(while Weisburd did not examine serious violence specifically, as we've
seen, serious violence concentrates even more than crime generally).
Next, he overlaid crime statistics with as many variables as possible,
including demographic, housing, employment, and voter participation data.[7]

What Weisburd and his colleagues found was striking: the social
data varied block by block as much as the crime data, with a few variables highly associated with chronic crime hot spots. Physical disorder
(litter, graffiti, overgrown weeds, inoperable cars on the street, and so
on) made a block twenty-five times more likely to be a chronic crime
hot spot. The presence of more employees and residents increased the
likelihood of crime by increasing the number of potential offenders
and victims. Being located on a major throughway made a block ten
times more likely to be a hot spot—and with each additional bus stop,
the probability doubled.

Policing and prevention programs are often delivered to entire
communities, but Weisburd and others argued that geographically
targeting these programs to hot spots could increase their success.
In addition to working less and costing more, Weisburd and his colleagues argued that community- or neighborhood-level approaches
might be "unnecessarily stigmatizing" to allegedly crime-prone communities. "If crime is found on just a small number of streets in a
neighborhood, it is misleading to label the whole area as a crime problem," they said, implicitly raising issues related to the perceived legitimacy of such efforts.[8]

The findings from Weisburd's first study confirmed what other
reviews had demonstrated: underfocused, overaggressive policing
does not work. Weisburd's second study broke new ground,

however, in suggesting that the same could be true for social programs, at least when reducing crime and violence is the goal. Rather than spreading scarce resources evenly across entire communities, narrowing the focus to provide higher doses in even smaller areas is likely to be more effective, and this is as true for prevention as it is for punishment. Focus and balance are complements when it comes to violence reduction; they cannot be substituted for one another. In terms of guiding policy, it should be both-and, not either-or, when it comes to putting anti-violence principles into action. Domestic affairs, like foreign affairs, require a balance of hard and soft power. To be effective, we must not only be focused; we must also be balanced.

Let's revisit Kleiman's concept of dynamic concentration in relation to the second fundamental of balance. As we learned, focused deterrence and hot spots policing both successfully apply the principles of dynamic concentration. That said, the initially impressive results of these efforts sometimes fade over time. When focused deterrence offers options to would-be shooters, it tends to work. When it promises only punishment, it tends not to. With hot spots policing, officers sometimes stop patrolling hot areas once they cool down, allowing crime and violence to creep back in.

In recognition of this reality, Kleiman's thesis should be modified. It is true that concentrating resources can turn dangerous targets into peaceful ones and that, once turned, fewer resources are required to keep the peace. That said, sustainability requires that some additional resources remain in place. In addition, dynamic concentration was originally concerned with amassing enforcement and deterrence capability, but resources must also be devoted to prevention. As originally described, dynamic concentration is all about the fundamental principle of focus. To sustain its success, it must incorporate the principle of balance as well.

VIOLENT PEOPLE AND places respond to both positive and negative incentives. Violence can be reduced using preventative and punitive approaches. Choosing one approach over the other runs contrary to the research and risks, fracturing the coalitions that are vital to sustainably stopping violence. As a matter of evidence and politics, then, policy makers need both tough and soft approaches. To be successful in reducing urban violence, we must be balanced as well as focused.

CHAPTER 5

NO JUSTICE, NO PEACE

ON AUGUST 9, 2014, AT 12:02 P.M., DARREN WILSON KILLED MICHAEL Brown. It happened in broad daylight, next to the Canfield Green apartments on a hot day in Ferguson, Missouri. Darren Wilson was a police officer with the Ferguson Police Department, armed with a SIG Sauer .40 S&W semiautomatic pistol. Michael Brown was an unarmed high school graduate, about to start a training program for heating and air conditioning repair.

According to the US Department of Justice, minutes before he met Wilson, Brown had taken several packages of cigars from a nearby convenience store. A toxicology report later showed that he was high on marijuana at the time. A police radio call went out, which Wilson heard as he saw Brown and a friend walking down the middle of Canfield Drive. Wilson passed the pair in his SUV, told them to get on the sidewalk, then stopped his vehicle at an angle ahead of them, blocking their path.

Wilson opened his door to get out, but it hit Brown. Brown reached through Wilson's open window and started to punch him repeatedly. Wilson reached for his weapon. So did Brown. While the two struggled over the gun, it went off, hitting Brown in the hand. Brown ran down the street with Wilson in pursuit. After a short chase, Brown turned and, for some reason, started back toward Wilson. Wilson fired: once, twice, ten times. Brown fell to the ground, dead.

Brown's killing was a tragedy, but was it a crime? Official accounts indicated it was not. The US Department of Justice, headed at the time by an attorney general widely credited with revitalizing civil rights investigations, conducted an exhaustive investigation of the incident. The department found no credible evidence indicating that Brown was shot in the back or that he had raised his arms in the "hands up, don't shoot" position, as many alleged. The department concluded that Brown had gone for Wilson's gun once, and so when he came at Wilson again, it was not unreasonable for Wilson to assume that there might be another struggle for his weapon. Brown was bigger and stronger than Wilson, who might reasonably believe that if there was a struggle, he would lose. Under the law, such circumstances could constitute a risk of "serious physical harm"—the Supreme Court's standard for the use of deadly police force. A Ferguson County grand jury investigated and came to the same conclusion. No charges—federal, state, or local—were brought by the authorities. Officially, no crime was committed.[1]

And yet Ferguson went up in flames, both literally and figuratively. Understanding why requires recognizing that the real story of Ferguson does not begin or end with what happened on August 9. It requires understanding the events leading up to and following that terrible encounter, because that context is essential in explaining why so many took to the streets to express their outrage and demand justice.

Months after Brown's death and the turmoil that followed, the Justice Department's official report was released to the public. That same day, a second report was released, surprising many. While the first report found Darren Wilson not criminally responsible for Michael Brown's death, the second was a scathing indictment of Ferguson's entire justice system.[2]

In its investigation, the Justice Department uncovered a system driven not by the pursuit of justice but instead by intense financial pressure. In March 2013, Jeffrey Blume, Ferguson's finance director, emailed John Shaw, its city manager. "Court fees are anticipated to rise about 7.5%," he wrote. "I did ask the Chief if he thought the PD could deliver a 10% increase. He indicated they could try." Demands like these—and there were many—formed a steady drumbeat for revenue that came directly from Ferguson's city management. These requests turned into informal directives that were passed through police ranks. Officers at all levels told investigators that the pressure was unrelenting. The constant need for more revenue resulted in a pattern of unconstitutional stops, citations, arrests, and use of force that disproportionately impacted the city's most disadvantaged residents, who were both poor and black.[3]

African Americans made up 67 percent of Ferguson's population but accounted for 90 percent of police citations. Over the span of two years, Ferguson's police department handed out four or more citations to a black individual seventy-three times, while only two individuals of other races received four or more citations. When the police used force, it was against African Americans 90 percent of the time, and when dogs were deployed that figure increased to 100 percent. In one case, police sicced a dog on a fourteen-year-old black boy who had allegedly refused to show his hands when confronted. He was bitten multiple times. The boy, who disputed the police's story, was unarmed and weighed 140 pounds. His offense: trespassing in an abandoned building.[4]

Ferguson's courts, rather than serving as a check on police practices, acted in concert with them to secure still more revenue for the city. The courts' primary interest was not doing justice but compelling payment. In 2013, the courts issued over nine thousand arrest warrants for missed payments and appearances, and, adding insult to injury, they imposed their own financial penalties as well. For Ferguson's poorest residents, minor offenses soon morphed into crippling debts, resulting in lost licenses, jobs, and housing, and even jail time. In one case, an African American woman illegally parked her car and received two citations along with a fine for $151. The woman, poor and occasionally homeless, struggled to pay. Over the next seven years, she was charged seven times for failure to pay and to appear, spent six days in jail, was arrested twice, and paid $550, all because she parked illegally once.[5]

The cumulative impact of these patterns, practices, and prejudices was devastating to the community, and it deepened long-standing mistrust of the police among Ferguson's African American population. In one instance, police responded to a report of a domestic disturbance but, once on the scene, issued a ticket for an occupancy violation. After that, the woman who had called told the responding officers that she "hated the Ferguson Police Department and will never call again, even if she is being killed." As the Justice Department observed, "As a consequence of these practices, law enforcement is seen as illegitimate, and the partnerships necessary for public safety are, in some areas, entirely absent."[6]

The unfair and illegal behavior of the authorities in Ferguson transformed its African American neighborhoods into tinderboxes. Against this backdrop, it seems obvious why Michael Brown's death sparked outrage among those living in the Canfield Green apartments. But what happened immediately after Wilson killed Brown fanned the flames further, turning what might have stayed a local matter into a national spectacle.

After he was killed, Brown's lifeless body lay in the street, face-down, in plain view for neighbors, friends, and relatives to see. Ninety minutes passed before his body was fully covered, and no less than four hours elapsed before it was finally removed from the location. The delay, a violation of standard police practice, both traumatized and infuriated those gathered at the scene.[7]

As unrest grew, local authorities refused to communicate with the protesters, media, and the public at large. Instead, they swiftly amassed an arsenal of military-grade weaponry, but without the necessary coordination and controls. Armored vehicles and snipers were deployed without clear justification. Tear gas was used without proper warnings or precautions. Dogs were used for crowd control in violation of standard police practice, producing images that hearkened back to the brutal repression of civil rights protesters in the 1960s.

Some officers acted inappropriately, even illegally, in other ways. One officer was captured on video yelling, "Bring it, you fucking animals, bring it." Another threatened demonstrators, pointing his semiautomatic rifle at them and shouting, "I will fucking kill you." Officers also made dozens of unnecessary, arbitrary, and unconstitutional arrests of activists and journalists.[8]

At every stage, the response from law enforcement undermined public confidence and stoked further resentment and rage. An after-action assessment conducted by the Justice Department's Office of Community Oriented Policing Services criticized Ferguson's responding agencies, finding that their militaristic response needlessly antagonized demonstrators. Leading public officials also expressed concern. "Those lawful, peaceful protesters did not deserve to be treated like enemy combatants," stated Missouri senator Claire McCaskill. President Barack Obama agreed: "There's . . . no excuse for police to use excessive force against peaceful protests, or to throw protestors in jail for lawfully exercising their First Amendment rights."[9]

Ferguson went viral. Social media was a key conduit of information about the original incident and the unrest that followed, shaping the local, national, and even international narratives. In the first five days following Michael Brown's death, Twitter users posted 3,648,032 tweets using the #Ferguson hashtag. On Facebook, a single page devoted to Ferguson received more than 117,000 "likes." In the mainstream media, Ferguson was easily the number one crime-related story in 2014, earning as much coverage in less than five months as the next four biggest stories combined. To many, Ferguson became a symbol for everything that they believed was wrong with the American criminal justice system: racial profiling, excessive and lethal use of force, and mass incarceration, among other issues.[10]

During the protests and their aftermath, there were alarming reports of increased crime and violence in Ferguson and neighboring St. Louis. From 2014 to 2015, violent crime in Ferguson surged

65 percent, with homicides increasing 150 percent. In the St. Louis metropolitan area, violent crime and homicide rose 8 percent and 18 percent, respectively. Tragically and ironically, the deadliest violence during the Ferguson unrest victimized not protesters or police but community members.[11]

Soon other cities saw similar spikes in violence after highly publicized incidents of police misconduct. A deadly pattern began to emerge: police violence begat community violence, with protests and publicity in between. On April 19, 2015, in Baltimore, a young African American man named Freddie Gray died in police custody. Protests began peacefully but then turned violent, resulting in rioting, looting, arrests, injuries, and destroyed property. As in Ferguson, the Department of Justice investigated the Baltimore Police Department, with similarly damning results. Investigators found a pattern and practice of unconstitutional stops, searches, and arrests, as well as excessive use of force. Violence skyrocketed in months that followed the riots, resulting in Baltimore's deadliest year on record at the time, with nonfatal shootings up 72 percent from the previous year and homicides up 63 percent.[12]

On November 24, 2015, demonstrations erupted in Chicago after the release of a previously suppressed video of a police officer fatally shooting Laquan McDonald, another young African American man. Yet again, the Justice Department investigation that followed found a pattern and practice of unreasonable police force in Chicago. The responsible officer was charged with (and ultimately convicted of) second-degree murder, the police superintendent was fired, but protests continued for months. In January 2015, homicides and shootings in Chicago began to soar. More than one hundred people were shot in the first ten days of the year. In 2016, nonfatal shootings increased 43 percent from the previous year, with homicides surging 58 percent.[13]

During the unrest in Ferguson, St. Louis police chief Sam Dotson gave an explanation for the recent spike in violence in his area. "It's the Ferguson effect," he said. "I see it not only on the law enforcement side, but the criminal element is feeling empowered by the environment." Dotson believed that in St. Louis, where crime was rising as arrests were falling, emboldened criminals were overcoming exhausted police. He called for more officers and resources: "If this is the new norm, the police department is not rightly sized," he said. "If these are the types of crime we're going to experience, we need a larger department."[14]

Conservative pundits and politicians seized on Dotson's words but made a somewhat different case. "The most plausible explanation of the current surge in lawlessness is the intense agitation against American police departments," argued commentator Heather Mac Donald. "This incessant drumbeat against the police has resulted in [their] disengaging from discretionary enforcement activity and . . . second-guess[ing] themselves about the use of force." Milwaukee County sheriff David Clarke testified before Congress, stating, "The constant bashing and maligning of the profession is starting to take its toll," with police officers refusing to "take that extra step" to do "self-initiated policing." During his presidential campaign, then-candidate Donald Trump called police "the most mistreated people in our country" and made defending them a central component of his platform.[15]

Progressives pushed back, accusing conservatives of fearmongering. The Center for American Progress labeled the so-called Ferguson effect a "myth," and the Brennan Center for Justice deemed it "simply wrong." Many in the media disputed the conservative case, but it was the *Atlantic*'s David Graham who did so most evocatively, writing, "The Ferguson Effect is the Bigfoot of American criminal justice: fervently believed to be real by some, doubted by many others, reportedly glimpsed here and there, but never yet attested to by any hard evidence." Liberals asserted that spikes in violent crime were isolated and, even if they weren't, root causes like poverty and unemployment were responsible, not demoralized police. A national debate on policing, protesting, crime, and violence had begun.[16]

As conservatives and progressives argued, a new explanation began to emerge. A few experts and academics, myself included, suggested there might be a "Ferguson effect" that caused crime and violence to spike, but not in the way conservatives claimed. Perhaps it was less about protesters and police and more about the communities they fought over. One thing was certain: as the two sides battled, it was neither police nor protesters who were dying; it was those in the neighborhoods themselves.[17]

Today we face a crisis of confidence in the nation's criminal justice system that is literally killing poor people of color. To meet this national moment, we must better understand the relationship between government and the governed, particularly between criminal justice institutions and the communities they serve. This is our best chance for understanding what went on in Ferguson and what has happened since.

No Justice, No Peace

Albert Einstein once said, "Peace is not merely the absence of war but the presence of justice." Over time, the statement has been repeated and rephrased, perhaps most famously by Martin Luther King Jr., who said, "True peace is not the absence of tension; it is the presence of justice." Protesters around the country echo this refrain when they shout, "No justice, no peace!"[18]

As quoted, Einstein's statement is clean and concise, but it also happens to be incomplete. Words frequently omitted from the statement make its original meaning clear: "Peace is not merely the absence of war but the presence of justice, *of law, of order—in short, of government*" (italics mine). Einstein was not making an abstract argument; instead, he was offering a concrete observation about the relationship between a government and its people. In short, he was talking about legitimacy. Without legitimacy there can be no guarantee of safety; with injustice comes the threat of violence.

What is legitimacy? According to one legal theorist, "Legitimacy is the recognition of the right to govern . . . justifying simultaneously political power and obedience." When an authority is seen as legitimate, people obey it voluntarily without being threatened or coerced. Beyond broad definitions like these, scholars differ in their descriptions of legitimacy, but there is an emerging consensus that it cannot be just one thing. According to political theorist David Beetham, "The key to . . . legitimacy lies in the recognition that it is multi-dimensional in character." Beyond this there is little agreement, and so for simplicity's sake I will consolidate the various descriptions of the phenomenon into two broad categories: legitimacy as effectiveness, and legitimacy as fairness.[19]

Effectiveness is judged by whether the primary purpose of the law—maintaining public safety and order—is achieved. A government's authority will not be respected if it cannot safeguard its citizens, especially so for those who live in neighborhoods where crime and violence are prevalent. Legitimacy therefore depends on effectively using the law to keep people safe from harm.

Fairness concerns both the letter and spirit of the law, in that true fairness requires the laws to be as trustworthy on the street as they are on the page. Fairness is both formal and informal; it relates to both processes and results. Laws are justified when they are created according to accepted constitutional and democratic processes. In addition, the impact of those laws should be felt equally across social groups. Importantly, laws must also be enforced according to widely accepted values, including transparency, impartiality, proportionality, and equality, among others. Laws must be fair as applied, not just as written.

While somewhat reductive, these simple notions of effectiveness and fairness are helpful to those who want to understand how legitimacy works in the real world. During my time working as a prosecutor in New York City, it was always clear that while what we did was important, *how* we did it was important as well, and that the two were connected. Convictions of criminals were legitimate only if we played by the rules. Moreover, it wasn't just about the end result—guilty or not guilty—it was also about the process that gave everyone involved a sense of whether justice had been done. The same is true for police, judges, corrections officers, and others—it's not just what you do but how you do it that matters.

Criminal justice officials cannot be fully legitimate unless they effectively address violence, crime, and disorder, follow the law themselves, and apply the law in a manner that is perceived to be fair. Each element is necessary but, on its own, insufficient. In the real world, individuals and institutions often fall short, acting legitimately in some ways but not others. "Lawful but awful" police shootings may be condoned by the courts but condemned by the community. "Zero-tolerance" policing might control crime in the short run but create racial disparities in stops, searches, and arrests. Community-based programming may generate goodwill but fail to keep the public safe. As Beetham recognized, "All [elements] contribute to legitimacy, though the extent to which they are realized in a given context will be a matter of degree. Legitimacy is not an all-or-nothing affair. [It] may be eroded, contested, or incomplete." Perfect justice may be unattainable, but reaching a reasonable measure of justice requires both fairness and effectiveness.[20]

On the streets of our cities, illegitimacy and violence are intimately associated with one another. The most brutal and controversial uses of police force frequently occur in our most violent communities. In these neighborhoods, we will see how a concept called legal cynicism plays out in deadly practice.

The Crisis of Community Cynicism

When officials abuse their authority, trust is undermined, especially in the communities that need them the most. Misconduct by a single officer is often imputed, appropriately or not, to a whole agency, or even to police in general. One rogue prosecutor can ruin the reputation of an office or stain the whole profession. Repeated patterns of misconduct cause even deeper damage. Unless addressed swiftly, official misconduct can poison the well of goodwill toward authority.

As Charlie Beck, former chief of the Los Angeles Police Department, told myself and others when we visited his department in 2017, "One bad apple can lose you the moral high ground."

Research indicates that high-profile instances of misconduct as well as everyday interactions contribute to what criminologists call "legal cynicism." Legal cynicism is defined as a "deep-seated belief in the incompetence, illegitimacy, and unresponsiveness of the criminal justice system [that] is thought to pervade many poor, minority communities." When people see law enforcement as unwilling or unable to help them, they withdraw from it, refusing to report crime, testify in court, or serve as impartial jurors.[21]

Until recently, most of what we knew about legal cynicism was based on interviews and surveys, not actual behavior. Studies measured how people answered questions, not what they did in real life. In 2016, our understanding of this issue took a step forward when sociologists Matthew Desmond, Andrew Papachristos, and David Kirk analyzed how police violence in Milwaukee impacted one of the most basic ways that communities engage with authority: by calling for help.[22]

On October 23, 2004, Frank Jude went to a house party hosted by a group of Milwaukee police officers. Jude was black; the officers were white. Almost immediately, he felt uncomfortable and decided to leave. Outside, Jude was confronted by officers who accused him of stealing. He was brutally attacked, first by nonuniformed officers from the party, then by uniformed police responding to the incident. Later, at a local hospital, his injuries were documented: a concussion, a broken nose, extensive cuts and bruises, impaired vision, and a possibly permanent disability in one hand.

What happened next? Nothing, at least until the *Milwaukee Journal Sentinel* exposed the incident in an explosive front-page story that detailed Jude's assault, his injuries, and police unwillingness to investigate and arrest their own. Protesters took to the streets demanding justice and the press covered the clamor for accountability. Eventually, charges were brought and, after an acquittal in local criminal court, seven of the eight officers involved were finally convicted of federal civil rights offenses.

For Desmond and his colleagues, the Jude case presented an opportunity to study illegitimacy in action. They collected and analyzed all of Milwaukee's 911 calls over a seven-year period: more than one million calls in total. They found that once the assault of Jude became public, 911 calls dropped by 17 percent, or about twenty-two thousand calls, for approximately a year. The results "kind of blew us away," Desmond said. "We weren't expecting to see such a big effect and an effect to last so long." When the public learned of misconduct, they called 911 less frequently. Not only did calls to police decline, but in the six months following the publication of Jude's story, Milwaukee suffered eighty-seven homicides—32 percent more than the same period in previous and subsequent years. The spring and summer after Jude's assault were the deadliest in the seven years covered by the study.[23]

Race was central to these findings. Most of the decline in 911 calls came from African American neighborhoods, and the effect was most durable there. While calls initially declined in all Milwaukee neighborhoods, calls in white communities bounced back quickly. Desmond and his colleagues argued that police brutality activated the "collective memory" of black people, meaning that recent abuses could be linked to a racially violent heritage that includes slavery, lynching, rioting, and other forms of racial oppression. Significantly, the decline in 911 calls was specific to crime reporting—calls for emergency assistance and other requests for service were unaffected.

The media mattered as well, both for raising awareness of police violence and for framing responses to it. Professional reporters made a difference, but citizen journalists who captured incidents on video and distributed them via social media had an even greater impact. Without them, news of these incidents might spread only by word of mouth and fail to reach a broader audience. Desmond and his colleagues also looked at instances of excessive police force in other cities and found that, with the assistance of traditional and social media, individual acts of police aggression could reverberate far beyond the neighborhood or city where the incident occurred.

Later, when discussing the study, Desmond commented that what happened in Milwaukee had "implications for what we're seeing in Cleveland, in Charlotte, in Baltimore, with very publicized cases of police violence. . . . I think that probably has a lot to do with the story." But it's not just violent abuse that produces cynicism. Mundane, everyday instances of unfairness also deplete reservoirs of trust, confidence, and goodwill. It doesn't take much—even a single instance of rude or poor treatment can seriously damage perceptions of legitimacy, beginning a chain reaction of disapproval and disengagement.[24]

If left unaddressed, cynicism can metastasize, encouraging refusal to provide the police with vital information. In 2004, a DVD entitled *Stop Snitching* circulated widely, partly because it included a brief appearance by basketball star Carmelo Anthony. Set in Baltimore, the DVD featured alleged drug dealers threatening informants and warning viewers against snitching. The ensuing press coverage introduced mainstream America to a culture of silence and intimidation that had been familiar to residents of high-crime communities for years.

When I asked Colonel Byron Conaway of the Baltimore police about this, he said, "Baltimore has this no-snitching policy. People want to handle things themselves. We have instances where we'll have a shooting and the victim will tell you straight up, I'm going to handle this myself, and then won't say anything else. The trust between the community and the police is broken." Deputy Chief Phillip Tingirides remembers difficult days when he first worked in Watts, Los Angeles. "I remember a homicide outside a party: guy walks through a crowd, shoots somebody in the head, then walks out. We get there and nobody saw anything," he told me. "The dysfunction between the police department and the community gave the gangs all the power in the world. We had literally zero legitimacy."

When illegitimacy encourages communities not to cooperate with the authorities, violence follows. Legal cynicism prompts residents to turn away from law enforcement and revert to self-rule via the "code of the street," an informal, brutal system based on respect and pay-back. In another landmark study, David Kirk and Andrew Papachris-tos focused on legal cynicism and its relationship to violent crime in Chicago.[25]

Kirk and Papachristos believed that legal cynicism could help explain why homicide rates varied among poor Chicago neighbor-hoods, where some viewed the police as more of a burden than a ben-efit. For those residents, self-reliance became necessary when dealing with potentially violent interpersonal conflicts. This was not the case for everyone in the community, but it was true for those most likely to commit violence.

Examining survey data from 343 neighborhood tracts of approx-imately eight thousand residents, Kirk and Papachristos compared residents' views related to legal cynicism with homicide rates. Further-more, they used data from the US census to control for complicating factors and found neighborhoods reporting high levels of legal cyni-cism had significantly higher homicide rates than those that viewed authority more favorably. In fact, legal cynicism was more closely cor-related with violence than poverty, inequality, or unemployment.

Residents of rough neighborhoods do not celebrate violence, but some do see themselves as having little choice but to embrace it for the purposes of self-preservation. In neighborhoods where cyni-cism runs high, if somebody beats up your cousin, you don't call the police; you reach out to friends and family to "handle your business." This is precisely what Colonel Conaway was referring to. In a related study, Papachristos and others analyzed an unusual survey of more than one hundred active gun offenders in Chicago and found decid-edly more negative views of the police among the offenders than among the public at large. They also found that among the offenders themselves, less favorable views of the police were associated with an increased likelihood that the offenders would carry a gun.[26]

Other studies have documented the link among legal cynicism, crime, and violence. One study found that young black men in New York City who had negative attitudes about the police were twice as likely to engage in criminal activity. Another analysis documented the same correlation between violence and cynicism in Chicago's poorest neighborhoods. Two scholars, looking to history, attributed the rising homicide rates of the 1960s and 1970s to the declining legitimacy of US institutions. To be sure, the study of legitimacy is plagued by the usual scientific challenges: inconsistent definitions, measurement problems, and the often-futile search for causality. That said, the association between legitimacy and urban violence seems well established, having been documented numerous times, in numerous contexts, and according to numerous methodologies.[27]

It is not only misconduct and misbehavior that diminishes legitimacy and drives cynicism. It is also the failure to effectively control crime and, most importantly, protect people from violence. While the country overall has enjoyed dramatic reductions in crime and violence over the past twenty-five years, high rates of crime and violence persist in many poor urban African American and Latino communities, isolating them from the rest of society. Residents of these neighborhoods can see the rest of society living in relative peace and tranquility, leading to a deep cynicism about how "the system" views and values people like them.

I have been to many community meetings where residents complain bitterly about the lack of public resources devoted to protecting them from harm. "They've got money to go to Iraq and Afghanistan—what about us right here in America?" they ask. People living in these neighborhoods know that the violence plaguing their communities kills thousands more than terrorism yet receives a fraction of the resources and attention. To them, the inescapable conclusion is that if society really wanted to stop the violence, it would, but it simply chooses not to because the victims of urban violence are somehow less important or worthy.

This raises an important misconception about people living in communities of concentrated poverty. While many well-meaning liberals who do not live in these communities worry about overpolicing and overcriminalization, community residents complain equally frequently about underpolicing and a lack of commitment to solving serious crime. Even Michelle Alexander, a leading critic of mass incarceration, acknowledges that "African Americans in ghetto communities experience an intense 'dual frustration' regarding crime and law enforcement."[28]

Not only does violence run especially high in such neighborhoods; clearance rates for violent crime run especially low. "Clearing" a case generally means arresting and charging an individual or group of individuals with a crime. In 2017, the national homicide clearance rate was 62 percent. This means that almost four out of ten perpetrators are literally getting away with murder. In cities like St. Louis, Baltimore, and Chicago, clearance rates are much lower, and lower still for the murders of young black and brown men.[29]

Information is the lifeblood of law enforcement. Unless a crime is committed in front of an officer or caught on video, authorities need information from the community in order to build cases and bring them to court. This is especially true for homicides, which leave no victims alive to tell their own stories. One criminologist has shown that whether information is provided by community members is highly predictive of whether a homicide case will ultimately be cleared. The "stop snitching" ethos that follows from legal cynicism perpetuates itself by preventing criminals who victimize communities from being brought to justice. This issue will be examined in more detail in the next chapter.[30]

Legitimacy deficits create a catch-22: to improve safety, there must be trust, but to improve trust, there must be safety. As the Justice Department noted in its review of the Chicago Police Department, "This breach in trust has ... eroded CPD's ability to effectively prevent crime; in other words, trust and effectiveness in combating violent crime are inextricably intertwined."[31]

The Perils of Police Cynicism

Legal cynicism is present not only within communities but among police, too, and with the same troubling potential for violence. While considerably less studied, it is clear that cynicism exists among many in law enforcement and that it likely impacts their performance in problematic ways.

There are many reasons why police might become cynical. Police know better than most that with regard to urban violence, today's victim is often tomorrow's perpetrator. As Colonel Conaway explained, "Officers who go from murder scene to scene, year after year, they get desensitized, and especially when they see people they've arrested before. When you respond to the homicide of someone who has been a thorn in your butt for ten years, it's a different reaction."

Just like residents of poor communities afflicted by violence, police officers are deeply discouraged by the ineffectiveness they witness inside the criminal justice system. Many see the system as a revolving door where criminals rarely receive real punishment. They also see a system starved for resources, not just for their own work but also for the work of teachers, social workers, health providers, and others dedicated to helping the poor. Officers receive the same message from society that residents do: that people in poor communities are not valued, and, by association, neither is their work with such people.

Police officers also feel misunderstood and mistreated—subject to arbitrary discipline from within their departments and exposed to criticism and abuse from without—and these feelings have only worsened since Ferguson. In 2017, the Pew Research Center surveyed a nationally representative sample of nearly eight thousand police officers concerning their attitudes and experiences. The results were striking. Owing to recent high-profile incidents between police and African Americans, 86 percent said their job was more difficult, and 93 percent were more concerned about their safety. Furthermore, 92 percent believed that those protesting and criticizing law enforcement were motivated largely or in part by anti-police bias.[32]

A majority of police officers also reported that they had also grown more callous during their time on the job. Disturbingly, officers who reported becoming more callous were also more likely to endorse aggressive and harsh tactics, to have been involved recently in a physical or verbal confrontation with a citizen, and to have fired their service weapon. Callousness, as measured by the Pew survey, appears to be the bridge between police cynicism and violence.

When officers succumb to cynicism, they are likely to engage in their own form of street justice, dispensing informal punishments in lieu of formal sanctions. These sanctions can be relatively modest—making someone wait longer than necessary to receive a traffic ticket—or much more severe—dispensing a brutal beating. This is certainly not the case for the vast majority of officers, but a few abusive cops can define a department, or even the entire profession, in the age of camera phones and social media.

As a young prosecutor in the 2000s, I felt this cynicism myself. I was personally responsible for prosecuting dozens of felonies and hundreds of misdemeanors, and it seemed impossible to see justice done in every case. Colleagues on both sides of the bar—prosecutors and defense attorneys—felt the same way. The crushing caseloads, poor working conditions, and low salaries all signaled society's collective unconcern about poor victims and perpetrators. Some colleagues would give in, passing on their perceived poor treatment to those they worked with, including victims, witnesses, opposing counsel, and even colleagues. And I witnessed all this from inside the Manhattan District Attorney's Office, one of the best-regarded and best-funded prosecuting offices in the nation.

When officials abuse their authority, community members lose confidence. When violence runs rampant, trust is undermined. Illegitimacy breeds cynicism among cops and communities alike, leading to violent street justice. When hope and reason fail us, we fall back on force.

Turning Vicious Cycles into Virtuous Circles

Social control is a term used by sociologists to describe the norms, customs, traditions, values, rules, laws, and structures that preserve social order. Formal social control is exercised by the state via the justice system to compel compliance with laws, regulations, and other rules.

Informal social control is exercised by the community, which applies social pressure to maintain shared norms. Generally speaking, people obey laws because they believe they must; they conform to norms because they feel they should.

The vast majority of social control is informal in nature. Overwhelmingly, people do not rob or steal even when they might get away with it. They refrain because they have internalized social norms, fear the disapproval of others who have internalized them, or both. The famous urbanist Jane Jacobs described informal social control in this way: "The first thing to understand is that the public peace—the sidewalk and street peace—of cities is not kept primarily by the police, necessary as the police are. It is kept primarily by an intricate, almost unconscious, network of voluntary controls and standards among the people themselves, and enforced by the people themselves."[33]

Legitimacy plays a key role in the interplay between formal and informal social control. When formal control is exercised legitimately, informal control is strengthened, lessening the need for further formal control. If police exercise their authority legitimately, they strengthen the community's capacity to police itself. Conversely, when the police act illegitimately, they create cynicism that reduces compliance and increases crime, thus creating the need for more compulsion. These patterns repeat themselves either positively or negatively, resulting in virtuous circles of peace or vicious cycles of violence.[34]

The law is most powerful when self-executing and self-perpetuating. It works best when citizens, not police, regulate their community's conduct. In a sense, if the law must be enforced, it has already lost. The brute force of formal social control is expensive: it requires funding for the police, court, and prison systems, and there are other costs—lost jobs and wages, fines and fees, and the separation of parents and their children, to name a few—faced by offenders, their families, and the community at large.

Formal control is largely reactive, acting after a crime has been committed. Informal social control is mostly proactive, preventing crime before it happens. Informed control works more efficiently than formal control. A healthy justice system minimizes the need for brute force by building and maintaining legitimacy within communities, especially those communities most at risk for crime and violence. It pays for government to promote virtuous circles and prevent vicious ones. The Enlightenment-era thinker Cesare Beccaria recognized this dynamic centuries ago: "To the extent that human spirits are made gentle by the social state, sensibility increases; as it increases, the severity of punishment must diminish."[35]

The Ferguson Effect Redux

The debate over Ferguson and the alleged Ferguson effect debate is now about five years old. Conservatives accused protesters of creating a climate that made policing impossible and caused violence to spike. Progressives countered with accusations of fearmongering. Who was right?

The rise in violence, unfortunately, was quite real. From 2014 to 2016, in the cities of Ferguson, St. Louis, Baltimore, and Chicago, homicide rose by 350 percent, 18 percent, 51 percent, and 84 percent, respectively. Even more disturbingly, homicide increased nationally by a shocking 21.8 percent. These increases were not, as some progressives claimed at the time, limited to just a few cities—murder rose in more than half of the nation's largest cities over those two years. That said, conservative claims of "American carnage" or a "new nationwide crime wave" were overblown. Even with the increases, violent crime and murder rates remained near historic lows for the vast majority of Americans, and property crime rates remained stable.[36]

What caused violence crime and homicide to surge? The conservative case for an alleged Ferguson effect turned out to be flawed. Yes, violence erupted as arrests plummeted in Ferguson, St. Louis, Baltimore, and Chicago, but this was not the case across the country. A new authoritative analysis from criminologists Richard Rosenfeld and Joel Wallman established that there is little hard evidence to support the conservative "de-policing" hypothesis nationally. That version of the

Ferguson effect, if it exists, appears to be highly localized, occurring in a few cities but not most. In other words, there was likely a Freddie Gray effect, and possibly a Laquan McDonald effect, but not a national Ferguson effect in the sense claimed by conservatives.[37]

At the same time, progressives were mistaken when they asserted that the rise in violence was nonexistent, random, or due to root causes such as poverty, inequality, or lack of opportunity. Whatever caused the spike should have increased at about the same time as the violence or just beforehand, but there is no evidence of any changes in those factors—if anything, the nation's basic conditions for the poor were improving during the relevant time period.[38]

The most powerful explanation for what happened in Ferguson and around the country lies in the pattern that was observed in city after city: police violence followed by community violence, with lots of protests and controversy in between. In some cases, the actions of officers were technically lawful, but they nevertheless provoked outrage because of a broader context of injustice and unfairness. For instance, in Ferguson, Baltimore, and Chicago, federal reports documented widespread abuses of authority that disproportionately impacted poor residents of color. Therefore the killings of young African Americans in these cities not only outraged these residents based on the facts themselves; they were also linked to deep and enduring resentment of racial mistreatment more generally.

In each city, police misuse of force activated long-standing legal cynicism among poor communities of color. Many in these communities pulled back from law enforcement, opting for street over courtroom justice. Street justice is not actual justice; it is simply revenge, which only creates more retaliatory violence. As violence skyrockets, police are pressured to resort to even more aggressive uses of force, and the vicious cycle repeats itself. Illegitimate formal social control weakens informal social control, which justifies more aggressive formal control, and so on. A deep cynicism sets in among both communities and cops, causing mayhem. This is the true Ferguson effect.

Politically, conservatives usually concern themselves with crime, while progressives tend to focus on justice. On the streets, however, the two are indivisible—sustainable crime control does not happen without social justice, and vice versa. There can be no choice between effectiveness and fairness in crime-fighting because both are necessary for true legitimacy. In the end, whether one sides with conservatives or progressives doesn't really matter, because the only way out of this national crisis in criminal justice is to push through it—we must reduce urban violence while restoring trust and confidence.

The Third Fundamental: Fairness

The first two fundamentals of anti-violence efforts—focus and balance—are intended to develop legitimacy by effectively preserving public safety. The third and last fundamental—fairness—is intended to build legitimacy by treating individuals and communities justly. The first two fundamentals concern what to do about urban violence, while the last concerns how to do it.

What can build legitimacy by bringing cops and communities closer together? Accountability for official misconduct is a must, as are systemic reforms to reduce racial disparities, but true fairness requires more. To that end, a key means of building legitimacy starts with a concept called procedural justice or fairness, which holds that legitimacy depends largely on whether the system's processes are believed to be fair, not just on the outcomes the system produces.

According to social psychologist Tom Tyler, one of the scholars who pioneered the concept's development, "views about legitimacy are rooted in the judgment that the police and the courts are acting fairly when they deal with community residents." His key insight is that perceptions matter—that legitimacy largely depends on the *perceived* fairness of the system. For Tyler, every time law enforcement officials interact with the public, there is an opportunity for a "teachable moment" in which people learn about the law and legal authority.

In these moments, the lessons learned by the public can be either positive or negative.[39]

What does procedural fairness mean in practice? According to legal scholar Tracey Meares, a colleague of Tyler's and another leader in this area, people want to be treated fairly, with dignity, and with respect. They want to believe that the decisions impacting them are well justified and without bias. They also want a say in what happens to them, the chance to tell their side of the story, even if ultimately decisions don't go their way. Finally, they want to believe that the authorities are acting in their best interest. When people believe they have been treated fairly by an authority—a police officer, a judge, or a boss—they see that authority as legitimate and will cooperate with it, even when an outcome might be contrary to their self-interest, such as a ticket, an arrest, or a denied promotion.[40]

Over the years, I have had countless conversations with perpetrators, victims, witnesses, community members, and others about specific cases and general policies. In almost every instance, I found that treating people respectfully, listening to them carefully, and taking the time to walk them through the process of how and why decisions were made were critical for getting their acceptance or buy-in. No one wants to be subject to the arbitrary whims of a distant authority. People want to know that if someone is making decisions about them, that those decisions will be made fairly and thoughtfully.

By improving the fairness of their processes, law enforcement agencies can increase their legitimacy among community members and thereby increase compliance with the law. Not one but two systematic reviews confirm that when police adopt procedural fairness strategies, they can improve satisfaction with their services as well as build community trust and confidence. There is also a significant body of evidence indicating that procedural fairness improves compliance with things like police orders and instructions. That said, there is relatively little rigorous evidence demonstrating that procedural fairness actually reduces crime and violence, although as the research continues to develop in this area, I expect that this link will eventually be confirmed.[41]

A key strength of procedural fairness is that it does not put the effectiveness of law enforcement at odds with its legitimacy. For far too long, a false choice has been promoted between effective crime-fighting and positive police-community relations. President Donald Trump calls for "law and order" police, while Black Lives Matter advocates push for the police to pull out of communities of color entirely. But as we've seen, legitimacy and security are mutually reinforcing, not mutually exclusive. Procedural fairness strategies can make criminal justice agencies more just and more effective *at the same time.* Using these strategies, law enforcement becomes more effective while simultaneously becomes more fair, transparent, and responsive.

Another advantage of procedural fairness is that it can be adopted by criminal justice agencies for both internal and external purposes remedying cynicism among cops and communities alike. For instance, improving the perceived fairness of processes within police agencies has been shown to improve job satisfaction, build commitment, reduce misconduct, and increase willingness to report misconduct. Improved fairness inside police agencies has also been linked to improved treatment of the public. In Seattle, when police supervisors met with their officers for a single session that was guided by the principles of procedural fairness, the officers became less likely to resolve incidents with arrests or uses of force, even when working in high-risk areas.[42]

A final and related benefit of procedural fairness is its versatility. It can be used internally and externally, but it can also be used by courts, prosecutors' offices, probation and parole agencies, and prisons and jails. The principles of procedural fairness should not be limited only to policing; they should be adopted and applied in every criminal justice setting.

Procedural fairness has been embraced by some forward-thinking law enforcement leaders and professionals, but it is still not emphasized enough. President Obama's Task Force on 21st Century Policing strongly endorsed procedural fairness, yet most police agencies have not incorporated these principles into their daily practices and procedures. Procedural fairness is also often labeled as a particular kind of policing program. This is a mistake. Procedural fairness should be understood not as a stand-alone approach but instead as the means for implementing *any* criminal justice strategy. In *Principles of Procedurally Just Policing,* a recently published manual on the subject, it states that "procedural justice is not a project or program to be completed, nor a goal to be achieved; it is a comprehensive change to the ways in which police departments do business and a constant work in progress." This should be true for policing and beyond.[43]

Some accurately observe that fairness is not just a matter of processes but also of outcomes. It is not just about perception but also reality. What about the racial disparities cited in the reports investigating the police departments in Ferguson, Baltimore, and Chicago? they might ask. What about the racial differences that plague almost every aspect of American criminal justice?

As will be discussed in chapter 9, broader efforts to reform the criminal justice system are entirely compatible with more targeted strategies to save lives in poor African American and Latino communities. More than that, these efforts need one another. Aligning the anti-violence, anti-racism, and pro-reform movements is essential to ensure fair and equitable treatment for poor people of color.

THE STUDY OF legitimacy is relatively new. Much of the work done to date has been theoretical, relying on surveys and interviews, conducted in artificial settings and with nonexperimental methodologies. Nevertheless, given the urgency of the legitimacy crisis in American criminal justice, policy makers do not have the luxury of waiting until academia comes to a consensus on these issues. They must act based on the best available evidence right now. The body of research in support of remedying legal cynicism with procedural fairness, while imperfect, is far stronger than any of the currently available alternatives.

Our diagnosis of urban violence began with the insight that violence is highly concentrated, clustering among a few powerful people, places, and things. We also learned that violent crime responds to both positive and negative incentives, i.e., the carrot and the stick. These discoveries led to two fundamental principles for reducing violence: focus and balance. In places like Ferguson, St. Louis, Baltimore, and Chicago, unfairness created cynicism, which led to violence, not just between police and protesters but also among those living in the communities they fought over. These events demonstrated the need for a third and final principle: fairness. In part 2, we will put all three principles into action.

Navigating this national crisis in confidence has not been, and will not be, easy. Building community trust is a slow, painstaking process, but it can be done. A crucial first step is recognizing that safety and justice, and effectiveness and fairness, are not at odds with one another. Shortly before he retired, Philadelphia police commissioner Charles Ramsey, an African American who had served as the co-chair for President Obama's Task Force on 21st Century Policing, paraphrased Albert Einstein's quote for a new time and context: "Public safety is not just about the absence of crime; it must include the presence of justice." The lesson of Ferguson is clear: We must attend to legitimacy and fairness in order to minimize violence. To bring about peace, we need justice.[44]

PART II

TREATMENT

CHAPTER 6

PACIFYING SHOOTERS

ERIK KING WORKS WITH KIDS. HE CREATES PROGRAMMING AND EVENTS for students at a high school in upper Manhattan that serves mostly poor African American and Latino children, where he works directly with some of New York City's most difficult youth. When a situation with a student becomes serious, Erik gets the call. One might wonder why kids who ignore most adults listen to him, or where his special ability to engage and connect comes from.

Erik and I have known each other for many years. When I approached him about this book, he wanted to help but had reservations. We agreed to use an alias so he could speak freely, and speak freely he did. As Erik described his childhood, it seemed as if he were running through a checklist of risk factors for future criminality and violence. Given where he started, what he went through, and where he is now, Erik's journey sheds light on how violence begets violence, and also on how the violence can finally come to an end.

Erik grew up in Alphabet City. Located on New York City's Lower East Side, the neighborhood is now home to hipsters, but decades ago it was infamous for poverty, drugs, and violence. When he was a toddler, Erik's parents separated and divorced after a brutal fight. He still vaguely remembers hearing the most intimate details of his life tossed around a courtroom by strangers as if he and his family were not present.

After that, Erik did not see his father much, but when he did, it left scars. For some reason his father favored his brother and had only contempt for him. "My father used to point to my brother and say, 'That's my son,'" Erik told me. "Then he would point to me and be like, 'And the fat one's his brother.' It hurt in a way that physical stuff could never compare."

Erik's father often fell behind on child support, forcing Erik's mother to work incessantly to provide for him and his brother. She worked multiple jobs—at a Fotomat, a medical billing firm, and others—just to make ends meet. Erik and his brother grew up poor and at times even went hungry. They wore their sneakers until the soles scraped off and their jeans had holes before it was fashionable.

After breaking her back figuratively, Erik's mother broke her back literally, leaving her unable to walk and bedridden for almost a year. Erik was nine. With his father out of the picture and his mother in the hospital, he and his brother were supervised at home by aides who stayed with them on a temporary basis. One of those aides was terribly abusive, beating Erik and his brother and forcing them to sleep on the floor as their beds lay empty in the next room.

The aide's abuse, coupled with his parents' absence, made a deep impression on Erik. "That nurse would dole out these endless fucking beatings," he recalled. "It made me feel like a throwaway kid, like nobody gave a fuck about me." Mistreatment and neglect shaped Erik's view of the world around him, and of himself. "I started feeling like there were two kinds of people: the wolves and the sheep." He would not be a sheep much longer.

Erik started fighting with kids in school. In sixth grade, when a boy from class teased him for being poor, he pushed the kid down a flight of stairs. "I felt verbal insults like they were physical attacks," he told me. "If you said something disrespectful, you got your teeth kicked in, because that was all I had."

Erik did not just experience violence at home and school; he also saw it on the streets of his neighborhood. "I saw people's heads get cracked open, people getting stabbed," he remembered. "It happened so much it seemed normal. Within my neighborhood, it just seemed like that was the way it was supposed to be."

During high school, Erik started lifting weights and made extra money by working as a bouncer at parties and bars. His reputation for violence grew—he started one gang, then joined another and finally another, becoming one of its most feared enforcers. "At that point in my life, I didn't have a lot of self-worth—I think it had to do with my dad not really claiming me as his son and the abuse from my childhood. So if I don't care about myself, and these guys say they love me when no one else does, then I'm going to sacrifice myself for them. If you were beefing with my people, I had no problem cracking your head open."

What began with fists escalated to knives and bats and then finally guns. Erik and his gang dabbled in all kinds of criminality, even traveling to other boroughs to rob drug dealers at gunpoint. The gang took full advantage of Erik's brutality, trading on his reputation and using him to settle scores. "There were people who would hang out with me because if they started something, I would finish it," he recalled. "People viewed me as a pit bull, an animal that could be sicced on people, and at the time I didn't mind that."

WE'VE ALREADY MADE the case for triage—addressing urban violence first in order to save lives and arrest urban poverty and decay. We've diagnosed the violence, showing how it concentrates among a violent few—small groups of people, places, and behaviors that disproportionately drive the problem. We've seen that violence responds to a wide range of incentives and strategies and that it is intimately related to the legitimacy of the criminal justice system generally and the police in particular. These observations led to the three fundamentals of effective anti-violence efforts: focus, balance, and fairness.

Now that triage and diagnosis are completed, it is time for treatment. This chapter and the two that follow introduce specific strategies and concepts that, taken together, can stop the bleeding in our most disadvantaged urban communities. Here we concern ourselves with the Erik Kings of the world—the "hot people" at the highest risk for killing and being killed. As we've seen, networks of individuals like Erik make up less than 1 percent of a city's population but account for the majority of its murders.

In this chapter we examine the three types of people who matter most when it comes to urban violence reduction: would-be shooters, someday shooters, and bona fide shooters. Would-be shooters are the adults and youths at the highest risk for violence as either perpetrators or victims. Someday shooters are the children who, absent some form of assistance, are at risk of becoming tomorrow's would-be shooters. Bona fide shooters are the adults who repeatedly turn down chances to change and persist in serious violent offending. Obviously, not every homicide is committed with a firearm, but urban killings are overwhelmingly shootings, which is why the term *shooter* is used here.

How should cities address each type of shooter? In brief, they must work with would-be shooters, offering assistance but promising punishment if they persist in violence. Someday shooters should be supported with intensive treatment now to avoid targeting them later for arrest and prosecution. Bona fide shooters must simply be separated from society. Before we discuss what to do with these people, however, we should know a bit more about who they are.

About Shooters

Even in the most dangerous, crime-ridden communities, most people stay away from serious violence. Shooters are usually young, poor, and members of a racial or ethnic minority group, but the same is true of many in their communities. What distinguishes the violent few from the equally disadvantaged many?

Erik was one of the first people I put this question to. He offered a number of insights into why shooters are different from those around them. He even divided shooters into categories (different than the ones laid out above). "There are three kinds of shooters," he told me. "There's one that just wants to please, the kid who may not be built that way but will do whatever he needs to do to be down." That's category one: the Wannabe. These shooters are so desperate for status or belonging that they will kill to get it.

"Then there is the guy who was born into it and the lifestyle has been normalized," Erik explained. "He has nothing else because that's all he knows." That's category two: the Legacy. These are boys who grow up in families that are deeply entrenched in criminal violence. These are shooters who are raised by other shooters.

"Then there are the kids who have been through real shit—foster care, beatings, molestation, rape. They have this empty look behind their eyes and you can tell they're willing to do anything." Here Erik could have been describing himself. This was category three: the Wounded. Emotional trauma suffered in childhood lives on long after physical injuries heal, often leading to violence later on.

There is a fourth category that Erik only hinted at. Even among shooters, there is a fraction of fearsome individuals who seem to celebrate violence for its own sake. Lieutenant Jose Lopez has spent the vast majority of his twenty-three years with the Chicago Police Department in gang and homicide units. "Out of a hundred guys, you have ten to fifteen who will step up if called upon or pushed, but every gang has those three to four hunters or killers that are not only willing to shoot, they like it," he told me. These are the Hunters. Many in the media fixate on these individuals, but keep in mind that, for the most part, those who commit murder do so for reasons we might understand, if not approve of or agree with.

I asked others about these four categories of shooters: the Wannabes, Legacies, the Wounded as outlined by Erik, and the Hunters as described by Lieutenant Lopez. Surprisingly, my interviewees agreed with each of these categories and added their own insights. Mario Maciel, director of the San Jose Gang Task Force, observed that for Wannabes, "there is that young kid who isn't violent by nature but who gets recruited and manipulated. He's a one-time shooter, while others have the possibility of multiple shootings."

Anthony Blockmon was a Legacy shooter himself. He was born into gangs—his father was a "shot-caller," or gang leader, in Los Angeles. He remembered a childhood full of wild parties, police raids, and violent attacks. "It's like a generational curse," Anthony told me. "Generation after generation of my family was all on the same page."

Like Erik, Raymond Solórzano was one of the Wounded. In high school, Ray joined a gang, and for seventeen years it was his life. For him the trauma of gang life built up over time, making him more and more violent. "For myself, when it came to the darker things I did, it was because of failed relationships, going in and out of jail, my friends dying or doing life in prison. This person I shot, this person I stabbed, I did those things because I was hurt."

These categories match what I've witnessed working in the field for over twenty years. I have questioned criminals in holding cells, stood across from killers in court, and sat down with former offenders to understand how they struggled, survived, and ultimately succeeded. I remember one colleague, a former shooter himself, describing what it was like to see the light flicker and die in someone's eyes as they passed away. I'm lucky—I've never witnessed that. But I have seen the light go out behind the eyes of far too many young men while they are still breathing.

These categories are fluid, of course, and most shooters belong in multiple categories, but according to my informal survey and my own experiences, these categories cover the vast majority of shooters. The violence perpetrated by these people makes more sense when you understand their circumstances. "One of the biggest things about street and gang violence is that it's happening for logical reasons, regardless of whether we agree with it or not," said Jon

Feinman, founder of Inner City Weightlifting, an organization that uses physical fitness to turn around some of Boston's most dangerous young men.

I have met plenty of shooters, even some killers. When I look carefully at what they have been through, in many cases I must admit that I might not have done things much differently than they did. Imagine that your early life was filled with deprivation, distrust, and trauma. Your main source of support is a small group of young men you grew up with. A rival kills one of them—your closest friend—and the police do nothing. Would you turn the other cheek? We all hope that we would make the right decision, but no one can be sure. David Kennedy once described these young men to me as "more trapped than evil," and I agree. Under the worst circumstances, we could all be killers.

Working with Would-Be Shooters

What works to stop would-be shooters before they pull the trigger? What can turn them around? The principles of focus, balance, and fairness provide some guidance. First, focus on only the would-be killers, and only on the specific behavior at issue: violence. Next, when engaging with these individuals, strike an appropriate balance between rewards and sanctions, offering help to stop the cycle of violence but also threatening punishment if it continues. Finally, embrace procedural fairness by offering shooters a say in their own recovery and treating them with honesty, dignity, and respect.

Three specific anti-violence strategies, rooted in these principles, stand out from the rest: focused deterrence, street outreach and mediation, and cognitive behavioral therapy. These strategies typically work independently and apart from each other, but an ideal effort would align and even integrate all three so they work seamlessly alongside one another.

IN THE UNITED States, nothing works as well to reduce urban violence as focused deterrence, a strategy briefly described in chapter 3. It does not work perfectly, it does not work every time, but it works better, on average, than anything else out there.

In 2016, sociologist Christopher Winship and I conducted a meta-review focused on which strategies worked best to reduce community violence. We examined forty-three reviews in total, which included more than 1,400 individual studies. From these reviews and studies, we identified thirty separate crime- and violence-reduction strategies. Of these thirty, focused deterrence had the strongest and most consistent anti-violence effects. According to the National Academy of Sciences, "Focused deterrence programs show consistent crime-control impacts in reducing gang violence, street crime driven by drug markets, and repeat individual offending. The available literature suggests that these programs have both short-term and long-term areawide impacts on crime."[1]

Focused deterrence originated in Boston in 1995 as a partnership among cops, communities, and academics from the Harvard Kennedy School. What started as the Boston Gun Project ultimately became Operation Ceasefire and was credited with a stunning 63 percent reduction in youth homicide and a 50 percent reduction overall. The effort became closely associated with "the Boston Miracle," a remarkable drop in violence in the city that happened during the 1990s. The "miracle" also involved other efforts such as police-clergy cooperatives and public health efforts, but it is clear that without the strategy, Boston's crime decline would have been decidedly less miraculous.

The strategy is known by other names, such as "pulling levers," although "focused deterrence" now seems to be the most common term. Focused deterrence has been used to address drug violence, domestic violence, and other forms of crime, but it is best known for and most effective in reducing serious gun and group violence. This particular form of focused deterrence is known as the Group Violence Intervention or Group Violence Reduction Strategy (GVRS). Relatively early on, focused deterrence initiatives dropped the term *gang* and replaced it with *group*—this may seem like an insignificant change, but it represents an important shift in thinking that will be described in detail later.

Over the years, I have seen the strategy in action from several angles—attending meetings, participating in programs, interviewing management and staff, and following its progress in city after city. I have helped fund and manage focused deterrence programs at the federal and state levels and have known David Kennedy, the criminologist who pioneered the strategy and has steered much of its development, for years.

The program has produced notable successes. For instance, in Oakland, a recently released rigorous evaluation indicates that the GVRS was a driving factor behind the massive drop in gun violence that the city has witnessed since 2011. That year, Oakland saw 93 gun homicides and 617 nonfatal gun assaults. In 2012, implementation of the GVRS began. In 2017, there were 63 homicides and 277 nonfatal gun assaults—a drop of 32 percent and 55 percent, respectively. I have seen many iterations of the GVRS, and the effort in Oakland is one of the strongest.[2]

In Oakland, the work begins with forming a partnership among police, prosecutors, key community members, and social service providers who can deliver under difficult circumstances. Each constituency is essential to the effort's effectiveness and legitimacy. Leave out law enforcement and you lose deterrence and accountability. Ignore the community and you lose legitimacy. Lose the services and you lose balance and forfeit the ability to encourage positive change, not just deter crime. Making sure these partners can work closely with one another is critical—without mutual trust, there cannot be collective action, and without collective action, the strategy fails.[3]

Once the partnership is created, it sets out to identify the key groups, group members, and group dynamics that are driving the violence. There a number of ways to do this. One is the social network analysis first mentioned in chapter 3, which systematically examines past shootings and killings in order to identify connections among the small number of individuals involved in serious violence. Here's a crude description of how social network analysis works in practice: Begin with one homicide victim and identify everyone they were criminally connected to. Then go on to the next victim and do the same thing, and repeat the process in order to generate a social network of individuals at the highest risk for violence. The more connections one has in the network, the higher the risk for shooting or being shot. Andrew Papachristos puts it bluntly: "Just because you don't see [the network] doesn't mean it's not going to kill you."[4]

Once the relevant groups and group members have been identified and resources have been marshalled, the partnership is ready to confront those driving the violence. This is done face to face, in group and one-on-one meetings, with a twofold message of caring and consequences. Group meetings are called "call-ins"—a hallmark of GVRS initiatives. "Custom notifications" are individual versions of the same thing. Call-ins are typically held in a neutral setting such as a church or community center where the partnership "calls in" group members to deliver their anti-violence message directly and in person. Many are required to attend as a condition of their probation or parole. At these meetings, the partnership voices its commitment to keeping group members alive and out of prison. It offers assistance and support while also clearly describing the sanctions that will be imposed should the violence continue.

These meetings are administered according to the principles of procedural fairness. Group members must feel they are being treated fairly in that they are being offered a clear choice with consequences spelled out in advance. The partnership expresses its concern for the well-being of the community at large, but also for the group members themselves. Getting the message right is essential at its simplest, it is this: "We are here to help you. If you do not let us help you, we are here to stop you."[5]

During these meetings, law enforcement officials provide the accountability component of the message, telling group members that they know that they are involved in violence and it must stop. If it continues, law enforcement will come down not just on them as individuals but on their entire group. Sanctions can range from major punishments, such as federal prosecution, to minor sanctions, like cutting off pirated cable. The message is clear: keep shooting and we will come down on you, all of you.

Members of the community then stand up to speak. Anyone with moral authority—neighbors, elders, preachers—can participate, but the most convincing are usually mothers who have lost sons to violence. Their testimonials are incredibly powerful, and they speak to the young men in the room as both potential perpetrators and victims. They talk about their love for their sons and remind group members to think of their own mothers. In the parlance of focused deterrence, these women represent "the moral voice of the community." This message, in my experience, is the one that hits home the hardest. As they listen to these women, I have witnessed tough young men soften visibly, the humanity and vulnerability that they hide from strangers suddenly revealed.

Last come the service providers, offering concrete and timely assistance. Got open warrants? We can help. Need an ID? We can handle that too. Often this message is doubly credible because it comes from a former offender who can honestly say, "Look, I used to be just like you, but I was able to make a change."

After the meetings end, the partnership must follow up relentlessly, following through on the promises that were made. The partnership must establish working relationships with group members, first to keep them safe and out of jail or prison, then to get them on a path to opportunity. To win their trust, the partnership reaches out tirelessly—calling, texting, and visiting—trying to connect with each member as frequently and for as long as possible.[6]

Once a relationship is established, safety concerns come first. Individuals who are most at risk for serious, potentially lethal violence are not simply "at risk." More accurately, they are "in crisis." The police may be looking for them. Someone may be out to hurt or kill them. The partnership must then do what is necessary to protect these people, arranging safe surrenders to law enforcement, mediating individual and group conflicts, and so on.

Once a person is safe and stable, longer-term planning can begin. A life plan can be drafted, with treatment, counseling, and mentoring provided, connecting group members to new peers and role models for making better life decisions. Access to formal services such as employment, education, and housing can be arranged. A key component of this work is making sure members are not caught up in endless bureaucracies—prior arrangements must be made to ensure they have quick access to the services they need.[7]

Finally, for those who persist in violent behavior, police and prosecutors use targeted law enforcement strategies to hold offenders and their associates fully accountable, sending a strong message that such conduct will not be tolerated. Law enforcement acts by "pulling every lever" to sanction violence among these members—anything from arrests to strict enforcement of probation and parole violations.

Why is the GVRS so successful? Research has not identified the specific components that drive its effectiveness, but I believe much of the strategy's success comes from a consistent application of the three principles already articulated in this book: focus, balance, and fairness.

First, focused deterrence is just that: focused. It is a highly targeted intervention that addresses a specific range of behaviors among a small set of groups and group members. Second, focused deterrence is balanced. While group members are punished if they persist in violent behavior, they are also offered opportunities to help them turn away from "the life." Third is fairness, or legitimacy. At the heart of the GVRS is a partnership among civic, criminal justice, and community leaders that builds legitimacy by embracing the principles of procedural fairness. When done well, the GVRS treats group members with dignity, offering them a clear choice that allows them to decide their own destiny.

The GVRS has another important strength: unlike most other anti-violence initiatives, it carefully accounts for the group dynamics that often motivate urban violence. In the call-ins, the entire group is warned: if you persist in shooting, there will be increased attention to everything you do until the shooting stops. Group members who attend the call-in convey this message to other members. When it is accepted, this message fundamentally alters the group dynamics around violence. Instead of being pressured into shootings, group members are pressured to avoid them in order to save the group from sanctions. When it works, the GVRS pacifies the groups responsible for much of a city's violence. These groups may remain involved in criminal activity, but they resort to gunplay far less frequently. When a city's most notoriously violent groups stand down, it lessens the need for violence among other criminal groups in the city, leading to less violence citywide.

The strategy is not without its challenges. Some see the GVRS as just another tough-on-crime measure. As one critic put it, "While the Ceasefire model of policing looks progressive, its reliance on collective punishment is anything but." On occasion, police and prosecutors have cannibalized the model, eschewing broader partnerships and relying only on its punitive aspects. Perhaps unsurprisingly, these efforts have failed. When the program is pared down to deterrence alone, it does not work.[8]

Some also criticize focused deterrence and the GVRS for a lack of long-term effects—often the strategy appears to drive violence down for a few years, only to see it creep slowly back up. This may be a valid criticism, but the same is true for almost every anti-crime intervention. Strategies can be successful in the short run, but if they are not sustained, it is more often than not a failure of governance, not of the strategy itself.

A SECOND NOTABLE anti-violence strategy revolves around street outreach organizations that directly engage with would-be shooters who cannot be reached by traditional law enforcement or social services. Often referred to as "credible messengers" or "interventionists," street outreach workers are known to and respected by the dangerous groups and individuals they work with. Often, but not always, they are ex-offenders themselves who leverage their own street credibility—their reputations, relationships, and inside knowledge—to maximize success.

A primary mission of street outreach is to mediate violent disputes, resolving them before they turn deadly. Outreach workers can also connect potentially violent individuals to services and other forms of assistance. Finally, some outreach organizations aim to change norms and attitudes about violence using media campaigns, rallies, and other forms of community activism.

Street outreach, particularly conflict mediation, happens any-where: street corners, crime scenes, funeral parlors, emergency rooms, prison visiting areas, or someone's apartment. It happens at all hours of the day and night. Outreach workers gather facts and intelligence about violent incidents to determine whether retaliation is likely, try to control rumormongering at crime scenes to prevent retribution based solely on hearsay or gossip, talk with victims of violence and connect them to services, organize peacemaking events and activities, and, most importantly, try to talk potential shooters out of shooting. Workers try to go wherever they have to, whenever they have to, often with little advance notice.

It's dangerous work. "There's only been a couple of street workers who got killed," Ronald Noblet told me. "But a bunch of them have gotten their asses kicked." Ron, an expert in mediating gang con-flicts, was among the first generation of street outreach workers in Los Angeles in the 1960s and 1970s. Street outreach is high-pressure, high-intensity, high-risk. Outreach workers, often survivors of vio-lence themselves, are constantly reexposing themselves to circum-stances that may trigger their own memories of trauma. The work is demanding, taking a mental, emotional, and physical toll on those who dedicate themselves to it.

Street outreach was initially developed in the 1950s and 1960s as a response to emerging gang-related crime and delinquency. These programs largely failed to reduce crime and delinquency—in several cases, they actually exacerbated it by unintentionally strengthening gang identity and the relationships among gang members, increasing what researchers described as gang "cohesion."[9]

The strategy fell out of fashion as criminal justice policy took a punitive turn in the 1970s. It reemerged in the 1980s and 1990s as an alternative to traditional tough-on-crime approaches. Most recently, street outreach has taken on the task of violence reduction explicitly. Its track record to date is positive but mixed: it has been evaluated numerous times in numerous cities, earning promising if uneven results.

In New York City, the best-known application of the strategy, Cure Violence, was associated with significant reductions in gun injuries and shootings. In Chicago and Baltimore, Cure Violence reduced violence in some neighborhoods but not others. In Newark, a street outreach effort had no effect on gun injuries, while in Pittsburgh and Boston, street outreach was actually associated with an increase in violence.[10]

As with focused deterrence and the GVRS, I have studied street outreach extensively, going out on the streets with outreach workers and engaging directly with the leaders of the largest outreach organizations. While working for Governor Andrew Cuomo in New York, I helped turn around a troubled statewide street outreach program.

When it works, the advantages of street outreach are clear: poor communities and especially the criminals within them are deeply disconnected from formal sources of authority. Outreach workers go where others cannot, trading on their status, connections, and street knowledge to stop shootings and killings. Where formal social control fails, outreach workers use informal social control to stop the cycle of violence.

Like the GVRS, street outreach incorporates the three fundamental principles of violence reduction. First, outreach focuses on those most likely to perpetrate deadly violence, and because outreach workers are not law enforcement officers, they can focus exclusively on preventing violence and not crime more generally.

Second, street outreach can provide much-needed balance to anti-violence efforts that focus exclusively on policing and prosecution. Outreach also connects tough-to-reach individuals with timely, urgently needed services, such as a meal, a ride, or a place to stay for the night. Outreach also workers also make referrals and attach those who will not ask for help to longer-term sources of assistance. "It was up to me," explained Raymond Solórzano when talking about his time as an outreach worker and getting individuals into treatment. "I had to use my relationships to kind of put my stamp on it."

Third, street outreach can improve community perceptions of fairness and legitimacy, serving as an invaluable bridge between criminal justice authorities and disconnected communities. In New York City, for instance, Cure Violence was associated with improved confidence in police and with increased willingness to report crimes. Outreach also empowers communities to voluntarily avoid bloodshed, and by strengthening informal social control it minimizes the need for formal social control in terms of arrests and incarceration.[11]

The potential benefits of street outreach are undeniable. At the same time, the risks are real. Some street outreach organizations unintentionally engage potential shooters in ways that reinforce their criminal and violent behaviors, increasing cohesion like earlier efforts did in the past. Outreach workers can accidentally encourage group solidarity by treating a set of loosely affiliated individuals like a close-knit community.

Street outreach workers sometimes model negative behaviors rather than positive ones. In trying to establish rapport with high-risk individuals, they may celebrate their own criminal and violent pasts, glorifying the very behaviors they are working to discourage. Some outreach workers even use their own violence, or the threat of violence, to stop the violence of others. "Guys who rely on their reputations as badasses are heading for a crash," Ronald Noblet told me. "Eventually you're going to get challenged, and it only takes a few pounds of pressure to pull that trigger." A related issue arises when an outreach worker is "fifty-fifty," meaning only halfway out of their former life. As Juan Carter, director of a street worker outreach team for the Institute for the Study and Practice of Nonviolence

(ISPN), told me, "To do this work, you have to be one hundred percent committed."

Outreach workers can also perpetuate the very illegitimacy that made their presence necessary in the first place. Independence is an absolute necessity for street outreach—if criminals think outreach workers will snitch on them, they won't talk to them, or worse. That said, there is a difference between being independent and being adversarial. Some outreach workers refuse to work with police at all and tell those in the community to do the same. In Pittsburgh, for instance, where the street outreach effort was associated with increased violence, researchers noted that there was "outright hostility" between outreach workers and law enforcement. When street outreach organizations aggressively position themselves as alternatives to a broken status quo, they can unintentionally reinforce the disconnect between the state and its citizens.[12]

In order for the field of street outreach to advance, it must be systematized and professionalized. Street outreach is not guesswork; there are right and wrong ways to go about it. Hiring should be scrutinized to ensure new workers are fully separated from any past criminality. Training should be expanded and improved to ensure that new workers understand the dos and don'ts of effective outreach. Supervision and management should be emphasized to keep workers active, focused, and on the right path. Finally, workers and supervisors need sufficient pay and benefits to support themselves, along with treatment and care for their own trauma. Finally, more attention should be paid to professional development—few people can or should do this work forever.

Perhaps no city has successfully implemented street outreach better than Los Angeles. The Urban Peace Institute (formerly part of the Advancement Project), in partnership with the Mayor's Office of Gang Reduction and Youth Development (GRYD), has professionalized the practice of street outreach, making it an essential part of a comprehensive citywide anti-violence strategy. In Los Angeles, outreach begins with a twelve-week certification course taught in an academy exclusively dedicated to training outreach workers. Among other things, workers are provided with response protocols that give them concrete guidance on their roles and responsibilities. After graduation, the performance of workers is monitored not only by their own street outreach organizations but also by the GRYD office. In 2014 and 2015, outreach workers in Los Angeles prevented an estimated 185 violent gang crimes, including 10 homicides and 175 aggravated assaults. Another promising model is the ISPN, which maintains working relationships with law enforcement while preserving its independence and street credibility. In addition to conflict mediation, ISPN offers in-house services and treatment to victims of violence—an invaluable resource for this type of effort.[13]

Street outreach is at something of a crossroads. The evidence in support of the strategy is promising but not yet proven. (The same is true for hospital programs that use outreach, treatment, and services to prevent violence.) Moving forward, the practice of street outreach must continue to improve. As with Cure Violence, street workers must be trained to use their relationships and reputations to stop the transmission of violence from person to person and group to group. As in Los Angeles, training academies should be established in every city that wishes to continue or adopt the practice. Also as in Los Angeles, there should be multiple street outreach organizations operating at the same time—it is unhealthy to give one organization a monopoly. Like ISPN, organizations should maintain professional but arm's-length relationships with law enforcement and provide, whenever possible, direct assistance to victims. A promising new effort in Chicago has brought together practitioners from GRYD, ISPN, Cure Violence, and others to revamp the city's approach to street outreach along these lines.[14]

It is often overlooked, but outreach workers played a critical role in the original GVRS effort in Boston, called Operation Ceasefire. Today, the two strategies are occasionally used in combination, but blending these approaches should be done more often, with more consideration given to how each can leverage the strength of the other. Too often, the GVRS and street outreach are seen as either-or strategies, when in reality they can and should be used together.

WOULD-BE SHOOTERS ARE highly associated with violent perpetration and victimization for many reasons, but one key factor putting them at risk is their own choices and behavior. A particularly common attribute among violent offenders is hypervigilance: they interpret ambiguous or innocuous social cues as hostile, leading to aggressive responses.

Violent behavior is often impulsive, so preventing such behavior is often a matter of keeping one's composure. For most, natural impulses are tempered by parents and other adult role models, but the same training can be provided clinically. Some believe that destructive thinking and habits become unbreakable unless they are addressed in childhood, but thankfully this is not true. Even for adults, poor decision-making can be changed through treatment, and that treatment has a name: cognitive behavioral therapy, often known simply as CBT. Along with the GVRS and street outreach, CBT is one of the best ways to work with would-be shooters.

Since the 1980s, CBT has been used in a wide variety of contexts, including as treatment for addiction, anxiety, and depression, but increasingly it has been used to treat criminal and violent behavior. Its core premise is straightforward: how we think shapes what we do. If flawed thinking leads us to antisocial or aggressive behavior, then correcting that thinking can improve our conduct. CBT is therapy, administered individually or in groups, that is designed to make people more aware of their own thoughts, help them better understand the consequences of their actions, and motivate them to adopt new strategies for both. It uses concrete techniques such as modeling and role playing, then provides feedback to help individuals practice new choices and habits.

Not one but several systematic reviews prove that CBT positively impacts criminal justice outcomes. Simply put, CBT works. It works for violent and nonviolent offenders. It works for adults and kids. It works behind prison walls and out in the community. It works by itself and when combined with other programs. Few interventions match CBT's reliability and versatility. In one particularly exhaustive review, CBT was associated with a 25 percent average decrease in criminal recidivism—a relatively large result—but when the most effective forms of CBT were used, recidivism declined an impressive 52 percent. These outcomes were not outliers—approximately one in five of the interventions studied produced such results.[15]

Of course, not all forms of CBT are equally effective. Key drivers of success include focusing on high-risk offenders and including programmatic components such as anger management and interpersonal problem-solving. Anger management helps people identify triggers and cues that arouse anger and teaches them to maintain self-control. Interpersonal problem-solving gives people skills for dealing with interpersonal conflict and peer pressure.[16]

In fact, almost every effective anti-violence treatment seems to contain, either formally or informally, some elements of CBT. In fact, efforts to reduce criminality and delinquency that lack a CBT component usually fail to achieve the desired results. This observation leads to an important insight: efforts to treat individuals at the highest risk for violence are likely to fail if they do not expressly address the individual's own thinking and behavior. This means that many of the most popular approaches to combating crime and reducing recidivism are unlikely to succeed without including some sort of CBT component.[17]

"Nothing stops a bullet like a job," Father Gregory Boyle, founder of Homeboy Industries, a well-known reentry program for former gang members, used to say. But Father Boyle no longer believes his own famous line. "When somebody introduces me somewhere and they say that, it almost feels creepy," Boyle said in an interview. "It doesn't get at what this is about. I would find somebody a job, sometimes even a career. But then a monkey wrench would get thrown and . . . next thing you know, he was back in the neighborhood and then returned to prison." It is easy to assume that employment can directly reduce violence, and there is a correlation between more jobs and less crime, but the track record for stand-alone vocational, employment, and work programs when it comes to preventing violent crime is decidedly mixed. The same is true for most education, arts, sports, music, and other programs advertising themselves as anti-violence efforts.[18]

Interestingly, CBT appears to be slightly more effective when combined with other services, rather than as a stand-alone intervention, so programs interested in increasing their effectiveness can add a CBT component to their efforts. An essential element of CBT is practice, and anything—a skill, a sport, or even a job—can be used as an opportunity to practice CBT techniques. That said, incorporating CBT must be done seriously and not as an afterthought. For example, arts and sports might be excellent ways to engage at-risk youth, but once they're engaged, concrete changes in thinking and behavior must be the goal.

In Chicago, the well-known Becoming a Man (BAM) program combines sports, youth engagement, positive masculinity training, and CBT. Over the course of an academic year, participants receive group CBT counseling in school once a week, along with one session of after-school sports programming. Two separate and rigorous studies found that after participating in the program, BAM students were 40 to 50 percent less likely to be arrested for a violent crime.[19]

Based largely on the success of BAM, private funders in Chicago have launched a new effort called READI Chicago, a CBT-informed employment program that explicitly targets would-be shooters. READI Chicago connects individuals at the highest risk for violence to transitional jobs and coaching. It also features CAD, which stands for Control-Alt-Delete, a CBT program that teaches participants to control their negative thinking, alter it, then delete it before they make a mistake. READI participants work in crews to develop job skills, practice conflict resolution, and change mind-sets and behaviors. The effort also uses street outreach workers to engage difficult-to-reach individuals.

CBT can be used to combat hypervigilance and other problematic thought patterns and habits, but where are these patterns coming from? For shooters, the short answer is trauma. As we saw with Erik King, traumatic exposure to violence as a child often leads to violence later on in life. Those at the highest risk for violence are usually not mentally ill, at least not in the way most people conventionally understand mental illness. Instead, they are traumatized. Most shooters are not crazy; they are hurt.

Post-traumatic stress disorder, or PTSD, is a term that describes the problems associated with witnessing or experiencing serious violence and other deeply distressing events. Symptoms include nightmares, flashbacks, guilt, shame, numbness, anxiety, depression, and avoidance. One of the most important symptoms in this context is hypervigilance, which keeps an individual always on guard, looking for threats, and quick to anger.

It is hard to overstate the salience and ubiquity of trauma when you work in the field of violence reduction. It touches everything and everyone. In one study, thousands of inner-city hospital patients in Atlanta, Georgia, were interviewed, and more than 30 percent met the medical criteria for PTSD. According to Dr. Kerry Ressler, the study's lead investigator, "The rates of PTSD we see are as high or higher than Iraq, Afghanistan, or Vietnam veterans." In another study, among recent releasees from Massachusetts state prison, half reported being beaten by their parents; 40 percent had witnessed someone being killed; 30 percent had endured family violence; and 16 percent had been sexually abused.[20]

A massive body of research has documented the tremendous impact of trauma over a lifetime. When pregnant women are exposed to violence, it increases the risk of premature birth and low birth weight. In children, it disrupts sleep, hurts the ability to concentrate, and impairs cognitive development. In adults, childhood trauma leads to risky behaviors such as smoking, alcoholism, drug abuse, and sexual promiscuity. It increases the chances of obesity, depression, and suicide. Late in life, it even elevates the risk for serious diseases such as cancer, lung disease, and heart disease.[21]

What links trauma to all these terrible symptoms? The answer is toxic stress. When threatened, the body releases large amounts of adrenaline and cortisol, causing people to react immediately with a "fight-flight-freeze" response. After the threat is gone, their bodies return to normal, but when this stress response is activated too frequently or for long periods of time, it can take a significant toll on the mind and body. When children perceive life to be generally, not just occasionally, dangerous, their brains stay on alert, continuously flooding their bodies with stress hormones.[22]

Not surprisingly, experiencing trauma in childhood is strongly associated with delinquent, criminal, and violent behavior in adolescence and adulthood. Adult criminal offenders are four times more likely to have experienced a high number of traumatic events than nonoffenders. A large body of research has found that exposure to violence is one of the strongest predictors of future violence. In fact, youth who suffer from chronic exposure to violence are *thirty-two times* more likely to become chronic violent offenders.[23]

Trauma also impacts those who respond to it on a daily basis. Police officers suffer from disproportionately high rates of substance abuse, depression, and even suicide. Emergency room doctors and nurses fight off exhaustion and depression. During my own time prosecuting violent criminals, I experienced a modest version of this myself. Spending every day speaking with victims, examining crime scene photos, and going over all the grisly details took a toll on me. I became easily irritated and quick to anger; one particularly bad outburst prompted my sister to confront me with the question, "Who are you?!" I offer this mild example only to illustrate how much worse the damage can be when exposure to violence is more direct and frequent.[24]

The subject of trauma also came up constantly in my interviews. Lieutenant Lopez has made over 135 homicide arrests in the course of his career. "Many of the kids I have arrested for violent acts had some sort of damage: post-traumatic stress, abuse, or apparent mental illness," he told me. "I've never arrested a healthy individual that just felt the need to kill somebody without motive." Former shooters like Erik King and Raymond Solórzano described what it was like to be the Wounded, individuals whose violence stemmed from their own victimization.

The impact of violent trauma is now well understood, but the practice of treating trauma related to urban violence remains in its infancy. Traditional services tend to focus on women and children, with young men of color seen first and foremost as perpetrators. Trauma is also a touchy subject—many do not recognize their symptoms or they see asking for help as a sign of weakness. Many would-be shooters absolutely refuse to see themselves as victims.

We need more evidence on how to treat trauma among those most likely to become involved in violence, but perhaps not surprisingly, CBT appears to be an important part of the solution. Trauma-focused CBT (TF-CBT) is perhaps the most well-supported treatment for PTSD in children and youth who have suffered one or more traumatic experiences. The treatment integrates CBT with more traditional therapies to help children talk openly about their traumatic experiences in a supportive environment. The treatment also involves parents or other caregivers, teaching them the skills they need to support their child's treatment and healing. TF-CBT can and should be adapted to work with traumatized young men who desperately need treatment but are deeply underserved. Despite tremendous need, there are only a few offering such services, and they are in their infancy. Street outreach programs like ISPN, perhaps in partnership with more traditional victim services agencies, are well situated to destigmatize trauma and provide such treatment to these traumatized young men.[25]

To turn would-be shooters around, the GVRS, street outreach, CBT, and other evidence-informed approaches tend to follow the same basic steps: First, they identify and engage those most at risk. Second, they stabilize those individuals and provide some measure of safety and stability. Third, once stabilized, they treat their misguided thinking, their unsafe and unhealthy behavior, and their trauma. Fourth, they offer opportunities for a better life. Fifth and finally, those who refuse help and persist in violence are punished with swift and certain sanctions. It all comes down to these five steps, followed more or less in sequence.

Supporting Someday Shooters

Working with would-be shooters is essential, but attention must also be paid to the someday shooters, the adolescents and children who might become shooters in the future. Someday shooters are in their early teens and younger, while would-be shooters are typically in their late teens and early twenties. Deviant and disruptive behavior among youth can lead to serious criminality and violence in adulthood, but early treatment can head off the high costs of yet another criminal career. According to one study, a high-risk fourteen-year-old who has already had six or more police contacts will eventually impose between $3 million and $6 million in costs on society—not to mention the unquantifiable costs imposed on victims, families, and communities.[26]

To support someday shooters, it is essential to help their families. Adolescents and children function within family units, and that unit must be healthy in order for those inside it to thrive. Having a strong, secure bond with at least one caring adult is extremely important in promoting resiliency. "Family" in this context should be defined as broadly as possible to include not only parents but also extended relations as well as trusted but not related caregivers.

Home visiting and parent training programs, both of which seek to improve child outcomes by helping caregivers more effectively socialize their children, are two effective strategies. Home visiting programs typically involve nurses, doctors, or social workers conducting in-home visits with mothers to educate them on how to properly care for their children. Parent training programs use individual or group training sessions conducted at clinics or schools, or in the community, to do the same.

Programs like these usually assess outcomes related to childhood behavior, but a few longer-term studies show concrete impacts on crime and violence. In Ypsilanti, Michigan, children who participated in an early education program that included home visits were less likely to have been arrested at ages nineteen, twenty-seven, and forty. Children in Elmira, New York, who received home visits had fewer arrests, convictions, and probation violations. Kids in Chicago who participated in an early education parent training program had lower rates of juvenile arrests and violent arrests at age eighteen. It is clear that these programs can help families get ahead of antisocial, delinquent, and even criminal behavior, but they have other benefits as well, including more educational achievement, less teenage pregnancy, improved economic outcomes, and better health.[27]

Functional family therapy (FFT) is another intervention proven to address aggression and violence. With FFT, therapists provide intensive therapy to a youth's entire family in order to correct patterns of interaction that contribute to their poor behavior. Together kids and caregivers learn communication, conflict resolution, and problem-solving skills. Once developed, these skills can be generalized to other areas, such as school, the community, and peer interaction. In one study, FFT recipients averaged 1.3 offenses over a twelve-month period, while the comparison group averaged 10.3 offenses. In another, youth who received high-quality FFT committed 35 percent fewer felony offenses and 30 percent fewer violent crimes.[28]

The most successful treatments for young children and adolescents share a number of elements. First, they incorporate elements of CBT, focusing on concrete changes in thinking and behavior with an emphasis on improving interpersonal relationships via anger management, impulse control, and interpersonal problem-solving. Second, like TF-CBT, they address the trauma that so many children and families from disadvantaged communities suffer from. Third, they treat the entire family (and define "family" broadly), leveraging strengths and addressing weaknesses.

Fourth, they are time-limited. FFT, for instance, generally runs for twelve to eighteen sessions over a period of about three months. Interestingly, just as with punishment, there appear to be diminishing returns to such treatments over time—more is not necessarily better in either context. Having time limits helps both the program and the family set and pursue concrete goals and reinforce family autonomy, independence, and agency.

Fifth, effective therapies are focused—they ensure that these interventions benefit the children and families most at risk for future violence. Generally speaking, the more these interventions focus on high-risk families, the more effective they are. More intensive (though still time-limited) programs tend to generate larger effects as well.

It is one thing to say, "Work with the toughest kids and families to get the best results." It is another thing to pull it off. These children and families are often the most difficult to work with. They can be uncooperative and disruptive, and they are more likely to drop out of treatment. It may not be easy, but the evidence does not equivocate: this is what it takes to successfully reduce crime and violence. Because small numbers of people are responsible for large amounts of crime and violence, successfully turning around a few can yield significant dividends.

Adolescents and children should have healthy attachments not only to their homes, but also to their schools. Contrary to what some believe, schools are generally safe places for kids. At school, students are protected from serious victimization and prevented from perpetrating crimes themselves. In the context of violence reduction, what matters most is keeping someday shooters physically present and engaged in school for as long as possible.

Sadly, for many years schools across the country adopted punitive school discipline policies that had disproportionate impacts on poor students of color, frequently suspending, expelling, and even arresting them for minor offenses. This is now known as the "school-to-prison pipeline." More kids out of school meant more opportunities for delinquency, crime, and violence, and this was especially so because youth at the highest risk for violence were also those most likely to be subject to such policies.[29]

During the Obama administration, the US Departments of Justice and Education launched a collaborative effort to end such practices. Unfortunately, that initiative ended when the next administration arrived. Nevertheless, proven programs are still available to foster safe and productive learning environments while still keeping kids in school. One particularly effective approach is called Positive Behavioral Interventions and Supports, or PBIS. PBIS is a school-wide strategy to reduce the student behavior problems that lead to suspensions, expulsions, and other forms of strong school discipline. Multiple studies have demonstrated that students in PBIS schools receive fewer school suspensions with improved perceptions of school safety. School-based programs like these have little impact on today's violence as few would-be shooters are actually attending school. That said, many someday shooters are still in school, and by keeping them there these programs prevent violence in the future.[30]

Putting Bona Fide Shooters Away

When all else fails, unlawful violence must be met with lawful force. By this I mean incarceration, preceded by arrest, prosecution, conviction, and sentencing. This is an unfortunate but unavoidable reality. There is no prevention or intervention strategy that works every time. If we fail to reconnect someday shooters to their families and schools, they may become would-be shooters. If we cannot turn would-be shooters away from violence, they may become bona fide shooters who must be separated from society. In public health, when all else fails and the danger of disease becomes too great, isolation and quarantine forcibly separate the sick from the healthy. The same is true for public safety.

My interviewees all agreed on this point. "You cannot save every-body," Mario Maciel told me. "If you had asked me this early in my career, I would have said yes, you could, but some individuals need law enforcement." Deputy Chief Tingirides came to the same conclusion: "At some point, we have to say you can't be in society anymore if you continue to victimize people, especially violently."

If chronic violent offenders cannot be changed, they must be stopped. One study estimates that the average murderer imposes almost $24 million in costs on their victims, the criminal justice and medical systems, and others. The most prolific killer in the same study murdered a total of nine victims, imposing a mind-boggling $150 mil-lion in total social costs.[31]

Interestingly, a former crime reporter has made the most persua-sive case for the firm punishment of serious violence. Jill Leovy cov-ered homicide for the *Los Angeles Times* for years. In 2015, her book *Ghettoside: A True Story of Murder in America* told a searing story of murder as seen through the eyes of a dedicated Los Angeles homi-cide detective, John Skaggs. The book also presented a powerful thesis on homicide in the United States: "The state's inability to catch and punish even a bare majority of murderers . . . was itself a root cause of the violence. . . . Like the schoolyard bully, our criminal justice system harasses people on small pretexts but is exposed as a coward before murder. It hauls masses of black men through its machinery but fails to protect them from bodily injury and death. It is at once oppressive and inadequate."[32]

Another former crime reporter, David Simon, believes much the same thing. Simon is best known as the creator of the powerful TV series *Homicide: A Year on the Killing Streets* and *The Wire*, but he began his career covering the local crime scene for the *Baltimore Sun*. Simon often speaks out about the violence that afflicts his hometown and the rest of the country, with views that are strikingly similar to Leovy's: "I watched the police department in Baltimore, and then I noticed it in other cities. . . . They were arresting people for drugs. . . . Meanwhile, the arrest rates for robbery, murder, were going down. And the one thing that makes cities safer is competent retroactive investigation of felonies. That actually can make a city safer."[33]

Leovy and Simon are from opposite ends of the country, but their opinions are informed by a similar set of professional experiences. Both, in their own words, advocate for perhaps the most targeted urban violence policy of all: just clear the cases. In 1965, police cleared 91 percent of all homicides. Since then, rates have slowly but steadily fallen to an all-time low of 59 percent in 2016. As mentioned in the last chapter, in 2017 the national clearance rate rose slightly to 62 percent, the third-lowest annual rate on record.[34]

Even worse, there are clear racial disparities in which cases get cleared. Kill a white person and you are more likely than not to be caught; murder a black person and you will likely evade capture. Over the past decade in Boston, police have made arrests in 90 percent of the homicides with white victims but in just 42 percent of those with black victims—the nation's largest and most egregious clearance gap. "There is no question that the African American community is victimized by this out of proportion," said former Boston police commissioner Ed Davis. "It's a tragedy of our time that we're not doing more to stop this."[35]

Find the killers and put them away. The idea is simple, powerful, and provocative. Why worry about potential offenders when there are actual offenders still roaming the streets? What's more, ineffectiveness leads to illegitimacy in the eyes of the community, so low clearance rates translate into less community trust and confidence in the police. According to Leovy and Simon, we could make communities safer and less suspicious of authority simply by solving more murders.

This is a tantalizing proposal, but there is a problem: there is little evidence to support the idea. "Criminologists, public health scholars, and other researchers who focus on gun violence prevention have largely ignored the challenge of improving clearance rates," criminologists Phillip Cook and Jens Ludwig wrote recently. "This is an unfortunate omission that should be remedied." I agree, but believe we should think of Leovy's argument as a call for balance, for remembering the fundamentals of crime and justice while promoting innovative approaches. We can catch more killers and support the other strategies discussed in this book at the same time.[36]

Improving homicide clearance rates can prevent murders in three ways. First, if more killers are brought to justice, people contemplating killing may think twice. Increasing the certainty of punishment produces a stronger deterrent effect. Second, if a murderer is caught the first time they kill, they will be incarcerated and unable to kill again as long as they remain in prison. Third, bringing murderers to justice eliminates the need and opportunity for others to take revenge, stopping the tit-for-tat cycle of retaliation.

There is reason to believe that increased attention to the investigation of homicides can improve clearance rates. In 2011, the Boston Police Department began to address their problematic clearance rates for homicides and other serious crimes. They worked to improve their rates through a combination of increased resources, additional training, and the adoption of improved investigative practices. In two years, the department was able to increase its homicide clearance rate by 18 percent.[37]

When it comes to clearing cases, manpower matters. One FBI analysis concluded that police departments whose detectives had fewer than five homicide cases per year solved significantly more cases. A forthcoming study indicates that the large differential between the clearance rates for homicide and for nonfatal shootings is mostly a matter of detective time and resources. During the economic recession that began in 2008, many police departments slashed staffing and budgets, and some have yet to fully recover from those years.[38]

It's not just about quantity; it's also about quality. During my time as a prosecutor, I worked with many detectives, and there was an enormous range of expertise, energy, capability, and commitment among them. I had the privilege of working with some of the New York Police Department's finest detectives and it often seemed as if there was nothing they could not do. They were dogged in their pursuit of proof: finding witnesses who appeared impossible to locate and persuading even the most hardened criminals to give information and testify. I also met John Skaggs, the impressive detective who was featured in *Ghettoside*, and speaking with him convinced me that while some of his abilities might be innate, many were transferable. I also worked with detectives who were lazy, dishonest, and incompetent—barely capable of the simplest investigative tasks. Not only did detectives like these do little to advance their cases, but they often damaged them with their ineptitude. The point here is that the quality of the investigator and the investigation truly matters when it comes to solving anything but the easiest cases.

In addition, building law enforcement legitimacy and investing in procedural fairness can make witnesses more likely to come forward and jurors more likely to convict. Improving the perceived fairness of the system can erode the "stop snitching" ethos that is pervasive in some communities. Finally, more support for the focused law enforcement strategies discussed in this book, particularly strategies like the GVRS that prioritize the most dangerous offenders and behaviors, will help hold more murderers accountable.

There is also a moral component to this. We have become hopeless and cynical about urban killing. We tell ourselves that nothing can be done, we blame the victims, or we avoid the subject altogether, fearful of "airing dirty laundry" about inner-city neighborhoods and of being perceived as disloyal, insensitive, or even racist. All these behaviors make violence seem normal when it should be anything but. We must retain our capacity for shock and rage at the act of murder. We should work intensively with those at the highest risk for violence, but society should never tolerate the act of killing itself.

With one exception (which will be discussed later), I never asked interviewees whether they had killed anyone, and they did not volunteer such information. There are some things better left unsaid, and there is no statute of limitations for murder. As a former prosecutor, if I had been given information about an unsolved homicide, I would be obligated to see that justice was done. I cannot absolve someone of such a crime. Only the state can do that, and possibly the family of the victim. It is not for me.

AFTER THE WOULD-BE, someday, and bona fide shooters comes everyone else. In poor, violent neighborhoods, many residents suffer, but only a few are violent. As we have noted, there is a strong tendency to conflate risk with need; that is, the risk of violence with the need for assistance. But for the purposes of violence reduction, focusing on the nonviolent poor is a costly distraction—a waste of time, energy, and resources.

This is a hard thing to say because it sounds as if I am suggesting that we ignore the needs of the poor. I am actually firmly in favor of all sorts of anti-poverty measures, but I support them on their own merits and not as anti-violence measures. It may also seem as if I am being soft on nonviolent crime. This is not true—I am simply calling for a more careful prioritization of crime, for focusing on the most serious crimes and criminals. We cannot do everything at once, so we should do what matters most, and do it first.

INTERVENING WITH THOSE most likely to kill or be killed is difficult, even dangerous work. But it has been done, and done successfully. To successfully reduce violence, we must connect with the Erik Kings of the world. We must engage, stabilize, treat, and then offer opportunities to them, working with would-be shooters, supporting someday shooters, and putting bona fide shooters behind bars.

This chapter focused on the hot people who commit the majority of urban violence. The next chapters focus on the hot spots where the majority of such violence happens.

CHAPTER 7

COOLING HOT SPOTS

IT IS MIDNIGHT ON THE CORNER OF WEST 70TH AND SOUTH MORGAN Streets in Englewood, a Chicago neighborhood that is notorious for violence. It's a Thursday in June and groups of young men are hanging out on nearby blocks, but here it is quiet. Not much foot or car traffic. An abandoned, boarded-up building sits on the corner, but beyond that, the area seems in relatively good order. The streetlights are working. The grass on the lawns has been mowed. There is little graffiti or trash. And yet, within just the past few weeks, there has been one murder down the street, another three blocks over, and five more shootings within a five-block radius.

A sergeant from the Chicago Police Department's Seventh District is taking me around. We discuss the city's challenges with violence as we go from hot spot to hot spot, responding to calls along the way. Most of the calls concern relatively petty disputes—a woman angry that her car is being repossessed, another arguing with her boyfriend over a cell phone—but there is a sense, even in these mundane interactions, of individuals under great pressure, ready to explode. Both women struggle to keep their cool as officers try to talk them down. Both women, fortunately, succeed.

The sergeant pulls up a map of the neighborhood on the console of his car. It displays recent shootings in the area and looks mostly empty except for the blocks around us and two slightly less deadly clusters to the east and north. Even here in Englewood, murderous violence is not everywhere.

AS WE'VE SEEN, there is clear and convincing evidence that violent crime clusters in and around locations known as hot spots. Even in the most infamous neighborhoods of the most dangerous cities, murder concentrates on just a few corners and blocks. If these hot spots can be cooled, the temperature of the entire city will fall.

In the last chapter, a series of people-based treatments were proposed: working with would-be shooters, supporting someday shooters, and, when all else fails, catching bona fide shooters and bringing them to justice. In this chapter, place-based treatments are recommended.

Hot spots can be chilled with a combination of policing, place making, and community building. Hot spots policing, executed properly, can suppress violence in places it happens most frequently, while an array of public and private partners can remake both the physical and social environment in and around these locations.

That said, there are challenges to overcome. These strategies come with risks as well as opportunities, and too often they are implemented in silos. To reduce violence in the most dangerous places, the best versions of each strategy must be used, and they must be used in a collaborative, coordinated manner.

In this chapter, we will sort through what works and what doesn't in order to identify the most promising paths forward. I'll also propose a way to bring these place-based strategies together. Before any of that, however, we need to ask an important question: What makes hot spots hot?

About Hot Spots

Hot spots, like hot people, are not hard to find. As Melvyn Hayward Jr. observed, "In communities across the country, you can go to hoods and you'll know, you don't even have to ask nobody." Melvyn, a former drug dealer and gang member himself, has worked for years in gang dispute resolution and serves as executive director of the H.E.L.P.E.R. Foundation, an organization he cofounded to serve youths and young adults at the highest risk for gangs and violence. If you lack Melvyn's expertise, just take a few years of violent crime data and map it out: you will see that homicides, shootings, and assaults clump together, not in neighborhoods, but in and around certain blocks, corners, and addresses.

Hot spots have been studied for decades now, and crime researchers have come to a few clear conclusions about the nature of crime concentration. First, hot spots are small in terms of geography, which is why academics often call them "microplaces" or "microlocations." A hot spot can be an individual address or group of addresses, or perhaps a single block or, at most, a small cluster of blocks.[1]

Second, hot spots may be small, but they are busy. City to city, hot spots take up only 3 to 6 percent of a city's geography but drive about 50 percent of all crime, with 20 to 25 percent of crime coming from the hottest 1 percent. Violent crime and homicides concentrate even more than other forms of crime.[2]

Third, hot spots are surprisingly durable. Chronic crime locations flare up, quiet down, then flare up again, year after year. In my hometown of Boston, criminologist Anthony Braga and colleagues examined violent crime data over a span of almost three decades. Over that period, he discovered that less than 3 percent of Boston's blocks generated more than half of all gun violence incidents. Furthermore, changes in these blocks drove changes in the city as a whole—when it came to urban violence, what happened in hot spots shaped what happened in the city at large, for better or for worse.[3]

We know that hot spots are small, busy, and stable over time. But why do they attract crime and violence in the first place? We know from academic research that physical disorder, foot traffic, and easy accessibility are all highly associated with crime hot spots. In the community, there are more answers. I talked with street outreach workers, cops, and former gang members, asking them first whether they believed that violence concentrates as the research says it does. There was clear consensus among my interviewees that the "law of crime concentration," as it applies to violent hot spots, is very real. Having settled that, I asked each of them, "What makes a spot hot?" The explanations fell roughly into three categories.

First and foremost, some hot spots are where hot people live, stay, or hang out. Violence may take place in a location, but it is committed by individuals. To illustrate, Erik King provided an example: "Let's say there is one guy, Mike, who lives in a building. Mike is crazy, so all the other crazy people go to his building, to his apartment, to hang out. Folks who continue to stay there are down with it, and the whole building becomes crazy, because Mike is bringing all these people there, attracting all this violence. Other folks, if they can move, they'll go to another building. That's a hot spot."

As Erik observed, when hot people move in, an informal sorting process begins. Melvyn made a similar observation: "It's about this territorial situation with the most notorious individuals. . . . People know not to fuck with them. It's about letting folks know where the power is—'This is where we at'—and rivals know that too." A hot spot can be where one dangerous individual or family lives, a known gang hangout, or a drug dealing location.

A second explanation is that some violent spots are hot because hot people pass through them frequently, providing chance opportunities for conflict and the settling of scores. These spots include nightclubs, bars, liquor stores, transportation hubs, and more. In many instances, rivals may not be actively looking for one another, but if they happen to be in the same place at the same time, it's on.

My own experience confirms this. When I was working with local experts to reduce youth violence in Detroit, there was a bus stop where a series of shootings had taken place. It was the only stop servicing a nearby school. When we investigated, we learned that when fights broke out at school between rival neighborhoods, disputes could turn deadly if older family members became involved. During school, fights were settled with fists; after school, relatives would bring in guns. When the bus was on time, after a fight in school, kids from outside neighborhoods could get home quickly, before relatives could react, giving everyone at least one evening to let tempers cool. On the other hand, if the bus was late, kids would wait on the corner like sitting ducks for relatives who came to finish the fight. This is also an example of how government services other than law enforcement, like transportation, can play a role in reducing violence.

The third explanation I heard had to do with the physical makeup of hot spots. Touring hot spots with officers, especially at night, I saw how impossible it was to police some of these areas. The challenges are many: public lighting is sparse or nonexistent, overgrown vegetation prevents clear sightlines, deserted properties serve as staging grounds for crime, and so on. Sometimes a setting just seems to invite violence.

The physical makeup of a hot spot can make violence easier to commit without getting caught. It can also send a signal that violence will be tolerated in such spaces. That being said, it is clear that environmental factors are secondary to actual interactions between people. If a shooter sees a rival and no law enforcement is present to intervene, there will be a shooting regardless of what the space looks or feels like.

No single feature forms a hot spot all by itself—they are always created from a combination of factors that slowly accumulate and then pass a tipping point. "It's not any one variable alone," gang task force leader Mario Maciel told me. "It's a combination of variables that breeds this." Having diagnosed these hot spots, we must now consider the treatments: policing, place making, and community building.

Policing

Criminologists have demonstrated that policing works best when focused on high-activity places. When there are more officers in an area, would-be shooters worry more about getting arrested and refrain from violence. They may even shy away from such areas entirely, limiting the opportunities for conflict even further.

The effectiveness of hot spots policing has been verified by independent researchers using the most rigorous methodologies. In 2004, the National Academy of Sciences concluded that "studies that focused police resources on crime hot spots provide the strongest collective evidence of police effectiveness that is now available." In 2017, the academy spoke again, this time in a more subdued tone: "The available research evidence suggests that hot spots policing strategies generate statistically significant crime reduction effects."[4]

Why the measured language? In the time between the two reports, more studies confirmed the effectiveness of hot spots policing, but with less impact than previously thought. Based on the studies available today, it turns out that the average effect of hot spots policing is somewhat modest. It tends to reduce crime and violence, but not by very much. It works, but it is no panacea.

What makes hot spots policing most effective? The anti-violence fundamentals of focus and fairness are a good place to start. In order to illustrate what police should do (and not do) at violent crime hot spots, we will look at hot spot interventions in two cities: Philadelphia and New York City.

Perhaps no city has experimented more with hot spots policing than Philadelphia. Beginning in 2008 under the leadership of then Philadelphia police commissioner Charles Ramsey, and with the support of a research team headed by Temple University's Jerry Ratcliffe, Philadelphia police have engaged in a series of tests to see which kinds of hot spots policing worked best.

In 2009, the partnership conducted a randomized controlled experiment, putting police foot patrols in hot spots, which led to a

23 percent reduction in crime. A year later, they conducted another experiment but this time went further, comparing several hot spot strategies against one another. The winning strategy was one that provided patrol officers with timely analysis and intelligence to help focus their attention on the serious repeat offenders who frequented the hot spot that officers were assigned to. This "intelligence-led" policing resulted in a 42 percent drop in crime in and around crime locations.[5]

Unfortunately, after the experiment's results were released, police leadership expanded the strategy widely, ignoring the lesson that when hot spots policing loses focus, it loses effectiveness and legitimacy. In 2010, the department was sued by the ACLU for engaging in a pattern and practice of racially biased stops and searches citywide. A year later the lawsuit was settled, with the department agreeing to collect additional data and conduct additional trainings. Since then, the number of stops and searches conducted by the Philadelphia police has dropped precipitously, but the parties disagree as to whether enough has been done.[6]

In 1996, New York City police commissioner William Bratton was featured on the cover of *Time* magazine under the headline "Finally, We're Winning the War on Crime. Here's Why," making the man and the strategy he championed—broken windows policing—world famous. The theory had first been introduced in a 1982 article by criminologists George Kelling and James Wilson, who argued that, in order to prevent crime, police should combat public disorder. Bratton brought a version of the theory to the New York Police Department (NYPD) and applied it enthusiastically, using arrests for low-level quality-of-life offenses to reassert control over public spaces that had seemed lawless to many. Initially, many in the media credited the strategy with producing the city's massive drop in crime in the 1990s.[7]

But broken windows policing ultimately became mired in controversy. The practice was associated with an enormous rise in stops and searches in New York City's poorest communities, popularizing a new term: "stop-and-frisk." Activists and advocates equated both broken windows policing and stop-and-frisk with oppressive, abusive, and racially discriminatory policing. The NYPD and its defenders responded that such tactics were a key component of the city's remarkable two-decade decline in crime and essential for maintaining public safety. However, after a lawsuit and the election of a new mayor in 2013, the NYPD moved away from broken windows policing and even the strategy's staunchest supporters appeared to have given up the fight. Contrary to what many expected, when stop-and-frisk numbers plummeted, crime levels stayed constant and then actually fell slightly.[8]

While policing in New York City was popularly defined by broken windows and stop-and-frisk, it also resembled an especially aggressive version of hot spots policing. As it turns out, NYPD's toughest tactics took place on the blocks in the city where crime was highest. These spots were flooded by inexperienced officers who used minor offenses and claims of suspicion to justify stopping, searching, and arresting large numbers of people.[9]

Like the police in Philadelphia, the NYPD acted increasingly indiscriminately over time, subjecting everyone (or at least most young men) in and around hot spots to high levels of scrutiny. Also as in Philadelphia, not only was the effort unfocused, but it was also widely believed to be deeply unfair.

Broken windows policing, as a strategy, has been relatively well studied, and the results confirm the lessons learned in Philadelphia and New York City. A systematic review of the approach examined twenty-eight evaluations and concluded that while the broken windows policing produced modest results overall, how it was implemented mattered greatly. When police collaborated with communities using problem-solving strategies, the results were considerably stronger and generated little if any resistance from citizens. When police used aggressive zero-tolerance tactics, the results were weaker and community resistance was strong.[10]

In sum, police can and should reduce crime by paying special attention to hot spots, but they must avoid casting too wide a net by supplementing their place-based focus with greater attention to people and behaviors that are genuinely dangerous. When police observe a known shooter in a hot spot, with a bulge in his waistband, hanging with associates, all of whom are drinking, they should be on high alert. In situations like these, most citizens expect the police to investigate and, if necessary, to intervene. At the same time, police should refrain from using these strategies in areas other than hot spots. As a matter of policy, law, and legitimacy, the most aggressive strategies should be limited exclusively to the most dangerous areas and people.

It is also crucial that policing of hot spots be carried out legally and in a procedurally fair manner. Transparency is especially important. For instance, when an officer approaches a group of young men and starts asking questions, the officer might be asked, "Why are you hassling us?" That question should receive a respectful answer, such as, "We've had a lot of shootings nearby, so we're paying special attention to this area. We just want to be sure everybody is being safe, so I'm going to ask you a few questions."

Cynicism and mistrust concentrate along with crime and violence. In fact, a recent study demonstrated that, in at least one city, rates of violent crime predict negative attitudes toward police even more than race. As we will see, improving police effectiveness and fairness in violent hot spots could be the best way to begin improving relationships between law enforcement and a community. If police can regain the trust of those in and around these areas, they are likely to improve their legitimacy overall.[11]

In violent hot spots, adopting the right policing strategy can pay dividends, but such strategies come with certain risks. Sometimes when crime falls, patrols are withdrawn as resources run low and crime creeps back up. Other times, patrols are ramped up, expanding beyond the hot spots where they are needed and appropriate. Finally, even when done properly, policing is no panacea. Consequently, in addition to policing violent places, we must invest in them.

Place Making

Like focus and fairness, balance is fundamental to place-based urban violence reduction. Pairing punishment with prevention, sanctions with rewards, and immediacy with sustainability is a hallmark of successful anti-violence efforts. Balance is also necessary for legitimacy, as communities tend to tolerate enforcement-only initiatives only temporarily. In order to be both effective and fair, we need police and prosecutors to curb violent crime in the short run while longer-term investments ensure that once violence goes down, it stays down.

In hot spots there are well-understood associations among crime, foreclosures, low occupancy rates, and vacant buildings and lots. Abandoned spaces serve as signs of a neighborhood in distress and decay. Physical and social disorder also closely correlates with crime and violence. But correlation is not causation: despite decades of study and effort, there are few place making interventions that consistently demonstrate strong if-then relationships to crime and violence. Targeted place-based investments that reduce urban disorder and blight should still play supporting roles, however, when it comes to violence reduction.

The epicenter of the nation's "cleaning and greening" movement is Philadelphia, where the city's horticultural society has transformed thousands of vacant lots into parks and gardens. In 2010, the city "remediated" abandoned buildings and lots by installing working doors and windows and by cleaning facades. In vacant lots, they removed trash and debris, planted grass and trees, and installed low fences with openings to create park-like settings. In total, the city fixed up over five thousand buildings and lots. Researchers found that fixing up abandoned buildings reduced firearm violence by 39 percent in nearby areas; doing the same for vacant lots reduced gun violence by 5 percent. These results are encouraging, but the overall evidence is not conclusive. One systematic review has concluded that urban greening efforts significantly decrease violent crime, while another cautioned that the evidence was too thin to support strong policy conclusions.[12]

Restoring and improving city services, especially street lighting, shows promise for reducing crime and violence. A systematic review of improved street lighting in the US and the United Kingdom revealed that better street lighting reduced crime by 21 percent, although for the US only the results were significantly weaker. Interestingly, because the modest benefits of street lighting were present both at night and during the day, the researchers suggested that these investments might increase community pride and improve informal social control as well as improve visibility.[13]

It is important to place these findings in context, however. Since the publication of C. Ray Jeffrey's *Crime Prevention Through Environmental Design* (CPTED) in 1971, interest in preventing crime by changing the physical environment has spawned dozens of organizations, associations, and networks; thousands of articles, reports, and studies; and billions of dollars in public and private investment. Despite massive amounts of attention and investment, the evidence for CPTED is mixed, showing only modestly positive impacts on crime generally and little to no impact on violent crime in particular. One promising exception, however, is that in Los Angeles, St. Louis, and Dayton, street closures and barricades significantly reduced drive-by shootings and other violent crimes.[14]

None of this means that CPTED or other environmental efforts to prevent violence are futile. It just means that they are unlikely to be transformative on their own. A key argument in favor of these strategies is their low cost and high potential return on investment. Philadelphia's greening effort cost only about $2,600 per building and $1,600 per lot, with maintenance costs of approximately $180 per lot per year. When offsetting these expenses against the high price of violent crime, researchers estimated that the effort saved Philadelphia taxpayers approximately $17,000 per building and $43,000 per lot.[15]

One key means of increasing the impact of these strategies is by improving their focus. Place making efforts are rarely targeted to the locations where violence concentrates most. To maximize the anti-violence impact of blight remediation and other place-based prevention, cities should target the hot spots where violence happens most frequently. It is not a coincidence that the street closures and barricade interventions that were directly focused on violence reduction had strong effects. Moving forward, place making efforts must be tightly focused on violent hot spots and not poverty, disorder, or crime more generally.

Community Building

The notion of community-based approaches is alluring are frequently mentioned in progressive policy circles. Community-based programs, community-based alternatives, and of course community-oriented policing. There's just one problem: nobody really knows what these terms really mean.

A common definition of the label *community-based* and a shared understanding of its role in crime reduction have proven elusive. For some, it means mobilizing the community itself. To others, it describes rehabilitating offenders "in the community" rather than sending them to jail or prison. To still others, it represents a philosophy, spirit, or set of values about how crime control should be conducted. Finally, some simply describe any anti-crime intervention physically located in a neighborhood as "community-based." To them, *community* simply means the setting where the work takes place. Under this last and broadest definition, almost all the strategies described in this book would qualify as "community-based" efforts, robbing the term of any practical use or meaning.[16]

The nebulous nature of the term is part of its appeal. Like the terms *holistic* and *comprehensive*, it forces no hard choices or difficult decisions—everyone can find something they like. Unfortunately, this lack of clarity has made it impossible to build up a strong base of evidence over time. New "community-based" programs and studies constantly reinvent the wheel by using bespoke definitions, terms, and measures. This results in outcomes that cannot be compared to one another. In any field, knowledge is cumulative, with new findings building on those that came before. For community-based crime prevention, such knowledge building has been severely limited by a lack of standardized approaches.[17]

Community-oriented policing, which is supposed to leverage partnerships with community residents in order to reduce crime and disorder, is a leading example of this problem. In 2015, criminologist Charlotte Gill and colleagues performed a systematic review of the strategy, analyzing twenty-five separate evaluations to see whether it was effective. Despite more than twenty years and billions of dollars in public investment, they found that community policing failed to have a significant impact on crime or violence and only modestly improved police-community relationships. These findings echo the conclusions of the National Academy of Sciences.[18]

That said, sometimes community policing does work. In Watts, for instance, the site of the infamous 1965 riots, Deputy Chief Tingirides helped establish the Community Safety Partnership (CSP). Under CSP, officers spend the majority of their time providing services to the community, not making arrests. In its first three years of operation, violent crime declined by 50 percent. Remarkably, arrests declined by the same amount. As a national strategy, however, community policing has failed to deliver less crime and has done little for police legitimacy. Why?[19]

In 1994, in response to rising rates of crime, President Bill Clinton promised to put one hundred thousand new community-policing officers on the streets. Over the next seven years, the newly established Office of Community Oriented Police Services (the "COPS Office") rushed more than $7 billion out the door to over ten thousand police agencies, more than half in the form of hiring grants. Little attention was paid to crafting a concrete, consistent model that could be perfected over time. As a result, a few police agencies launched impressive efforts to connect their work to the communities they served, but many more paid only lip service to the strategy.[20]

Ask any major police department if they are committed to community policing and they will assure you that they are. Look behind the platitudes, however, and you will find that even for police departments actively engaged in community policing, the term means different things in different jurisdictions. Not only does this hurt the strategy's effectiveness, but it also prevents us from understanding what has worked, what has not, and why.

Many nonpolice, community-based approaches purport to increase informal social control in communities, making them more resilient to crime and violence. There is a case to be made for this notion—high levels of social disorganization are associated with crime and violence. Unfortunately, this idea has not translated into concrete crime-fighting success. Neighborhood watch programs generate only modest benefits at best, while citizen patrols do not seem to work at all. More broadly, there have been no systematic reviews of community mobilization or other engagement strategies. While many like the idea of a community pulling itself up by its bootstraps, there is little evidence that it actually happens in the real world.[21]

In 1997, sociologist Robert Sampson and colleagues introduced the concept of "collective efficacy" in order to capture how social cohesion among community members translates into their "willingness to intervene for the common good." Collective efficacy is a means of measuring a community's capacity for informal social control. Keeping an eye on strangers, mediating disputes between neighbors, calling the police when warranted, and attending local council meetings are all forms of collective efficacy. It is not a passive concept; rather, it describes the extent to which a community will take actions in its own interest. It also explains why, other things being equal, some communities are better than others at resisting crime, violence, and disorder.[22]

Around the globe, studies have shown that communities with higher levels of collective efficacy tend to have lower levels of violence, yet the concept has been difficult to put into practice. In the more than twenty years since its introduction, few anti-crime interventions explicitly premised on increasing collective efficacy have been developed, implemented, rigorously evaluated, and found to be effective.

In sum, the evidence indicates that neither community policing nor any other community-based programs have consistently reduced crime or violence. In fact, most allegedly community-based programs that successfully reduce violent crime focus on the community only indirectly, if at all. Perhaps the notion of community is simply too amorphous to translate into specific policies. Instead of abstract notions of collective action, we should focus community- and relationship-building efforts on violent spots, just as was recommended for place making efforts. Instead of trying to rehabilitate communities separate and apart from the state, we should be emphasizing legitimacy and fairness in order to promote a positive, mutually reinforcing relationship between communities and the law enforcement agencies that are supposed to serve them.

To reduce urban violence, we need a new notion of community, one that is tightly focused on the hot spots where such violence concentrates. Hot spots are not simply geographic locations; they are also social settings. In addition to being microlocations, they are microcommunities. Rather than organizing partnerships across whole neighborhoods, we should begin with a block or two. We should focus on the collective efficacy of hot spots, enhancing local willingness to intervene in and around the places where crime and violence concentrate most.[23]

Importantly, this new concept of community should include rather than exclude the police. Recent studies indicate that hot spots policing, when implemented in a procedurally just manner, can actually increase collective efficacy and improve informal social control. Additionally, asking communities to rescue themselves from high rates of crime and violence is not only ineffective; it is profoundly unfair. Racially discriminatory governmental policies were essential to

producing concentrated poverty in many communities of color, and
it is from that poverty that crime and violence arose. Having played
a role in creating violence-ridden urban communities, the state must
now play a role in liberating them.[24]

Partnership-Oriented Crime Prevention: Pairing Policing, Place Making, and Community Building

An emerging practice holds promise for uniting the hot spots policing, place making, and community building strategies identified
in this chapter. In criminology, it is called *third-party policing*, but
partnership-oriented crime prevention may be a broader and more
appropriate term. With partnership-oriented crime prevention, police
engage residents, landlords, business owners, regulators, inspectors,
licensing authorities, and others, encouraging them to help prevent
the crime and violence that happen in hot spots.[25]

In Chula Vista, California, police successfully collaborated with
the local chamber of commerce along with code enforcement, planning, and building officials to pressure owners of nuisance motels to
address the crime, drug use, and prostitution that were concentrating
in these locations. In Chicago, police reduced drug- and gang-related
crime by working with city attorneys and inspectors to force landlords
to clean up properties where drug dealers and gang members were
operating. Business improvement districts, which often utilize private
security personnel to supplement police services, are another well-
known example of this approach. While only a few of these efforts
have been rigorously evaluated, the early results are encouraging.[26]

Partnership-oriented prevention works by bringing police together
with non–law enforcement organizations to bring additional resources,
expertise, and authority to bear. Rather than resorting to arrests, police
and their partners can use fines, orders, injunctions, and evictions to
address crime-producing conditions in violent hot spots. Another important benefit of partnership-oriented crime prevention is that when
police and community partners work together, legitimacy is enhanced.[27]

These principles can be used to guide policing, place making, and community building in violent hot spots. Hot spots policing, properly executed, can quickly bring a measure of safety and stability to dangerous places—it is the tourniquet to stop the bleeding. Then police can partner with others to change the physical makeup of crime locations—this is the stitches to close the wound. Finally, by using the principles of procedural fairness to bring impacted residents into these efforts, police can build legitimacy and foster a stronger sense of community to promote long-term healing and recovery.

EVEN IN NEIGHBORHOODS like Englewood, deadly violence is not everywhere. Instead, it clusters in a few discrete locations where hot people hang out or pass through and where the environment signals that such violence will be tolerated. To reduce urban violence, place-based strategies need to be deployed according to the principles of focus, balance, and fairness. We need hot spots policing, but only when done properly. We need investment, but it needs to be the appropriate type of investment. Finally, we must narrow our notion of community, limiting it to the microcommunities in and around violent hot spots. At the same time, we should expand it to include police and prosecutors, other city officials, property and business owners, civic leaders, and, of course, residents. We must put the right strategies together in the right ways.

CHAPTER 8

GUNS, GANGS, AND DRUGS

WE'VE SEEN THAT URBAN VIOLENCE IS STICKY, CLUSTERING AMONG small groups of violent people, places, and things. The last two chapters outlined people- and place-based treatments to reduce violence among hot people and in hot spots. This chapter examines the things that drive violence—guns, gangs, and drugs—but with an important twist: to complete the three-pronged approach, we must analyze them as behaviors, not objects. To maximize effectiveness, policy makers and practitioners should focus on what hot people actually *do* in hot spots.

Guns, gangs, and drugs get a good deal of public attention, and that is warranted, but why they caused concern in the first place is often overlooked. Guns are an issue because of gun violence, gangs because of gang violence, and drugs because of drug abuse, overdoses, and violence. They are best understood not just as static objects but also as dynamic behaviors that facilitate violence. Instead of guns, think illegal gun carrying; instead of gangs, gangbanging; instead of drugs, violent drug dealing.

Gun Carrying, Not Guns

Many believe that the US has more crime than other high-income countries. This is wrong. Many believe that it has more violent crime; also wrong. The US is not significantly more criminal nor more violent than its wealthy peers, but it is more deadly. While the United States' rates of nonlethal crime and violence are fairly unremarkable, its homicide rate is roughly seven times higher than the high-income-country average, driven by a gun homicide rate that is twenty-five times higher.[1]

Americans own about 265 million firearms in total—more than one per adult. The US has less than 5 percent of the world's population, but almost half its civilian-owned guns. In 2017, almost forty thousand Americans lost their lives to gun violence—more than whose who died in traffic accidents.[2]

Firearms facilitate the act of killing. To commit murder, one must have the means, motive, and opportunity to do so. Guns do not create the intent or the opportunity to kill, but once a killer is in the presence of their intended victim, guns provide a quick and easy means of completing the act. Firearms are used in about 70 percent of all homicides, and crimes committed with guns are about three times more lethal than those committed with knives and almost forty-four times deadlier than those committed without any weapon at all. By making it easier to kill, guns ensure that more people are in fact killed. Over thirty peer-reviewed studies confirm that higher rates of firearm possession are associated with an increased risk for violence and homicide; studies that say otherwise have been debunked.[3]

In one sense, the story is quite simple: the US has more gun violence because it has more guns. In another sense, the story is more complicated. The overwhelming majority of firearms in the US are in the hands of citizens who own their weapons lawfully and use them responsibly. Only a minuscule percentage of these weapons will ever take a human life. Sound firearm policy depends on reconciling these two truths: more guns means more gun deaths, but few guns are actually used to kill people.

To complicate matters further, many see gun violence in the US as a crisis, but in fact the nation is facing at least four separate but related gun crises. In 2017, there were more than fourteen thousand gun homicides, caused mostly by urban violence, followed by violence among intimate partners and family members, along with a small number of murders due to mass shootings. Gun suicides caused the largest number of gun-related fatalities at almost twenty-four thousand.[4]

These four crises—urban gun violence, domestic gun violence, mass shootings, and gun suicides—share many common elements. Most obviously, they all involve guns. Almost all the perpetrators are men. Suicidal thoughts can serve as precursors to homicidal violence, and some domestic and mass killers commit suicide after their crimes. Many mass shooters have histories of domestic violence; perpetrators of urban violence often do as well. When examining the interactions among these four phenomena, it becomes clear that violence learned in one context can lead to violence in another—a deadly contagion effect.

While there are connections between these crises, they are also independent and different from one another in important respects. Urban gun violence primarily occurs between disadvantaged young men of color, while rates of gun suicide are highest among older white men. Mass shooters often target strangers, while domestic offenders kill those closest to them. Urban and domestic homicides as well as suicides take lives with numbing regularity, while mass murders happen relatively rarely (though still far too frequently).

The clearest disconnect among different forms of firearm violence is between urban violence and all the others. The difference boils down to how perpetrators get their guns: domestic homicides, mass shootings, and suicides are usually committed with legally purchased firearms, while urban violence is perpetrated with guns that are loaned, stolen, or bought on the black market. Relatedly only about one of every six guns used in the commission of a crime is legally obtained.[5]

When it comes to how we should respond to gun violence, this difference is critically important. Federal law bars those convicted of felonies or domestic violence misdemeanors from purchasing or possessing a firearm. It also prevents those subject to domestic violence restraining orders, those found by the courts to be mentally ill, those who are fugitives from justice, and those who are addicted to drugs from getting and keeping guns. Finally, federal law sets the minimum legal age for possessing a handgun at eighteen and the minimum age for purchasing a handgun from a federally licensed firearms dealer at twenty-one. Many states have additional prohibitions and standards for gun possession and ownership that go beyond federal law.[6]

For those most likely to shoot or be shot on the streets of our cities, one or more of these prohibitions typically applies, which means that reducing urban gun violence depends mostly on the enforcement of laws already on the books. Curbing illegal gun carrying—hot people, carrying hot (illegal) guns, in hot spots—is crucial. This behavior is perhaps the most important proximate cause of urban homicide today.

WHETHER A HOT person carries a hot gun in a hot spot depends on, among other things, supply and demand. To reduce the demand for illegal firearms among dangerous people in dangerous places, the risk of apprehension must be high. Strategies that increase the risk of being caught with a gun in high-crime locations can deter criminals from carrying weapons in those places.

In 2012, criminologists Christopher Koper and Evan Mayo-Wilson conducted a systematic review of police strategies designed to reduce the illegal carrying of firearms. Surprisingly, they found only four studies that were sufficiently rigorous to be considered, three of which were conducted in the US. One of these studies was the Kansas City Gun Experiment.[7]

In 1995, Kansas City began directing police patrols to local hot spots where homicide rates were roughly twenty times the national average. Officers focused their attention on detecting and recovering illegal firearms through car and pedestrian stops. Over six months, officers issued 1,090 tickets, checked 948 cars, stopped 532 pedestrians, and made 616 arrests. They also seized twenty-nine guns—65 percent more than in the previous six months. Most importantly, total gun crime fell by 49 percent. Interestingly, when the effort was stopped and restarted five months later, the target areas experienced another significant decline in gun-related crime. In Kansas City, officers did not focus on stopping all crime in the hot spots they patrolled. Instead, they focused only on gun crime, and specifically only on one behavior: the carrying of illegal firearms. The lesson was that it is critically important to focus not just on specific people and places but also on specific activities and behaviors.[8]

Koper and Mayo-Wilson observed that in all four studies gun crime was reduced but nevertheless cautioned against drawing definitive conclusions based on their limited number of studies. That said, in 2018, a report on policing from the National Academy of Sciences favorably commented on the Kansas City experiment and other efforts to reduce gun crime in hot spots. Koper and Mayo-Wilson were careful to note that interventions that reduced illegal gun carrying did little to address the underlying societal conditions associated with gun violence, but they argued that such strategies could help break the cycle of such violence and establish baseline conditions for future improvement. "To use a medical analogy," they wrote, "one must stop the bleeding before one can heal the patient."[9]

Some object to any form of "crackdown," even on guns in violence-prone locations, due to the controversies with stop-and-frisk policing and the potential for abuses of authority. These concerns are warranted but can be addressed. As we have seen, when police conduct stops and searches in a limited, targeted manner and in consultation with impacted communities, they can reduce violence without triggering significant opposition. Emphasizing community buy-in is essential; in Kansas City, for example, extensive community outreach was done before police patrols began, and when residents were surveyed later, they expressed support for the patrols.[10]

The Group Violence Reduction Strategy (GVRS) and street outreach are also important evidence-informed approaches to reduce illegal gun carrying. Both of these strategies are not only people based;
they are also behavior based, meaning that they work with the riskiest
people to turn them away from the riskiest behaviors, including but
not limited to illegal gun carrying.

Another means of reducing illegal gun carrying is to limit supply
by reducing the number of guns that end up in the wrong hands in the
first place. As criminologist Anthony Braga recently observed, scoff-
law gun dealers, private buyers and sellers, illegal gun traffickers, and
criminals all regularly exploit the weaknesses of the nation's "incredibly leaky" system for buying and selling firearms.[11]

There is emerging evidence that local efforts to disrupt illegal
firearms trafficking can limit the flow of new weapons to criminals.
That said, there is little evidence that these supply-side efforts actually reduce gun violence. The path by which criminals illegally acquire
firearms is an intentionally murky one. Most get guns from people
they know: friends, family members, and fellow criminals. The impact
of anti-trafficking strategies is limited because they cannot easily
identify and target the people and weapons most likely to be involved
in violence. In fact, the best-known supply-side strategy is famously
ineffective for precisely this reason.[12]

Gun buyback policies have been widely discredited among criminologists yet remain popular with the press and policy makers. Buybacks encourage citizens to voluntarily surrender their firearms, usually
in exchange for gift certificates or small amounts of cash. Photo
opportunities abound as community members happily hand over old,
inoperable, and obsolete firearms that are highly unlikely to be used
to commit actual crimes, which is why the impact of these buybacks is
minimal at best.[13]

And yet these efforts continue, even flourish, the evidence against
them notwithstanding. I remember a tense meeting with law enforcement officials outside of New York City at which I was briefed on

local strategies for reducing gun violence. At the time, I was heading up GIVE, the Gun Involved Violence Elimination initiative, a statewide effort in New York to reduce violent gun crime. (For more information about GIVE, see appendix A.) When the officials enthusiastically described their gun buyback program, I informed them of the evidence against the strategy. The lead official hesitated, then his expression hardened. He replied, "Well, we get great press off these things, so we're doing them." I responded, "You can do what you want, but not with our money." The meeting ended shortly thereafter.

Because criminals do not get guns the way noncriminals do, it is easier to deter them from carrying firearms than it is to stop them from acquiring such weapons. Plugging the holes of our leaky gun markets is critically important, but to reduce urban violence right now, it is better to focus on reducing the demand for illegal weapons by dangerous people in dangerous places.

WHAT ABOUT BROADER measures to control the supply of firearms? Many legislative reforms aim to limit access to guns in one way or another. Prohibiting individuals with histories of domestic violence from possessing guns reduces domestic homicides. Banning high-capacity magazines limits the lethality of mass shootings. Campaigns to promote the safe storage of guns, particularly when they provide free safety devices such as trigger locks, have reduced suicides and accidental shootings.[14]

Another strategy aims to reduce all forms of gun violence simultaneously. Permit-to-purchase (PTP) laws do what their name suggests: they require a person to have a permit before purchasing a firearm. Ten states currently have some form of PTP requirement. In those states, before individuals can receive a permit, they get fingerprinted, pass a criminal background check, complete a firearms-safety course, or meet some other condition.

Over a series of rigorous studies, public health researcher Daniel Webster and colleagues have amassed a sizeable body of evidence supporting PTP laws. In one study, they found Connecticut's 1995 PTP law was associated with a 40 percent reduction in the state's homicide rate over ten years. In another, Missouri's 2007 repeal of its PTP law increased firearm homicide rates by 23 percent annually, leading to more than fifty additional deaths per year. A third study demonstrated that in large urban US counties, PTP laws were associated with an 11 percent reduction in firearm homicides.[15]

Licensing gun owners makes good sense, just as it makes sense to license automobile owners. As public health researcher David Hemenway has argued, we should regulate guns the way we regulate cars. Since the 1950s, auto fatalities have fallen by as much as 85 percent. It did not happen all at once, and it did not happen by banning cars. It happened incrementally, little by little, by making cars and roads safer, with seat belts, airbags, padded dashboards, improved street lighting and signage, speed limits, crackdowns on drunk driving, and so on.[16]

While these and other supply-side measures will do some good, and a few will do considerable good, few if any address urban violence directly. Most of the public discourse on gun control revolves around new gun laws, but new laws are unlikely to stop the killing happening in the streets right now. These measures should be considered complements to, not substitutes for, the strategies identified in this book to reduce urban violence.

ASIDE FROM SUICIDES, urban gun violence kills more people than any other form of gun violence. It is also the most addressable form of violence based on the evidence available today. Yet urban violence is not at the center of the gun violence conversation. Why not?

Various distortions in the public debate work against a strong focus on urban violence. The first and most important distortion concerns mass shootings, which capture the public's attention more than any other form of gun violence. Sadly, many Americans still do not recognize that mass shootings constitute a minuscule portion of gun violence in this country. Since the famous Texas Tower shooting in

1966, approximately 1,135 persons have been killed in mass shootings. Over that same period, there have been almost a million firearm homicides in total.[17]

Our national preoccupation with mass shootings warps our understanding of urban violence. Three-quarters of mass shootings are carried out with legal firearms; the vast majority of urban homicides are not. Mass shootings are usually committed by white perpetrators against white victims, while urban homicides are typically carried out by black perpetrators against black victims. Mass shootings are episodic, acute events that are difficult to study or predict; urban homicides are chronic events that happen all the time, making them more amenable to research and analysis.[18]

When mass shootings dominate the conversation, the policy discussion on gun violence is perverted. The right stonewalls while the left favors measures with little regard for targeting or risk. When broad-based measures to limit access to firearms encounter resistance, politicians look to politically palatable measures that often do more harm than good. For instance, it is politics and not evidence that is the driving force behind most school safety and mental health proposals that claim to prevent gun violence. Schools, despite the headlines, are quite safe places for children to be—in terms of probability, a typical school will see a student homicide only once every six thousand years. Billions have been spent on measures to make schools more secure, despite the fact that there is no evidence that they significantly reduce the risk of school shootings. Similarly, some mass shooters display signs of mental illness before their massacres, but most perpetrate their crimes for terrible but all-too-human motivations—seeking revenge or fame, for example. If all major mental illnesses were miraculously cured, experts believe this would result in a mere 4 percent decline in gun violence overall.[19]

Further impeding the public conversation is the fact that we know far too little about guns, gun violence, and gun control. The reason for our lack of knowledge is simple: there's just not enough research. A recent study compared the thirty leading causes of death in the US to the amount of funding and number of publications dedicated to them. The study found that gun violence research was dramatically underfunded: based on the number of fatalities associated with gun violence, researchers predicted that nearly $1.4 billion in funding and 38,897 publications would be devoted to the issue. In actuality, gun violence received only $22 million in funding and was the subject of approximately 1,700 scholarly articles—1.6 percent and 4.4 percent, respectively, of the expected total. In fact, relative to mortality rates, gun violence is the most underfunded and understudied cause of death in the nation.[20]

For years, any effort to seriously study the connection between guns and gun violence has been met with intense resistance from the National Rifle Association and other gun rights organizations, and they have been stunningly successful in their efforts to either shut down or muddy scientific inquiry in this area. Gun rights advocates lobbied for the Dickey Amendment, a rider to a 1996 spending bill that prohibits the CDC from engaging in gun control advocacy, which has also had a chilling effect—as was its intent—on gun-related CDC research. They also also secured the Tiahrt Amendment, which prohibits the Bureau of Alcohol, Tobacco, Firearms and Explosives (ATF) from releasing information from its firearms database to anyone other than law enforcement agencies in connection with a criminal investigation, effectively blocking the use of gun trace data for research.

This opposition creates a situation where evidence is lacking for the effectiveness of gun control policies, not because such policies do not work, but because they have not been studied. No one would argue that studying labor markets is intended to do away with jobs or that the goal of traffic safety studies is to do away with cars, yet gun violence research is opposed because any effort to study guns is perceived as one small step down a slippery slope to banning all guns.

There is hope. While the impasse over guns in Congress remains, states are slowly but steadily making more reforms. In 2018, California launched the first state-funded center to study gun violence, and Arnold Ventures, a philanthropic foundation, launched a multiyear research collaboration with $20 million in seed funding. An ever-growing cadre of journalists have dedicated themselves to providing the public with a more complete picture of gun violence across the nation. Finally, the school shooting in Parkland, Florida, the deadliest ever in a high school, unleashed a wave of student and youth activism.[21]

These young activists made a series of wise choices to enhance the impact of their advocacy, but most importantly, they seemed to understand intuitively that their struggle was linked to the struggles of so many urban teenagers today. Instead of ignoring urban violence, they acknowledged and highlighted it, even criticizing the media for not paying more attention to it. Linking the constituencies suffering from urban violence, domestic violence, mass shootings, and suicides may be the best recipe for constructive and concerted political activism on these issues moving forward. Solidarity among those who have lost blood, limbs, friends, and family members is a sound strategy for broadening and deepening the coalition to prevent all forms of gun violence.[22]

THE WAR OVER guns will rage on, but the battle to save lives in urban America can be won right now with policies that do not require new laws or regulations. The strategies in this book—the GVRS, street outreach, and targeted crackdowns on gun carrying—have been demonstrated to prevent gun violence not by limiting supply but instead by reducing the demand for firearms among the people most likely to use them, in the places where they are most likely to be used.

Gangbanging, Not Gangs

Erik King has the dubious distinction of having belonged to three separate gangs, one of which he founded. "Most gangs are formed as a response to another gang," Erik told me. "If you can't be safe by yourself, gangs give you safety and belonging." It may begin with mutual

protection, but as gangs grow they need a means of supporting themselves and their members, and that is where crime comes in. "There's
a Venn diagram between gangs and crime. Guys are hungry—who's
paying for food? Guys want to go out and party—who's covering the
tab? That's when it's like, 'Hey, we could sell weed or coke.' That's how
it starts. It happens to every crew, and the bigger you get, the more
money you need."

Just like the myth of easy drug money—many dealers make less
than the minimum wage—gangs offer but do not deliver protection.
"Shit goes awry—you get involved in all these beefs," said Erik. "You
joined up for self-defense, but then you become the dudes you hated."
Once the cycle of violent retaliation has started, it is difficult to stop.
"Now you're a target because people know you. Now you can never be
alone—you always have to be with your people." Gang members are
at elevated risk for violence not just as perpetrators but also as victims.
The grim reality is that youths who join gangs in pursuit of safety only
place themselves in greater jeopardy.[23]

Like guns, gangs facilitate violence. Gang members make up less
than 1 percent of an average city's population but are involved in as
much as 20 percent of its homicides. In cities like Boston, Chicago,
and Los Angeles, gang-related killings account for 30 to 60 percent of
all homicides. That said, gangs cannot be equated with violence. Not
all gangs are equally violent, and as we've seen, not all gang members
are equally violent. "Most kids just want to be down," Erik observed.
"It's only a few guys that are the real dogs, that do the real work." Also,
while a glance at the evidence seems to show that gangs cause violence, a deeper look also reveals the opposite: violence causes gangs.[24]

We have been looking at gangs all wrong, and we have been doing
so for decades. We fetishize gangs, obsessing over the details of their
rituals, rites, and ceremonies. We exaggerate their numbers and their
crimes. We stereotype them, grouping all gangs and gang members
into a monolithic whole. And, despite all this attention, we have yet to
find any specifically gang-oriented policy that consistently works to
reduce crime or, more importantly, violence.

Police create gang units, prosecutors build gang cases, and politicians pass laws prohibiting all manner of gang activities. Nothing has worked. Some activists coo over gangs, mistaking them for nascent community groups. That has not worked either. We have been so wrong about gangs, for so long, that an entirely new approach is needed. We have to start over and refocus our efforts not on gangs but on gang violence. If a gang or a gang member is violent, they deserve our anti-violence attention. If they are not, our time and energy are better spent elsewhere. With gangs, the issue is not the group's identity; it is the group's behavior. Gangs are not the problem; gangbanging is.

Rejecting the very notion of gang prevention, intervention, and suppression may sound counterintuitive, but leaders in the field have been calling for it for years. Connie Rice, a legendary civil rights activist in Los Angeles and founder of the Advancement Project, recently told an audience, "If you attack gangs, they get stronger. You must declare war on violence and trauma."[25]

THERE ARE A number of persistent myths, misunderstandings, and gaps in knowledge concerning gangs in the United States. First, many assume that gangs in the United States are large, organized, hierarchical organizations with elaborate rituals and structures. Generally speaking, people who believe this have watched the classic 1988 movie *Colors* too many times. Most gangs in the United States are small, informal groups that have limited capacity for highly organized crime. There used to be a few large gangs, but most have broken down into smaller, less organized groups. "The structure has loosened tremendously," gang intervention expert and former gang member Melvyn Hayward Jr. told me. "You got some Bloods and Crips working together now, and some Bloods and Crips fighting their own." Gang expert Ronald Noblet made an intriguing observation about this trend: "The new norm, worldwide, is the flattening out of authority. Gangs are just one manifestation of that—it simply reflects society." These observations are confirmed by research. For instance, while the dominant narrative about gangs is that they are well-organized groups in competition with one another, one study found that when gang members were killed by another gang member, the perpetrator was often someone from their own gang.[26]

Second, many members of the public assume that all gangs, and all gang members, are equally dangerous. They are not. Gangs vary greatly in terms of the intensity and scale of the violence they generate. Furthermore, only a small number of individuals within any gang will actively engage in the most serious violence. "Everybody's involvement in the gang is at a different level," former gang member and gang worker Raymond Solórzano told me. "There's some that go all the way, there's some that get in but don't get too deep—they don't commit murder or go to prison. Out of a whole gang, maybe five percent commit the real serious crimes." Gangs and their members are simply more complex than is commonly understood.

Third, we simply have no idea how many gangs and gang members there are in the United States. Gang statistics are notoriously unreliable, yet they're often cited authoritatively. The problems begin with a lack of a universal definition. There is no agreement on what constitutes a gang and a gang member. Who gets counted varies from state to state and city to city.[27]

From there, the issues multiply: law enforcement officials creating gang databases can add individuals without an underlying arrest, conviction, or a hearing. Most individuals join gangs for relatively short periods of time, a few years at most, yet once an individual is identified by the police as "gang-affiliated," it can be extremely difficult to remove the designation. As a result, these databases grow and grow and simultaneously become less and less accurate. Increasingly these designations are being challenged in court, and many jurisdictions are abandoning these databases in favor of more accurate, less controversial strategies.

In 2012, before it was discontinued, the National Youth Gang Survey indicated that there were approximately 850,000 gang members in the United States. In 2015, another survey estimated that there were well over 1 million youths aged five to seventeen who were involved in gangs, or about 2 percent of all such youths nationally. The bounds of their estimates were huge, however—there could have been as few as 675,000 or as many as 1,535,000. It is important to note that even the highest estimates of gang membership are still tiny compared to the national population. Even in neighborhoods plagued by gang violence, the majority of youths generally remain unaffiliated.[28]

We know even less about the number of crimes committed by gang members. According to the FBI, gangs account for approximately 5 to 7 percent of all murders each year, but that number cannot be accurate because this data is reported by police departments, which usually underreport gang killings if they report them at all. New Orleans, for example, reported zero gang murders in 2015. So did Baltimore. In fact, more than two-thirds of all reporting police agencies reported either zero gang killings or one.[29]

Strikingly, the majority of reported gang killings come from just two cities: Los Angeles and Chicago. In Chicago, gang crime must be motivated by gang concerns, meaning that it must achieve some gang objective to be labeled a "gang crime" by the authorities. In Los Angeles, any crime committed by a gang member is considered "gang-related," whether or not it had any other connection to the gang. These definitions matter: one analysis compared these two definitions and found the former yielded twice as many gang crimes as the latter.[30]

Fourth, research has identified various risk factors for becoming a gang member, including experiencing a traumatic life event, displaying antisocial tendencies, having low levels of parental supervision, having pro-delinquent attitudes, and associating with delinquent peers. These factors make sense, but as gang expert Scott Decker has noted, "there are no risk factors that uniquely predict the probability of gang membership, as the same factors . . . also predict other antisocial outcomes." Switch out the term *gang* for *criminal* or *juvenile*, in other words, and you will get the same results.[31]

In addition, while risk factors may be useful in terms of understanding gangs, they offer little in terms of concrete guidance or assistance on how to actually address gang violence. We know that various factors are loosely associated with elevated rates of delinquency and criminality, but which ones are most important? How much do they elevate risk, and for whom? There are few reliable answers. The scholarship on risk factors, despite decades of effort, has not revealed a clear path forward.[32]

Fifth and finally, we know little about what actually works to reduce gangs, gang membership, and gang-related crime. Almost every serious effort to survey the field for best practices has resulted in disappointment and frustration. In particular, the prestigious Campbell Collaboration has tried not once or twice but three times to systematically examine the state of gang prevention, with all three efforts failing for lack of sufficiently rigorous studies. As Decker has concluded, "The state of research and practice in responding to gangs has not advanced to the point where it is possible to identify 'best practices' based on advanced research designs."[33]

G.R.E.A.T., or Gang Resistance Education and Training, is perhaps the best-known gang prevention program of all time. And it doesn't work very well. G.R.E.A.T. was originally developed as a nine-lesson anti-drug curriculum taught by police officers to students at school. The approach was based on the Drug Abuse Resistance Education (DARE) program, another effort that has maintained popularity despite strong research demonstrating its ineffectiveness.

After initial evaluations described G.R.E.A.T. as a promising strategy, researchers took a hard look at the program and found it wanting. G.R.E.A.T. program leaders responded admirably by overhauling the program and evaluating the effort again. In its new iteration, G.R.E.A.T. improved attitudes toward law enforcement and modestly reduced gang membership but failed to have any impact on delinquent or criminal behavior. G.R.E.A.T. failed for many of the same reasons other gang reduction strategies have: it did not target violence or those most at risk for violence. Ultimately, G.R.E.A.T. did not deliver because of a fatal flaw: its strategy was based on gang identity, not gang behavior.[34]

Not only has the emphasis on gangs been ineffective, it's actually made the problem worse. No one has learned this lesson better than Father Greg Boyle. Early on in his career, Father Boyle was instrumental in negotiating several gang truces in Los Angeles, but then he changed his approach. "I have learned that you work with gang members and not with gangs; otherwise you enforce the cohesion of gangs and supply them oxygen."[35]

This word, *cohesion*, was first mentioned in chapter 5 in reference to street outreach efforts, but it also comes up again and again when discussing the unintended effects of gang policies. Researchers have written extensively about the dangers of increasing gang cohesiveness or togetherness. "The more you go against gangs, the stronger you make them," said Ronald Noblet. "The gang is strengthened and their cohesiveness increases from the attack."

Gangs thrive on reputation. When gangs are engaged or attacked directly, their reputations and status are enhanced. We should never ignore the violence gangs perpetrate, but we should acknowledge gangs themselves only when absolutely necessary. President Donald Trump is fond of calling out the transnational gang MS-13 and discussing its horrific crimes in detail. By doing this, Trump is actually providing the gang with free publicity, playing up its power in the eyes of local communities, making them easier to intimidate and control.

REFOCUSING OUR GANG-RELATED efforts is actually easier than it seems. Remember that the nation's leading anti-violence strategy, the GVRS, targets group not gang violence. Early on, the strategy discarded *gangs* as a loaded term that distracted from the reality of what was happening on the street. "'Gang' means something pretty particular to people—structure, purpose, cohesion, leadership. It's a myth, almost always," says David Kennedy. "Most street groups don't have much of any of that. . . . The core reality [is] it's all about the groups." The GVRS recognizes that while group dynamics play an important role in violence, those dynamics should be used to change *behavior,* not *identity*. By focusing on group-oriented violence, not the group itself, the strategy can pacify gangs while draining them of their status, power, and reason for existence. Street outreach, when done properly, can do the same thing.[36]

Crime and violence prevention strategies that do not focus on gangs can also be substituted for those that do. "In many cases, delinquency prevention programs should be implemented over gang programs," a recent systematic review of anti-gang strategies concluded. A recent evaluation examined whether Functional Family Therapy—the delinquency and violence prevention program described in chapter 6—could be adapted to work with gang-involved youth. One year after treatment, high-risk program participants were arrested less frequently, had fewer felony charges, and were less likely to be deemed delinquent by courts. The authors of the study concluded, "For too long, gang programming has been divorced from the broader movement of prevention science. . . . Evidence-based gang programs based on rigorous scientific standards can and should be developed."[37]

We have already identified strategies like FFT that are proven to keep high-risk kids out of trouble, whether they are in a gang or not. If we focus on keeping kids from becoming involved in violent crime, the gang problem will take care of itself. Stop the violence and the gang loses its reason for being. "A gang needs enemies," Ronald Noblet told me. "If a gang has no enemies, there is no gang." We have been fighting gangs, hoping to end violence, but we had it backward. We should be fighting violence in order to end gangs.

Violent Drug Dealing and Abuse, Not Drugs

Drugs are a deadly serious public health concern. Over seventy-two thousand Americans died from drug overdoses in 2017—three times the number from a decade and a half earlier. This increase has been driven by a fourfold increase in the number of deaths from opioids, including heroin, fentanyl, and prescription pain relievers. The opioid epidemic is a public health crisis of truly massive proportions, deserving of a similarly massive response from our government. Sadly, a truly proportionate response to the nation's distress has yet to materialize.[38]

In relation to urban violence, however, the connection between drugs and violence is nowhere near as clear as it once was. The rise of crack cocaine in the 1980s was closely associated with intense competition and violence between rival sellers. Today's opioid epidemic is just as deadly but much less violent. Dealers go to war over "turf" less frequently; instead they sell via couriers using mobile phones and the internet. The transactions occur in private, via networks where the parties are more likely to know each other, rather than out on the street with exchanges between strangers. Another crucial distinction is that the opioid epidemic began with a form of legalization: drug companies were permitted to sell opioids and doctors were allowed to prescribe them, but abuses piled up quickly as pharmaceutical companies relentlessly pushed sales to broader and broader groups of people. The crack epidemic, on the other hand, began as and remained a criminal endeavor. Finally, one epidemic began in white suburban and rural communities; the other began in black urban communities. Many commentators have appropriately observed that this may be why today's epidemic is viewed so much more sympathetically by mainstream (that is, white) America.[39]

For all these reasons, drugs and drug dealing are not as useful as proxies for violence as they once were. We must be mindful that today, it is violent drug dealing, or violent drug markets, and not all drugs or drug dealing, that should be addressed for the purposes of violence reduction. Violent drug dealers and markets were, and are, suitable targets for aggressive law enforcement efforts. Nonviolent drug dealing and drug consumption are better addressed by the public health system.

Once again, the principle of focus is crucial. Targeting violent dealers and markets for enforcement sends a message to the criminal community about what conduct is most likely to land them in prison. The immediate goal is not to end the drug trade but to influence it, pacifying it wherever possible.

This conclusion is reinforced by the evidence. It is well established that drug treatment and specialized drug courts can significantly reduce addiction and recidivism. Drug enforcement, however,
appears to have limited impact and may actually increase violence by
destabilizing drug markets and creating violent competition among
dealers. Taking a killer off the streets reduces violence, but incarcer-
ating a dealer often just opens up an opportunity for a new dealer.
Focused deterrence has had some success in reducing violent open-air
drug markets, but even that strategy is most effective when focused
squarely on violence.[40]

In sum, drugs are no longer central in the fight against urban violence. When rivalries among drug dealers spark shootings and killings, then those rivalries must be addressed, but generally speaking
drugs should not be the focus of anti-violence efforts.

Drug abuse, not just drug dealing, contributes to urban violence, but in narrower ways than one might think. In my interviews,
the issue of drug and alcohol abuse came up again and again, but
more so in relation to those already predisposed to violence. For hot
people with histories of substance abuse, treatment may be an essential step toward recovery, not just from drugs or alcohol, but also
from violence.

In fact, more attention needs to be paid to the substance most
closely and frequently associated with violence: alcohol. Alcohol
interferes with the region of the brain responsible for self-control. An
inebriated brain is a less inhibited one that is more prone to aggression and violence. More crimes are committed under the influence of
alcohol than under the influence of all illegal drugs combined. In recognition of these realities, criminologist Mark Kleiman has suggested
that tripling alcohol taxes could reduce the murder rate by 6 percent.[41]

Studies also indicate that violence can be reduced substantially
by regulating the availability and use of alcohol, either by managing
the hours, prices, and locations at which it is sold or by providing
evidence-informed treatment for alcohol abusers. Several countries
have reduced violence by regulating alcohol sales and distribution,

most commonly by restricting selling hours and days, limiting sales to specific sites, establishing a minimum drinking age, and establishing sobriety checkpoints. One systematic review found strong evidence that preventing bars and restaurants from selling alcohol late at night can lead to substantial reductions in violence. The anti-violence effectiveness of such strategies can be enhanced with additional focus on violent crime in hot spots. We need not restrict excessive drinking everywhere, only where it is most dangerous.[42]

TODAY'S PUBLIC NARRATIVES are often framed in absolutes: Ban guns. Put gangs out of business. Legalize drugs. Anything less seems like an act of political surrender. Such talk might sound good, but it doesn't do much in terms of reducing urban violence. Absolutist answers on urban violence are often impossible to implement in reality, mostly because they ignore the practical yet pressing reality of the violent few. All guns are not the problem—guns in the hands of the most dangerous people and places are. All gangs are not the problem—the most violent gangs and gang members are. All drugs are not the problem—violent drug dealers and substance abusers are. The more we fetishize guns, gangs, and drugs, the more we miss the subtle truth that it is the behaviors, not the items themselves, that drive most of the danger. It is violence itself, not the instruments of violence, that should command the majority of our attention.

PART III

PROGNOSIS

CHAPTER 9

HOW TALK INFORMS ACTION

IN PART II WE REVIEWED TREATMENTS THAT ARE AVAILABLE, AFFORD-able, and proven to stop the bleeding caused by urban violence. Those treatments could begin today, without new laws or big budgets, yet few cities have adopted these approaches. Despite the fierce urgency of urban violence and the accessibility of demonstrated solutions, progress remains slow, uneven, inadequate. Why hasn't success been sustained and spread about the nation? Why do policies proven to work still lack attention and support?

As we turn from treatment to prognosis, we must look forward. How we talk about a problem shapes how we solve it. Previous chapters addressed aspects of the national conversation around urban violence, but this chapter takes the topic head-on, examining what is wrong with how we talk about crime and violence and what can be done about it.

This chapter also analyzes how politics often obscures our best options for saving lives. Political parties polarize discussions of urban violence, pushing false narratives and presenting false choices. Political leaders listen selectively to poor communities of color, hearing only what they want to hear. All of this leaves the public with a series of superficial either-or choices when it comes to reducing violence, when the best solutions are mostly both-and.

Even with politics out of the picture, the best evidence- and community-informed strategies are not always easy for the public to grasp. Outside of a small set of experts, few truly understand the science of reducing urban violence. When people don't know what works, they assume that nothing does, leading to pessimism, hope-lessness, and cynicism.

Moving forward, the national dialogue on urban violence should be about solving problems, not winning arguments. But in addition to talk, we need action. Changing the conversation takes time, and poor urban communities need relief right now. A small but vocal constitu-ency must be created to ensure that the best-proven strategies get the support they deserve soon. Even as we push to change the narrative, we must get to work right away.

Rejecting Race-Based Rhetoric

Eric Garner was an unarmed civilian who died in Staten Island, New York, after a New York Police Department (NYPD) officer applied a prohibited chokehold to Garner's neck in the course of arresting him for selling loose cigarettes. In response to the uproar caused by Garner's death, former New York City mayor Rudy Giuliani argued that "police officers can misbehave [but] 96 percent of the problem is black-on-black crime."[1]

In reaction to demonstrations protesting the death of Michael Brown and other African Americans killed by the police, television host Bill O'Reilly contended that "much of the violent crime in Amer-ica is being committed right now by young black men. . . . There is a violent subculture in the African American community that should be exposed and confronted."[2]

In labeling urban violence "black on black," politicians and pundits like Giuliani and O'Reilly were not so subtly advancing an enduring narrative of racial inferiority, where disparities in rates of violent offending are cited as evidence that urban violence is primarily a "black" problem.[3]

Looking only at the data, there is a kernel of truth to these arguments: between 1980 and 2008, African Americans were 3.76 times more likely than the average person—and 6.18 times more likely than white people—to be victims of homicide. They were 4.14 times more likely on average—and 7.64 times more likely than whites—to commit homicide. During that period, black people accounted for 47 percent of all homicide victims and 53 percent of all homicide perpetrators despite representing only 12 percent of the US population.[4]

Nevertheless, characterizing such disparities as evidence of "black-on-black" violence is deeply misleading. Violent crime is mostly intraracial, meaning that it happens mainly between members of the same race. Ninety-three percent of African American homicide victims were killed by a member of their own race. Likewise, 84 percent of white homicide victims were killed by another white person, yet such violence is not labeled "white on white."[5]

While African Americans are disproportionately represented among victims and perpetrators of violent crime, this crime is no more inherently "black" than financial crime is inherently "white." One socioeconomic context promotes violence among those living in concentrated poverty, while another affords opportunities for white-collar theft among the wealthy. In both cases, the offenders are largely from one race, yet large majorities of both races are uninvolved. Both black and white people live their lives largely free from crime, yet with black people and violence, there is an assumed connection, while with white people and fraud, there is not.[6]

Behind the "black-on-black" label is an implicit assumption that urban violence is the result of chronic lawless behavior enabled by community tolerance for criminality. That assumption is wrong. Most

African American people, even if they live in poverty, share the moral standards of mainstream society and are no more tolerant of crime and violence than any other racial group. Those who have lived with the criminal justice system's ineffectiveness and unfairness, if not outright brutality, may be cynical about law enforcement's ability or willingness to help them, but that cynicism should not be confused with amorality.[7]

The related accusation that African Americans ignore the issue of urban violence is also baseless. Poor communities of color have campaigned for years against the mayhem they witness in their neighborhoods. Over the summer of 2018 in Chicago, for example, groups of predominantly black demonstrators repeatedly stopped traffic on major city expressways to demand that lawmakers do more about the bloodshed they were seeing on their streets. Calls from black communities for more assistance and resources have gone largely unheeded, however, except when those calls include requests for aggressive law enforcement.[8]

Labeling urban violence as "black" also perpetuates deeply harmful stereotypes about African Americans. As described by historian Khalil Gibran Muhammad, beginning in the late nineteenth century, claims of cultural inferiority replaced the outright bigotry of biological inferiority, with rhetoric of black criminality becoming a new proxy for advancing old claims. Crime among European immigrant groups was explained away while crime among African Americans remained racialized as a matter of community or family values. Over time, this narrative became an accepted basis for prejudicial thinking, discriminatory treatment, and even racial violence. Black people were portrayed as a race apart, distinct and allegedly dangerous, but in reality quite vulnerable.[9]

As we've seen, it was racism, not culture, that produced high rates of criminality and violence among isolated and poor African Americans. Racial segregation created concentrated poverty and disadvantage, which then produced crime and violence. Cumulative and simultaneous disparities in housing, education, and health, among other factors, drive racial differences in victimization and offending to this day. African Americans (and Latinos, for that matter) are no more violent than any other group, but in far too many cases, their circumstances are.

Ignoring this, "black-on-black" proponents argue that African Americans are at fault for urban violence, so it is their responsibility to stop it. Suspiciously, most only raise these concerns in response to allegations of abuse and misconduct by law enforcement. In multiple ways, "black-on-black" arguments are weaponized to absolve broader society of responsibility not just for urban violence but also for police violence, placing the onus for addressing such issues squarely on the communities suffering from them the most. This is the same tactic deployed by many of those arguing for an alleged "Ferguson effect"— using urban violence to turn the tables on advocates and reformers calling for change.

Worse still, some on the right go further, appealing to the racial fears and resentments of their political base in order to maintain support. In his speech announcing that he was running for president, Donald Trump called Mexican immigrants "rapists" who bring "drugs" and "crime" into the country. During the first debate of the general election, he described African Americans and Latinos as "living in hell because it's so dangerous. You walk down the street, you get shot." In his inaugural address, in a reference to "crime and gangs and drugs," he stated, "This American carnage stops right here and stops right now." Now in office, he has threatened to "send in the Feds" to stop the "carnage" in Chicago, and he continues to falsely claim that loose immigration laws have created an "infestation" of Latin American gangs.[10]

There is nothing wrong with calling attention to urban violence, but the way Trump talks suggests that he is more interested in politics than problem-solving. Trump portrays immigrants as criminals, but every study to seriously examine the issue shows that immigrants, even illegal ones, commit fewer crimes than citizens. He suggests that we live during an especially bloody era in the nation's history, when in fact most Americans have never been safer. Trump claims to be concerned about the violence in Chicago but then blocks millions in funding for Chicago police when the city refuses to fall in line with his anti-immigrant policies.[11]

When pressed for solutions, Trump typically calls for a return to the outdated tough-on-crime policies of the 1990s. He has repeatedly cited the NYPD's discredited stop-and-frisk policies with approval. His first attorney general, Jeff Sessions, championed aggressive prosecution efforts like Project Exile—an aggressive federal gun violence effort from Richmond, Virginia, whose results were called into question once rigorously evaluated. In response to crime and violence, Trump argues for more law enforcement, conducted more brutally. But the record of the past three decades amply demonstrates that such policies do not work, because they are unfocused, imbalanced, and deeply unfair. Trump is a crime dinosaur, peddling policies that went extinct years ago.[12]

The dishonesty and superficiality of his views on violent crime reveal that Trump's positions and policies are better understood as pretexts for a broader culture war waged to win political support by keeping Americans angry and afraid of the "other"—immigrants, blacks, Muslims, and so on. Trump's slogan may be Make America Great Again, but the reality is closer to Make America Scared Again.

Embracing Efforts to Reduce Urban Violence

In 2010, *The New Jim Crow,* a book written by legal scholar and civil rights lawyer Michelle Alexander, was published. The book argued that the primary purpose of today's American criminal justice system is the subjugation of African American people. "Like Jim Crow (and slavery)," Alexander wrote, "mass incarceration operates as a tightly networked system of laws, policies, customs, and institutions that operate collectively to ensure the subordinate status of a group defined largely by race." The book has been dubbed the "secular bible" for progressives seeking criminal justice reform and spent more than a year on the *New York Times* bestseller list.[13]

In 2017, law professor Paul Butler, in his book *Chokehold: Policing Black Men,* wrote in a similar vein, "Cops routinely hurt and humiliate black people because that is what they are paid to do. . . . The police, as policy, treat African-Americans with contempt." Progressives in academia, advocacy, and the media continue to echo similar refrains.[14]

According to Khalil Gibran Muhammad, in response to the false narrative of racial inferiority, "researchers and reformers rewrote black criminality in terms of racism in the criminal justice system," where high rates of crime and violence among poor African Americans are attributable to their treatment at the hands of the white power structure.[15]

It is understandable why Alexander, Butler, and others make such claims. Historically, they are accurate: the criminal justice system was indeed a favored tool used by whites to keep blacks and other racial minorities separate and unequal. Even today, at the front end of the system, police stop, search, arrest, and use force against African Americans in disproportionate numbers. On the back end of the system, black people are disproportionately represented in jails, prisons, and among those on probation or parole. In 2014, the last year for which national data was available, black people were arrested at a rate that was double the national average. For the past three years, the percentage of black people killed by police was double their proportion of the US population. In 2014, African Americans represented 35 percent of those in jails and prisons, roughly triple their number in the US population.[16]

The recent wave of progressive criticism of the US criminal justice system is important. More than that, it is necessary. The system remains replete with racial disparities, and, not surprisingly, poor people of color view the system decidedly more negatively than white people do. As we saw in Ferguson, Baltimore, and Chicago, illegitimacy leads to violence, not just between police and protesters, but also inside the community itself. Critiquing and ultimately addressing these issues through reforms in policing, prosecution, courts, and corrections can slowly build legitimacy and decrease violence over time.[17]

Still, when progressives define the current criminal justice system exclusively in terms of racism, when they label all law enforcement as illegitimate, and especially when they call for the system's abolition instead of its reform, they overlook the fact that the very same people who bear the brunt of the system's inequities and injustices are the ones who need that system most of all. Such extremism hurts, not helps, poor communities of color. For the sake of those for whom safety is not a given, our current system must be improved, not eliminated. In addition, sustainable advances in legitimacy and safety depend on communities and criminal justice authorities better understanding and working with, not against, one another.

Painting police, prosecutors, or the criminal justice system at large with a broad brush is neither fair nor accurate. Overt racial discrimination and abuse, once commonplace, is now rare. Some officials, as we have seen in this book, remain racist, corrupt, and brutal, but they do not represent most of those working in law enforcement today. According to former gang member Anthony Blockmon, "Some people hold a grudge against all officers. All officers ain't the same, just like all of us. Just like the race thing, you got good and bad in each." Gang task force leader Mario Maciel agreed: "Within law enforcement you have bad apples, but nobody in the media talks about the ninety-eight percent that gave a solid day's work with empathy and compassion. . . . That messaging makes you believe that all cops are racist." Maciel argued it is the same for the young, mostly Latino men he works with. "If I don't believe that all brown boys are bad, then I shouldn't believe that all cops are bad. And let me tell you this," he confided, "there was a time in my life that I would've said all cops are terrible."

Almost every serious, empirical review of the role of race in criminal justice finds that, while it plays an important part in determining outcomes, other factors play significant roles as well. With policing, critics point to disproportionate numbers of stops, searches, arrests, and, of course, use of force as evidence of a racist system, yet recent rigorous reviews have found the if-then, causal connections between race and racial disparities to be weak or unclear. When it comes to sentencing, multiple reviews come to a similar conclusion: racism is not the determinative force in punishment that some seem to believe. In a systematic review of seventy-one published and unpublished studies, criminologist Ojmarrh Mitchell found that "discrimination in the sentencing stage is not the primary cause of the overrepresentation of African-Americans in U.S. correctional facilities." Criminologist Cassia Spohn recently reviewed a similar body of literature and observed that while "most studies conclude that [racial disparities] result 'to some extent' from discrimination," such disparities "result primarily from racial differences in crime seriousness, prior record, and other legally relevant factors."[18]

Racism continues to influence criminal justice outcomes, but disparities inside the system are also driven by disparities outside the system. According to psychologist Phillip Atiba Goff, an expert in racial bias and discrimination in policing, "Before anybody's had contact with law enforcement, they've had contact with schools, with jobs, either getting them or not, with the health care system and the housing systems, all of which suffer from many of the same and sometimes even worse forms of bias than does law enforcement. What we are frequently picking up on is not the prejudice or discrimination by law enforcement, but rather the symptoms of a society that is still sickened and toxified by the prejudices and discrimination of our current society, and from generations past." In the US, the criminal justice system is no outlier when it comes to race—education, health, and housing systems all have similarly troubling disparities. Even if it were possible to eradicate racial bias entirely within the criminal justice system, troubling racial disparities would persist.[19]

I do not raise these points to minimize the importance of race and racism—progressives (and everyone else) should continue to care deeply about racially disparate treatment in the criminal justice system and elsewhere. These points serve only to rebut the most extreme and unsupported critiques by advocates and activists who believe that our current system is so infected with racial prejudice that it must be discarded entirely. Based on the evidence, this naïve and dangerous view is unsupported by the facts.

Characterizing all of criminal justice as irredeemably racist or illegitimate does not actually advance a broader social justice agenda. In America's cities, keeping safe is a top priority for poor people of color—freedom from violence is one of their most immediate and urgent needs. In 2016, three organizations—the Joint Center for Political and Economic Studies, the Joyce Foundation, and the Urban Institute—took the obvious but overlooked step of surveying 1,200 African Americans and Latinos about the key criminal justice issues facing the nation, speaking with them about their experiences and views concerning gun violence, mass incarceration, and police misconduct.[20]

For many of those surveyed, these issues were not abstractions—they directly impacted their lives and the lives of those closest to them. Forty-two percent of African Americans surveyed had been personally affected by gun violence. Seventy-five percent knew someone who had been sent to jail or prison. Fifty-six percent had had previous negative interactions with law enforcement. For Latinos, the ratios were almost as high at 29, 58, and 34 percent, respectively. Perhaps surprising to some, 80 percent of African Americans stated that gun violence was an "extremely serious problem"—more so than mass incarceration (69 percent) or police misconduct (50 percent). Latinos ranked these issues similarly at 54, 43, and 24 percent, respectively.

In the ongoing national shouting match on race, crime, and justice, those actually living with the realities of crime and punishment are often hard to hear over the din. Progressives claim to speak for those who disproportionately bear the burdens of both crime and punishment, but too often they listen selectively, elevating only those concerns that align with their previously held political agendas. Like conservatives who cherry-pick the concerns of African Americans and Latinos when they call for more law enforcement, progressives hear these constituencies when they call for less incarceration and less police brutality, but not when they cry out for relief from deadly violence.

Not surprisingly, 57 percent of African Americans and 45 percent of Latinos surveyed believed that "most people in America don't care about the gun violence that is affecting communities of color." Large majorities also believed that addressing such violence could reduce incarceration and increase community confidence in the police, reflecting a keen awareness of the connections among urban violence, mass incarceration, and police legitimacy, and an understanding that these challenges must be addressed together. Politicians, pundits, advocates, and activists must listen to the whole story that poor people of color are telling when it comes to crime and punishment in their communities.

The evidence clearly shows that law enforcement is an essential element of any realistic anti-violence strategy. Many of the most effective anti-violence strategies described in this book depend heavily on the active involvement of the police. If progressives cannot overcome their suspicion of law enforcement, they will be unable to provide the security that the constituencies they claim to care about so desperately need. As we've seen, balance is fundamental to reducing violence, which means that rewards must be balanced against sanctions, prevention balanced against enforcement. Most poor people of color want cops in their communities, but they want the right ones, acting in the right ways.

Progressives must also be careful not to perpetuate the illegitimacy they hope to address by using language that vilifies police and other criminal justice officials. Criticism of the criminal justice system is warranted and needed, but that criticism should be responsible and mindful that ultimately there must be reconciliation between communities and criminal justice officials. When the system falls short, it must be called to account, but in a manner that results in positive reforms, not poisoned relations.

Some on the left are concerned that by elevating urban violence as an issue, they lend support to the racist narrative that poor people of color are disproportionately criminal and violent. This concern is understandable but misplaced. Denying that high rates of violence exist in urban communities does not do anyone any good, least of all the residents living in those communities. Violence must not be a dirty secret, because treating it as such could be seen as an implicit admission that "black-on-black" arguments have merit. Instead, progressives should consistently reaffirm that people do not differ in their predilections for crime and violence, only in their history and circumstances. This does not absolve individuals or communities of responsibility for violence, but instead broadens that responsibility to include society at large.

Some progressives also worry that paying attention to urban violence will distract from their broader reform agenda or trigger public fears that could derail progressive reforms, prompting a return to the oppressive "law and order" policies. Like conservatives, but for different reasons, progressives often see a zero-sum, either-or choice between crime and justice, effectiveness and fairness, safety and legitimacy. Just the opposite is true, however: reducing violence and promoting reform are entirely compatible goals. In fact, sustained progress toward one goal is unachievable without similar progress toward the other. Those representing the political left cannot credibly claim to have a complete social justice agenda if that agenda ignores the life-and-death struggles of their core constituencies.

There is a deep irony here: most of the successful strategies set out in this book were originally conceived, developed, and implemented by progressives. For example, the originator of focused deterrence and the GVRS, David Kennedy, is a progressive. The creator of Cure Violence, Gary Slutkin, is one as well. Progressives have a strong track record when it comes to fighting crime and violence, yet these accomplishments are ignored by the top tiers of progressive leadership. Instead, when the subject of crime and violence comes up, it is addressed only indirectly, through gun control, police and prison reform, and root causes. As we have seen, all of these strategies are commendable on their own merits but are unlikely to impact urban violence significantly in the short run. The political left has a strong story to tell on urban violence, yet it mostly remains silent.

To recap, poor African Americans and Latinos are not to blame for urban violence—we all are. "Black-on-black" rhetoric urges us to shirk our collective responsibility for this devastating problem. Poor communities of color are not to be feared or hated because of urban violence; this demonizing plays to the darkest side of American history and society. Similarly, not all members of law enforcement are to blame for the actions of a corrupt and brutal few. Characterizing the current criminal justice system as a tool for racial subjugation is not constructive. Cops and communities plagued by violence need one another, and politicos in both parties should recognize that.

Getting the Word Out on What Works

When it comes to reducing urban violence, experts are fond of saying, "We know what works," but that "we" generally does not include the public, policy makers, or the media. When it comes to violent crime in America's cities, the reality is that most people are woefully unaware of what actually keeps the peace in urban America. Why don't more people know about the science and successful practice of violence reduction?

Evidence-informed strategies do not oversimplify the complex challenge of urban violence. Because such approaches do not dumb violence down, they can be difficult to digest quickly. They may also challenge us to think and feel differently. For these reasons, they are often overlooked: we usually want solutions that can be evaluated using our own intuition and common sense. The media caters to this, telling us what we want to hear rather than what we need to know.

Unfortunately, easy answers and quick fixes turn out to be of limited usefulness when it comes to solving complex social challenges like urban violence. To paraphrase the journalist and critic H. L. Mencken, for every complicated problem there is a solution that is clear, simple, and wrong. The public is open to new and better ideas, but those ideas need to be packaged in an understandable way. The same is true for the media—if reliable evidence on crime and violence were more accessible, more reporters would write about it.

The good news is that we have a large body of scientific research on urban violence. The bad news is that most of it is hidden behind publisher paywalls, written in academic-ese, divided across disciplines and sectors, and of varying quality. Too much research is produced in a bubble. Too many scholars have limited contact with those with actual exposure to crime, leading to studies that pursue abstract academic queries with little relevance to real life.

Advances have been made. Systematic reviews address some of these shortcomings by bringing together the best evidence on certain important questions. Think tanks and policy shops frame academic ideas in engaging ways while producing research of their own. Some in the media are becoming increasingly sophisticated in their reporting on urban violence, and some leaders have championed evidence-informed crime policy. Still, too much knowledge remains trapped in academia's ivory tower.

None of this is easy. To paraphrase Einstein, everything should be made as simple as possible, but no simpler. The challenge in explaining complex phenomena like urban violence lies in striking an appropriate balance between simplicity and accuracy. Sacrifice too much simplicity and you lose your audience; give up too much accuracy and you mislead them.

Persuading people to get excited about evidence-informed violence reduction is challenging for a few more reasons. The idea that cities should target the highest-risk places, people, and behaviors can be difficult to accept. Such approaches may not seem fair at first glance because they devote extra assistance—or unwanted attention—to a select few. Many are skeptical of giving special treatment and favor more universal approaches, even when those approaches are not particularly successful.

Another challenge is proportionality. Common sense suggests that big problems require big solutions. Urban violence imposes tremendous costs on poor communities and the public at large, but because it is highly concentrated among a few people, places, and behaviors, it is actually "small" in terms of policy. That we can do a lot with a little on this issue can be hard to believe.

All of this makes understanding urban violence a bit harder. As the writer Malcolm Gladwell put it, "Our usual moral intuitions are little use, then, when it comes to a few hard cases. . . . We can be true to our principles or we can fix the problem. We cannot do both." The evidence for what works is strong, but most of us tend to make decisions with our hearts, not our heads.[21]

While researchers must do better in bringing their work to a wider market, the media can share more stories about the complex realities of urban violence and how best to address them. Mainstream, new, and social media matter, both in terms of raising awareness of urban violence and in framing potential policy responses.

Driven to maintain and expand viewership, news organizations often sensationalize crime coverage with "when it bleeds, it leads" reporting, or they repeat the standard story lines—violence is all about guns, poverty, or values—without analysis or scrutiny. When reporting what happens, the media often leaves out how often it happens and why. For instance, articles with headlines like "50 Shot over the Weekend in Chicago" do not mention that Chicago, being one of the largest cities in America, has larger numbers of everything, including but not limited to shootings. Chicago's violence problem is real, but smaller cities that are perennial "murder capital" contenders, like Baltimore, Detroit, New Orleans, and St. Louis, have homicide rates that are twice as high yet receive a fraction of the media's attention.

In addition, in order to keep the public reading, watching, and listening, the mainstream media provides extra space and time to crime stories that are new, unusual, and dramatic. In 2016, the most-read stories on the *New York Times* website involving crime and violence—the Pulse nightclub and Dallas sniper shootings—were not representative of the problems of crime and violence in general, giving the false impression that crime is far more evenly distributed among the populace than it actually is. Emphasizing the unusual suggests to people that violence is happening everywhere, all the time, and at random. This creates public concern for atypical victims of violent crime, but not enough for those whom violence visits regularly. Distorted coverage can also create an atmosphere of racial threat, reinforcing narratives like the "American carnage" that is touted by Trump.[22]

While the mainstream media caters to the general public, new media tailors its information to target audiences. As a result, it feels less obliged to provide a representative sampling of what is actually happening in the real world. Instead, news websites, blogs, podcasts, and other new-media outlets often shape their stories and coverage to suit the preconceptions of their core audiences. Social media platforms go even further, curating the news feeds of their users in order to present them with items that they're more likely to like, share, and post. This means that, with the advent of new and social media, less and less challenging information is reaching the public. Previously held beliefs are constantly reinforced, leading individuals to believe that their views are more representative of mainstream opinion than they actually are.

In addition, new and social media often lack the ability or willingness to verify the accuracy of the information they provide. Mainstream media is far from perfect but most traditional news organizations hold themselves to certain professional standards of objectivity and accuracy. With new and social media, users are not only being selectively fed accurate news, but unverified and often inaccurate news is served up as well. Information-filtering processes feed polarization, creating echo chambers in which voices we agree with are amplified while contrary views are silenced.

In such a sensationalized, polarized environment, evenhanded stories about everyday violence often find it hard to compete for attention. And it is these stories that can celebrate the successes of treatments like cognitive behavioral therapy and explore the science supporting them. The media—mainstream, new, and social—must do a better job of getting the word out on such stories.

Changing the Conversation

Moving forward, we need to change the way we talk about urban violence and make evidence- and community-informed solutions a bigger part of the public conversation. Both sides of the political spectrum must move away from trying to win arguments and toward working to find solutions. A problem-solving mind-set is essential for sound policy making in urban violence—or any other area, for that matter.

For the last few years, an increasing number of conservatives have collaborated with progressives to pursue comprehensive criminal justice reform. Republican leaders, supported by conservative organizations like Right on Crime and the Prison Fellowship, have strongly advocated alongside progressives for more sensible and humane criminal justice policies. These collaborations have led to a number of significant reforms at the state level, with conservative states like Texas leading the way. In Congress, this collaboration recently resulted in the passage of the First Step Act, a law that reduces certain mandatory minimum sentences and expands "good time credits" to reduce sentences for well-behaved prisoners, among other things. Even President Trump supported the bill in the end and signed it into law.[23]

That said, the rise of Trump marks a return to the dark days of Republican politics when the specter of black criminality and violence was raised to scare white voters into supporting conservatives at the polls. For instance, during the 1988 presidential campaign, Republicans aired ads attacking Democratic candidate Michael Dukakis as soft on crime. These ads prominently featured ominous images of African Americans, including, most famously, Willie Horton, who had recently committed several heinous crimes while participating in a prison-release program in Dukakis's home state.

Such tactics were reminiscent of the Republican "Southern Strategy," which was created after the passage of the 1964 Civil Rights Act to win over southern white Democrats by appealing to their racial fears and resentments.[24]

Republicans must disavow racial fearmongering and continue with progressives on the path to criminal justice reform. Many traditionally conservative principles are consistent with sound crime policy: limited government, fiscal responsibility, and the Christian belief in forgiveness and redemption. Conservatives must push back on those in their own ranks who advocate only for more police, prisons, and tough tactics. One-sided policies of pure punishment have not worked, and there is a real relationship between the perceived fairness of the system and its ability to keep the peace. Until they emphatically reject those outdated and discarded ideologies, conservatives' role in reducing urban violence will remain limited.[25]

While conservatives must stop exploiting the issue of urban violence, those on the left must go further than just pushing back on the right. Progressives must embrace the issue of reducing urban violence as an essential means of serving their poor constituents of color. Addressing racism in criminal justice remains crucial, but vulnerable African Americans and Latinos are demanding freedom from violence as well as freedom from discrimination. The same is true of society at large—some fears of violent crime are reasonable, and unless progressives address such fears directly, they will continue to leave a void that will be filled by opportunists from the other side of the political spectrum.

Progressives must be more than just critics—they must offer an affirmative vision of what law enforcement should do, as well as what it should not do. They must address urban violence directly and not just through poverty reduction, gun control, or police reform. The anti-violence principles of focus, balance, and fairness are entirely consistent with progressive values. They ensure that aggressive policing is limited, that enforcement is paired with prevention, and that building community trust and confidence remains a top priority. Progressives should lead the way by demonstrating that urban violence can be controlled with strategies that are neither brutal nor indiscriminate, that lives can be saved with minimal collateral costs, and that these policies can enjoy strong support from the communities directly impacted by them.

To better inform the public about urban violence, scientific research should be conducted in consultation with criminal justice practitioners and community members. The most relevant and reliable studies must then be brought out from behind the paywalls, summarized in language that an eighth grader can understand, and broken down into bite-size chunks that are digestible by the general public. We also need the media to be more willing to take the science and bring it into the public square.

Changing the public conversation tends to be difficult and slow. Policy proposals that depend on immediate and sizeable changes in public opinion are likely to fail. In addition, such proposals must be pushed through our decentralized political and bureaucratic systems of fifty states, more than three thousand counties, and almost twenty thousand municipalities, each with its own set of independent elected and appointed officials. Our federalist system is not designed to quickly convert public opinion into governmental action—quite the opposite, in fact. The system's complexity tends to frustrate the will of the silent majority and reward only the most dedicated interest groups. That is why the NRA has been so successful to date—not because of its broad appeal, but because its high level of organization has enabled it to apply relentless pressure on public officials to coerce them into action (or inaction). Because broad-based change is difficult and slow, a new strategy is needed to push for the policies that can reduce urban violence right now.[26]

Creating a New Constituency

If you've seen real violence up close, ideology comes in a distant second to solutions. Poor communities of color want an end to income inequality, concentrated poverty, lack of opportunity, and pervasive discrimination, but they also desperately want to live in peace. Now.

While the standard answers—it's all about culture, guns, or poverty, for instance—appeal to base supporters on the right or the left, they offer little relief from the violence that is happening on the streets of America's cities at this very moment. The strategies outlined in this book do just that, but they fail to fall neatly into one political camp or the other. Because there is no ready-made constituency for successful anti-violence strategies, one must be created. Thankfully, this group need not be large—it just needs to be loud.

To build support for evidence- and community-informed anti-violence strategies, a massive shift in public opinion is not necessary. Instead, we need to change only enough hearts and minds to support those who are already deeply dedicated to advocating for anti-violence policies that are focused, balanced, and fair. These supporters would organize locally and nationally, creating awareness, building support, engaging the media, and lobbying politicians and policy makers. We need a small but committed group of peacemakers to demand serious solutions to urban violence.

Given their relatively low cost and scale, support for anti-violence efforts is a relatively small request of government, but the ask must be made again and again. Anti-violence advocates must organize to apply public pressure until their demands are met and be vigilant against backsliding. Politicians must understand that there will be consequences if they fail to address this problem. Journalists must be educated to help hold officials accountable for their actions, or lack thereof. Communities must be engaged to ensure that their political support is conditioned on concrete commitments to address these challenges.

Who are these peacemakers? What groups make up this anti-violence coalition? In my view, members should be drawn first and foremost from residents living in affected communities. Next are the dedicated practitioners working alongside them, both inside and outside law enforcement. After that, academics, researchers, and analysts offering additional expertise should be added. Lastly, outside allies should be recruited to bring additional political muscle and dollars to bear. The first two groups are already deeply engaged in the struggle to save lives. The next group is involved, but could be more closely connected. The last group is largely absent.

Poor communities of color often lack the political capital necessary to move these policies on their own, so additional support needs to come from other socioeconomic and racial groups. More middle- and upper-class people, many of whom will be white, need to engage with the plight of lower-class people, most of whom are black and brown. To bring more attention and resources to the cause of reducing violence, more Americans must cross class and color lines in support of communities suffering from high rates of violence. The young activists from Parkland are one hopeful example of this.

It must be remembered that violence does not concentrate in poor communities of color by accident. Disparities in crime and violence that were created by white racism are now perpetuated by white indifference. Today, racial apathy, not racial hatred, is a major obstacle to progress. Hatred may be the greater sin, but it is less pervasive. White people's collective unconcern for their fellow black and brown citizens is more prevalent and more damaging.

Today's racial disparities might not reflect, for the most part, an ongoing intent to oppress or discriminate, but they do indicate an unwillingness to revisit a racist past that remains relevant to this day. According to the writer Ta-Nehisi Coates, "It is as though we have run up a credit-card bill and, having pledged to charge no more, remain befuddled that the balance does not disappear." While racial hatred may no longer be central to a proper understanding of urban violence, racial indifference remains important. The past privileges some and penalizes others to this day. White Americans benefit from a legacy of racial advantage, whether or not they or their ancestors participated in racial persecution. While racial disparities may not be the fault of most white people today, those disparities still confer benefits, and with those benefits come responsibilities.[27]

To be sure, race represents only one kind of privilege, and white people living in poverty rightly resent the notion that they are, in any absolute sense, privileged. For them, class-based disadvantages trump any race-based advantages. Similarly, the socioeconomic benefits that accrue to affluent African Americans may outweigh any disadvantages based on race.

To convince well-off white Americans that they have a responsibility to remedy problems that they did not actively create is no easy task, and the current conversation on race and criminal justice only makes it harder. As Comedy Central's Trevor Noah observed in an article decrying the polarization of American politics and society, "Either black people are criminals, or cops are racist—pick one. It's us versus them. You're with us, or you're against us." Race blaming from either side drives people to assign culpability rather than accept responsibility. For this reason, a productive public conversation on urban violence cannot begin and end with race.[28]

I have worked on reducing urban violence with hundreds of individuals from all races, backgrounds, and walks of life. Many of them are from crime-ridden communities, but others are not, yet they share the same sense of purpose.

"Growing up, I had a very sheltered existence," Elizabeth Banach, executive director of Marylanders to Prevent Gun Violence (MPGV), told me. "I was never exposed to anything that might cause me to worry about my safety." Liz grew up in rural Virginia with a father who was an avid hunter. Guns were part of her everyday life, but gun violence was something that happened far away, to unfamiliar people.

That began to change on December 14, 2012, when twenty young children were gunned down in their own classrooms at Sandy Hook Elementary School in Newtown, Connecticut. Liz was deeply shaken by the tragedy. She started to worry about the safety of her own kids but continued her quiet suburban life in Columbia, Maryland.

A turning point came on January 25, 2014, her daughter's birthday. Liz asked her husband to take the children out to the mall so she could get the house ready for her daughter's party. An hour after they left, her mobile phone rang. It was Liz's mother, asking where she was. Liz told her mother that she was home, getting things ready. Thank goodness, her mother said, because there's an active shooter at the mall right now.

"I can still feel the adrenaline running through my body," Liz recalled. "I called my husband and he didn't pick up. It was probably only a few minutes before he called back, but it felt like an eternity." Liz's husband had taken the kids to the park instead. They were safe, but a disturbed young man killed two strangers at a nearby mall that day and then took his own life. Liz signed up to volunteer with a national gun control organization that night.

Her work with the organization went well at first, but as Liz learned more about the issues, she became frustrated. "Sandy Hook is what brought me to the table, but when I looked at the numbers, I learned the vast majority of gun violence was urban violence and suicides." She asked her organization for more information, but they were slow to respond, so she began visiting nearby Baltimore to learn more, meeting with mothers who had lost children to gun violence. "I especially remember meeting Phyllis," she told me. "One of her kids had been killed, two had been shot." As Liz became close with Phyllis and a few other women, her feelings grew stronger. "We can't do this work in Baltimore and not talk about urban violence," she told her organization. "All we're talking about is Sandy Hook." Ultimately Liz left the group and joined MPGV so she could work on urban violence more directly.

Mass shootings made Liz aware of gun violence, but it was her relationships with other mothers that committed her to the urban side of the issue. "It's one thing to read something," she said, "but it's an entirely different thing to sit down and talk to someone who has lived it." Now Liz works in Baltimore every week, participating in meetings, attending memorials, and helping out wherever she can. She also visits Annapolis, Maryland's capital, to lobby elected officials. The women she works with are now her friends.

"I don't worry about my children being shot anymore," Liz said. "I do worry about them growing up in a country that doesn't care about people getting shot." It bothers Liz that she can protect her kids in a way that her colleagues in Baltimore can't. "The reality is, my kids have advantages. They'll always have a safety net, and I need them to know that there are children out there that don't have that net." Liz wants her kids to understand their privilege and take responsibility for it. "I don't want my kids being sheltered like I was."

Her work is deeply rewarding, but aspects still aggravate her. "We try to make it safe for people of color to come work with us, but we won't go into their spaces," Liz said. "It makes me angry that a lot of well-meaning white people don't make the effort to really know where these people are coming from. I've been doing this for five years, and almost nobody is willing to go to Westport or Cherry Hill or West Baltimore. Jen and I are in those communities all the time." (Jennifer Pauliukonis is the president of MPGV.) Perhaps this is not surprising: "This work takes a financial, emotional, and mental toll," Liz told me. "But the good parts outweigh the bad."

Liz's experiences mirror many of my own. I too come from a privileged background. Speaking and working with those who have lived through violence can be sobering, and spending time in the nation's deadliest neighborhoods can be frightening, at least at first. That said, my life has been enormously enriched by my time spent with these people and in these communities.

Raymond Solórzano and I talked about this. I asked him how he felt about outsiders coming in to work with him and his community. His answer was practical. "If you're honest, and your heart's in it, then where you're from doesn't matter. If you're here, I respect you for that, I respect what you do, because you're here with us."

"If we do the work, we might have setbacks on both sides, but we have to look past them," Ray continued. "The way to do that is by showing up to the next meeting, saying that the past incident doesn't represent all of us, and by continuing to work on the problem." Deputy Chief Tingirides of the LAPD agreed. "By working through the issues, you start building relationships. And you do that by taking a lot of crap. You gotta get yelled at, screamed at, you gotta hear what people are saying to put yourself in their shoes," he told me. "The way we get through this crisis is by building relationships and doing the hard work of keeping them."

This jibes with my experience as well. The best way to create empathy and understanding is to get people from different backgrounds problem-solving in close contact with one another. Rather than waiting for a reconciliation that might never be fully realized, just get to work and stay committed. If racism created segregation, which produced concentrated disadvantage, which finally led to violence, then we must begin with violence and work our way backward. We don't need a lot of new people to create this anti-violence constituency, we just need the right ones, those who are willing to dedicate themselves to the difficult but gratifying endeavor of saving lives.

I AM OFTEN asked, "Why are we as a nation not doing more about urban violence?" This chapter represents my best answer to this question, along with my best recommendations for what to do about it. To summarize: Change the narrative on violence, but don't wait to take action. Bring people from diverse backgrounds together and get down to business.

Changing the conversation on urban violence is important. The standard political positions and talking points must be challenged. Researchers and the media must make solutions to urban violence more accessible and easier to understand. But it is also important to keep in mind that we don't have to convince everybody. A small set of peacemakers can bring change if they are sufficiently committed and organized. Talk must be accompanied by action.

CHAPTER 10

REDEMPTION AND RECOVERY

THERE IS A SACRED QUALITY TO THE STORIES I WAS TOLD WHILE researching this book. When people related the most intimate details of their lives, conveying their crimes, injuries, and losses as well as their aspirations and dreams, sometimes all I could do was sit in quiet reverence.

This chapter offers stories of redemption and recovery to demonstrate that even when a person delves deeply into darkness, it is possible to return to the light. Some say that rehabilitation is impossible once a person is caught up in the cycle of violence. "If you don't get to these kids early, they are lost forever," they say. "Focus on the next generation," they advise. These stories show this simply is not so.

This chapter also identifies themes that were repeated in story after story. While every person's path to redemption and recovery was different, there were strong similarities among them. These themes provide a road map for rehabilitation: reconnecting to family, finding faith and religion, making the most of prison, serving and helping others, and treating trauma.

This chapter continues with a brief discussion of the evidence demonstrating that far more people succeed in leaving crime behind than is commonly understood, then concludes with a final story. As we near the end of this book's journey, it is best to allow the people who have survived urban violence to speak for themselves.

OVER THE YEARS, Erik King gave and received his share of abuse. He was beaten, stabbed, and shot. On his belly he bears a two-inch scar from a .380 round. Just above that scar lies another from a .25-caliber slug. On his side, three small pockmarks show where he was partially hit by a shotgun blast. Across his hands, arms, legs, and body, he bears no fewer than eight scars from stab wounds.

Despite everything, there were a few positive people who stayed connected to Erik: a football coach, his aunt, a girlfriend. "My girlfriend unconditionally loved me. I came home one night, blood all over me, and the first thing she asked was if I was okay. I was so hyped up on adrenaline, I couldn't even tell whose blood it was." His girlfriend started to cry. "I was like, don't cry for that motherfucker, and she said I'm not crying for him, I'm crying for you. . . . It got to me."

Erik actually considers himself fortunate. "I had a small group of people who said to me, 'We know what you've done, and it doesn't define you, but at this point, you have to make a choice.' That hit me hard, because for a long time I thought I didn't have a choice." He was also lucky that, despite a string of arrests, he was never convicted of any serious crime, never went to jail for more than a week or two, and never saw prison.

With help from people like his girlfriend, Erik slowly began to separate from his gang. Fights became less frequent, but the separation wasn't happening fast enough. He needed a bigger change if he was going to escape his past life. After a particularly bad incident landed Erik in the hospital, his old coach decided to get him out of town. "He came to me with a one-way ticket to London and a thousand dollars and was like, 'You have twenty-four hours to decide—the plane leaves tomorrow.'"

In England, away from those who valued him for his violence, Erik made friends with people who appreciated him as a person, not a weapon. He replaced negative sources of self-esteem with positive ones: photography, music, and, most importantly, working with youth. When he returned to the United States two years later, he began working in Red Hook, Brooklyn, helping kids who came up hard like he did. He was good at it. "I can hear shit that other people can't," Erik told me. "If you haven't missed five meals, then you don't know what it's like to be hungry." From there, one job led to another, and to new life based on service, not violence.

Today Erik does not talk much about his past, but he does not run from it either. A lot of bad things happened to Erik, and Erik did a lot of bad things—he feels a responsibility to make up for his part in it all. Toward the end of our conversation, Erik asked me, "What would be the point of my journey if it didn't wind up meaning something?"

RAYMOND SOLÓRZANO GREW up in a working-class Mexican neighborhood in Los Angeles. He joined his gang at sixteen years old. For Ray, the trauma of gang life built up over almost two decades, making him more and more violent over time. He used drugs and alcohol to help him cope. "I masked my emotional trauma with alcohol," he told me. "All those things I did, it wasn't because I was hard, it was because I was hurt—a hurt individual releasing hurt."

In 2008, Ray was back in the community after serving a six-year sentence for carjacking. Soon he was back to his usual routine. "I found myself thinking, 'Here I am all over again,' but I was addicted to meth, addicted to alcohol, and I didn't know how to leave." Things started to spin out of control. "It got ugly. People got killed, crazy things were happening. I was high, drunk, driving around at two in the morning without a license, with a gun and four parolees in my car." At that point, Ray decided to make a change. "'I gotta try something,'" he recalled thinking, "'because I'm not gonna make it.' Deep down I didn't want to get killed or do life in prison."

Ray checked himself into a Christian halfway and drug recovery home, where he found God and stayed for over three years. "It was something that worked for me." When Ray was ready to move on, he left the home and got a job helping ex–gang members like himself. He also stayed active in his church, which was where he met his wife. Today Ray is a husband, a father, and a pastor. He also operates a recovery home for former gang members and drug addicts. "When they see me, it's like an example, a model. I tell them, 'You can make it dude. Learn from my mistakes.'"[1]

ANTHONY BLOCKMON INHERITED his gang affiliation from his father. "What I saw was my dad gangbanging," Anthony told me. "It wasn't like he was telling me to do it, but in a sense he was because that was all I saw." When he was nine, his father was murdered. "That was where all that anger and hurt and pain and rage built up in me," he remembered.

Growing up in the Venice neighborhood of Los Angeles, Anthony acted out early. In elementary school, he started fighting classmates, writing graffiti, and causing trouble. At eleven years old, he was "jumped in" to his father's gang. At eighteen, he started selling drugs and went to jail for the first time. From then on, Anthony was never out of jail or prison for more than a year. "As I was growing up, I tried to mimic my father. I was walking in his shoes."

At twenty-five, Anthony went to prison for selling crack cocaine. While there, he learned that his girlfriend (now his wife) had also been locked up for the same offense. He decided to make a change. He wrote to her, and together they turned to religion. "Before I changed my life, everything was offered to me," he told me. "I worked child care, peer mediation, a job at McDonald's. My mom even sent me away to Mississippi for a while. None of that helped until I talked to the Lord, then everything turned around for me."

When Anthony was released from prison in 2006, he and his then-girlfriend stayed with her mother. Within a few weeks he had a job at a construction site, and he has been working steadily ever since.

Anthony is now a committed husband and father who serves on the board of a local gang prevention organization, Venice 2000. He and his wife attend church every Sunday.

Anthony smiled as he talked to me about his life now. "Living that way was just so much stress. Before, I always had to watch my back; now I walk with peace. Police used to be my worst enemy; now they wave at me. I love the freedom of being a citizen." As Anthony spoke, I was reminded of Proverbs 28:1: "The wicked flee when no man pursueth, but the righteous are bold as a lion."

THE FIRST THING that struck me about Eddie Bocanegra was his thoughtfulness. Sitting in a clean and comfortable meeting room a few doors down from his office, Eddie was careful with his choice of words in order to be sure his story would not be manipulated or mischaracterized. Today Eddie is successful, educated, and professional. Many would be surprised to learn where his journey began.

Eddie witnessed his first homicide at thirteen years old. It happened in broad daylight, right in front of him, just a few yards away. Eddie grew up in Little Village, Chicago, where gangs were a constant presence. Before the killing, Eddie knew about gangs, but he mostly stuck to sports. Afterward, he began to see things differently.

If he joined a gang, Eddie thought, he could better protect himself and his family. Danger was all around him, and the police were no help. Eddie had seen his friends get bullied by the cops and had heard stories of much worse treatment. As a younger kid, he had called the police whenever his dad beat his mother. From now on, Eddie decided, he would handle things himself. "I wasn't forced in," he told me. "I just went up to a gang member I knew and said, 'I'm ready.'"

By fourteen, Eddie was a full-fledged member. The gang he joined was well-known in Chicago, and his chapter had an especially violent reputation. A few years later, Eddie started to see that he had made a mistake. "I was eighteen and already knew that the direction I was going would not lead me to anything, but I didn't know how to get away."

Alberto and Ricardo were from Eddie's gang. They were older and had always looked out for him. One evening, they decided to meet some girls in the next neighborhood over. While they were waiting in a parking lot for the girls to arrive, a young man rode up to their car on a bike and opened fire. Alberto was shot in the leg, but he turned out okay. Ricardo got hit in the back and was paralyzed for life.

Eddie raced over to see his friends in the hospital. Afterward, he got into their car, still with its shattered windshield and bullet holes, and went looking for revenge. "I was so angry and hurt," he recalled. "I didn't know what to do with it, how to process it." That night Eddie couldn't find anyone responsible, but two months later, he received some information. "Somebody told me, 'Hey, those guys are a few blocks away,' so I decided to go over and retaliate."

It was July 17, 1994. "It was about ten or eleven at night, and I see this young guy in the middle of the street," Eddie told me. "I came out of the car and shot three times—twice at him, once at his guys. I tried to shoot him in his back, in his spinal cord, to paralyze him the same way Ricardo was paralyzed."

For a moment, Eddie felt like he had completed his mission. "I felt like I was able to avenge my friends, but that was very short-lived, because I found out the next day that he was dead. His name was William and he was eighteen years old. I realized right away that I had taken something that wasn't mine."

About a month later, when the police called Eddie in for questioning, he confessed. "I felt like the right thing to do was to step up and take responsibility." Eddie understood the consequences he was facing. "I knew that if I signed that confession, my life could be over. But I felt sick with guilt—I had spent weeks wondering whether God would ever forgive me. That's not to say that a part of me didn't justify it, telling myself, 'This is part of being in a gang—we're at war,' but then you realize it's just a bunch of bullshit. I mean, a war about what?"

Eddie was convicted of first-degree murder and received a sentence of twenty-nine years in prison. When he left the county jail to start his sentence, he had an epiphany. "I remember thinking to myself: 'I have an out date. I need to make sure that I come home as a better person, but I don't know what that means and I don't know how to get there.' I'll never forget that."

In prison, Eddie got his GED, his associate's degree, and took correspondence courses in economics. He learned how to paint and sold his work to inmates and correctional officers. "Change happened to me in different ways. It wasn't one thing and it didn't happen overnight," Eddie explained. "When I was in prison, I had to time to reflect. You're going to find this hard to believe, but I spent almost two years in segregation—three months here, six months there—and I loved being in the hole. It gave me time to think. To dream."

Eddie paused. He didn't want his story to send the wrong message. "I want to be careful about this," he told me. "It's not that everybody comes out better. My aunt came to visit me. Every month she sent me a hundred dollars. Other family members sent money, letters, and visited too. For the most part I had good support. That's rare for most folks in prison."

After fourteen years in prison, Eddie was released on parole. When he went in, he was eighteen years old. When he came out, he was thirty-two. "I still felt this tremendous sense of guilt—who was I to take someone's life? It may sound weird, but I feel extremely grateful to William because his death—his sacrifice—pushed me to atone by helping others around me."

Eddie began volunteering, working to turn around youths from his former gang. From there, he became a street outreach worker for Cure Violence and was profiled in the well-known documentary *The Interrupters.* He traveled the country giving talks on promoting peace and reducing violence. A few years later, he was running his own violence prevention programs. In addition to all that, Eddie earned his bachelor's and master's degrees, both in social work.

In 2017, Eddie joined the Heartland Alliance as a senior director in order to lead READI Chicago, a massive new job-training antiviolence effort. "Ten years ago, I was in prison. I never would have thought that I would be where I'm at now. Today I work for a large nonprofit, have a nice home and a beautiful family."

It would be difficult to imagine a more successful trajectory than Eddie's—he went from convicted murderer to senior executive in about a decade. His story serves as a reminder that redemption is possible and recovery is never entirely out of reach. On the other hand, no one is more careful than Eddie to point out that in many ways his story represents the exception, not the rule. He was intelligent, charismatic, and supported by a strong family that refused to disavow him despite everything he had done.

Eddie, now a committed Christian, also pointed out to me that his redemption will never be final or complete. He works incessantly, often up to and past midnight. "For a lot of people like me, we do this work to repent, to atone. Our salvation is literally dependent on this," he said. "Everything I do, it's just my way of paying the tab, of paying back William and paying back God."

AFTER LISTENING TO these stories, along with dozens more like them, I noticed a number of subjects that came up again and again. Five themes—family, religion, prison, service, and trauma—were consistent refrains in the stories told by survivors of urban violence.

Over and over again, I heard that family was central to why people became involved in violence—and also to why they left it behind. For Erik, abuse and neglect suffered at home led to violence in the street. Anthony inherited his gang affiliation from his father. The support of Eddie's family was crucial to his recovery. For many, their decisions to change were motivated by loved ones. They became better people not for themselves but for those they cared about. For those who were parents, the desire to protect and leave a better legacy for their children provided a particularly powerful incentive.

For many I spoke with, redemption had a strong religious component. For Ray, Anthony, and Eddie, their faith in God was instrumental to their recovery. This is not unusual—many rely on religious faith to recover from all kinds of addictive and destructive behaviors, so it should not be surprising that some sort of spiritual conversion is common among those who were once serious criminals.

Churches, mosques, and other houses of worship often play significant roles in anti-violence efforts. African American clergy in Boston were critically important to the "miracle" that dramatically reduced urban violence there in the 1990s. More recently, hundreds of faith congregations across the country have joined LIVE FREE, a faith-based campaign working to end gun violence and the mass incarceration of young people of color. The campaign has been a strong advocate for the GVRS, supporting its implementation in over a dozen cities since 2012, including Oakland's successful initiative.[2]

Another theme from my conversations was the positive role that prison often played in rehabilitation. For Eddie, for instance, prison provided him with time to reflect and build the skills that would be necessary for starting a new life. As Mario Maciel explained, "Prison might be the only way to reach a kid, to get them cleaned up, medicated, dealing with their issues, and receiving services. The services are minute, but there can be even less out there in society." He continued, "Prison can do wonders for those who need a hiatus. All I ask is that we not throw away the key."

A common misconception about American prisons is that they are revolving doors through which people cycle in and out, becoming better criminals in the process. According to one frequently cited statistic, more than half of all offenders released from state prison return within three to five years. Unfortunately, the usual measures of recidivism give a misleading impression by including individuals who churn in and out of prison multiple times, thereby driving up recidivism rates. In actuality, only one in three offenders returns to prison, and only one in ten returns more than once.[3]

Service was another essential component of redemption for many I spoke with, particularly those who had perpetrated violence themselves. Service was seen as a way to seek forgiveness. Erik, Ray, Eddie, and many others I interviewed felt a tremendous obligation to give back by helping others avoid the mistakes they once made.

Such people are invaluable—they are gold—when it comes to preventing violence and saving lives. Credibility is currency in urban violence reduction, and former criminals are often rich with it. Some of this capital comes from reputation, but more comes from the ability to empathize, to connect with those in desperate situations. "I really listen, and when kids wonder if I'm hearing them, I tell them I understand," Erik explained. "I don't try to story top, like, 'Yo, I was stabbed, I was shot,' because they can tell by the way I listen that I know about beatings, I know about starving, I know about gluing sneakers together." United Playaz, a violence prevention and youth development organization in San Francisco, has a motto that sums it up well: "It takes the hood to save the hood."[4]

Finally, recovering from trauma was a consistent refrain in my conversations. Researchers have only recently begun to appreciate the extraordinary depth of the trauma that many of those exposed to violence endure, and only recently have those living with such trauma felt safe enough to begin talking about it publicly. In addition to being evidence- and community-informed, strategies to address urban violence must be sensitive and responsive to the issue of trauma.

REDEMPTION CAN BE conveyed through stories, but it can also be seen in the data. After examining the criminal histories of over eighty-eight thousand people arrested in New York, criminologists Alfred Blumstein and Kiminori Nakamura found that after about a decade of staying clean, people with criminal records were indistinguishable from the general public in terms of their likelihood of being arrested. They described this phenomenon as "redemption"—if a person could stay clear of the law for ten years, they were statistically redeemed, or no more likely to get into legal trouble than anyone else.[5]

Consider the power of this finding, then consider how contrary it is to standard criminal justice practice. In every state, there are thousands of legal provisions that deny people convicted of crimes access to public housing, welfare assistance, certain occupational licenses, and the right to vote. Few of these "collateral consequences" are time limited. Contrary to the findings of Blumstein and Nakamura, people with criminal records are often treated as permanently dangerous, forever marked with a scarlet letter of shame and suspicion.[6]

This permanent branding of people is also inconsistent with traditional notions of punishment itself. When a crime is committed, the perpetrator takes take something from their victim and from society at large, creating a debt that must be repaid. Time spent behind bars is one conventional means of repaying that debt, and once a person's sentence has been completed, that debt should be considered paid in full. There's a popular saying "Don't do the crime if you can't do the time." But the expression is misleading, because many continue to pay a heavy price for past mistakes even after they have completed their sentence. Too often, redemption is withheld, despite the evidence, logic, and morality.

KIM ODOM NEVER stopped searching for the meaning in her son's death. She even met with the young man who provided the gun to Steven's killer. She needed to see him, she told me. "I wanted to know who did this, and what happened in their life that could bring them to that point."

They met in February 2016 in the Old Colony correctional facility in Bridgewater, Massachusetts. The young man told Kim about his life, his family, and his time in foster care, but a question kept coming back to her. "How do you go from ten years old carrying skateboards to seventeen being involved in a murder?" He told her that he had been a victim too. At fourteen, he had been shot, and then somebody told him how he could get even. From there, he was on his way.

Kim told him, "I know you can't bring Steven back, but what you can do is make every effort not to spit on his grave by returning to that life." Kim needed to know that Steven's death would not be in vain. "This young man has to take ownership, and if he's willing to do that, then there's got to be help for him, because we all know that when folks go into prison and then come back out, that it's not an easy thing. People have already written folks like that off."

Almost exactly ten years after Steven's death, Kim and Ronald went to a cookout. When they arrived, a woman they didn't recognize got up abruptly and left. A few minutes later, she returned and approached them. "I'm sorry for your loss," she said awkwardly. They thanked her and the woman left again. It all seemed a bit strange, but Kim and Ronald thought little of it until Kim's friend told them who the woman was.

It was the mother of the boy who allegedly murdered Steven.

A few minutes passed, then her friend told Kim that the woman was outside, waiting. If she and Ronald wanted to talk to her, they could. Kim and Ronald went outside. The woman was standing there. They hugged.

> She's crying, we're crying. "I've always wanted to talk to you," I told her. "I want you to know we don't hold any ill feelings." She kept saying, "It hurts, it hurts" and I said I know it does. Then as we're talking, I'm realizing that just as we're getting to come upon ten years without Steven, she's coming upon ten years too, because her son was murdered on October 14, ten days after Steven died. I told her, "You know, this is complicated, but both of our sons' lives matter." She hugged us, said, "Thank you," and then left.
>
> I'm hurt, but I don't hold anything against her. I'm a mother, and no mother wants to be that mother whose child took another mother's child, or the mother who has lost a child. One hopeful thing we can do is come together and heal, even if we're not buddy-buddy, but mother to mother.

The city of Boston is building a serenity garden in Steven's honor, just a block or two away from the Odoms' home in Dorchester. On a cold and gray afternoon in December, just before this book was finished, Kim and I visited the site. Work on the garden was not nearly finished, but there was a gravel yard, two benches, and several potted plants. It felt peaceful. We sat down and talked.

We talked about grief, resilience, and hope. About the need to stay dedicated while practicing self-care. I asked Kim why she remained close to issues that were so hurtful to her and Ronald. "It's too important to give up," she told me. "We have to continue to care, because it's not just about us, it's about others as well. You need to lend your voice whenever you can."

For Kim and others like her, helping is a form of healing. "When you share your story and someone lets you know it helped them, that's the blessing. That's the reward."

I thought for a moment. Kim and I had met for the first time almost a decade before, when the memory of Steven's death was recent and raw. Her story, and other stories like hers, had moved me deeply.

I turned to Kim and thanked her. I said that without her, I might not have stayed focused on the issue of urban violence. I might not even have written this book. Kim smiled, and her eyes glazed over with tears. Mine did too. We sat for a moment in silence, listening to the wind.

THIS CHAPTER RECOUNTED personal stories of redemption and recovery. The next chapter concerns how we move forward as a country, redeeming ourselves and recovering as a nation by saving the lives of thousands of the nation's most disadvantaged and disenfranchised young people.

CHAPTER 11

GETTING STARTED

LET'S RETURN TO THAT YOUNG MAN LYING UNCONSCIOUS ON THAT gurney in the emergency room. As the trauma surgeon on duty, you recognize right away that he is bleeding out, hemorrhaging from that wound in his leg. You know immediately that unless this patient receives urgent medical attention, he will die.

You and your team swing into action. A nurse applies direct pressure to the young man's leg to control the bleeding. You insert a balloon catheter into his femoral artery, then inflate the balloon to completely but temporarily stop the hemorrhaging. From there, your team races the young man to the operating unit, with you jogging alongside his gurney, holding the catheter in place.

The young man is quickly prepped for surgery. An assistant takes the catheter so you can scrub in. The catheter is replaced with vascular clamps, which are applied to the artery on each side of the wound. You inspect the artery and discover it is partially severed.

You decide on a synthetic vein graft to repair the damage and carefully sew the graft into place. Once finished, the clamps are released and blood flows through the graft. An X-ray confirms the graft has been successful and that normal blood flow has been restored. Thanks to you, this young man will live. With time, he will recover. With care and support, he may even thrive.

WE MUST STOP the bleeding in urban America. Too many of our young men die needlessly in an undeclared but unrelenting civil war among members of their own communities.

To stop the shooting and killing, we must take action, addressing violent injuries collectively as urgently as we treat them individually. We must approach urban violence as if it were a patient in the emergency room, going stage by stage, from triage to diagnosis, treatment, and finally prognosis.

Urban violence is the linchpin of concentrated urban poverty, holding all the other conditions of such poverty—joblessness, homelessness, poor education and health—in place. That's why we must triage urban violence, putting it first in terms of sequence, if not importance. Until we pull this pin, poverty in our cities will remain as resilient as ever.

Next we should study urban violence, being careful to diagnose it appropriately. We must recognize three fundamental truths about urban violence: that it is sticky, concentrating among small numbers of people, places, and behaviors; that it responds to both positive and negative incentives; and that it is closely related to the legitimacy of the state. These basic truths lead us to the fundamental anti-violence principles of focus, balance, and fairness.

Having diagnosed violence, we can treat it with a series of people-, place-, and behavior-based strategies. We can work with would-be shooters, support someday shooters, and bring bona fide shooters to justice. We can cool hot spots with a combination of policing, place making, and community building. Finally, with hot people in hot spots, we can focus on the most dangerous behaviors: illegal gun carrying, gangbanging, and violent drug dealing.

If we take these steps, our prognosis will be a positive one. Modest reductions in violence each year, multiplied across communities all over the nation, can save thousands of lives, avoid billions in costs, speed progress on poverty, and reduce racial strife.

FORMER SPEAKER OF the House Tip O'Neill famously said that all politics is local. The same is true for urban violence. Whether they are small municipalities like Flint, Michigan, or huge metropolises like Houston, cities form the front lines of the war on community crime and violence.

In our decentralized federalist system, criminal justice is largely, though not exclusively, a local matter. The same is true for other fields implicated in the prevention and control of violence, such as health, human services, housing, and education. Also, while urban violence looks similar from place to place, local differences matter, making homegrown knowledge and know-how essential for adapting strategies to local contexts. For these reasons and more, addressing urban violence is first and foremost a local endeavor.

In this book, I have provided a new paradigm for reducing urban violence, one that treats urban violence in cities like a gunshot in the emergency room. But would it actually work in practice? How would a city get started? What would it cost? How many lives would it save? And what if we did this not in one city, but in every city suffering from serious violence across the nation?

Triage

Before a local anti-violence effort is launched, city leaders must reach consensus on some basic ideas and principles. Nothing else should be done until there is agreement in principle on a few basic concepts.

Everyone must agree, up front and in advance, on the nature of the problem to be solved. This means coming together around a common definition of the challenge. The clearest possible definition of urban violence would be this: unacceptably high rates of lethal and potentially lethal violence, committed in public spaces, as measured by the number of homicides and shootings that result in injury. At this early stage, details are not important—broad agreement on the ends and means is what is required—but moving too far away from this definition risks watering down the effort before it even begins.[1]

Care must be taken to ensure that everyone is truly on board with an effort that reduces violence by focusing on violence itself directly and not indirectly by alleviating poverty or addressing crime more generally. An anti-violence effort might offer economic and other opportunities to poor people and places, but it does so as part of its anti-violence mission. For example, creating jobs and providing parks might be useful in this context, but only if they can be linked to less violence. The same is true for guns, gangs, and drugs—they are important matters in their own right, but here they matter only in relation to violence.

Once general agreement is reached on the problem, the group can turn to solutions. Again, details are not necessary at this point. What is important is agreeing that the path to peace will be, generally speaking, evidence- and community-informed. *Evidence-informed*, in this context, means drawing on the best data and evidence currently available. It also means that key decisions should be determined not by politics but instead by what empirical information shows will save the most lives. *Community-informed* means the effort will also give voice to those most impacted by urban violence by listening carefully and inviting participation according to the principles of procedural fairness.

What does this look like in practice? The leaders and stakeholders of this effort agree to devote themselves to an anti-violence initiative that addresses violence directly and specifically. These leaders and stakeholders also agree to a process that is driven by data and evidence and that offers impacted individuals and communities a meaningful say along the way.

It is important to note that this process, while inclusive, should not be open. An open process inevitably becomes a political one, and politics is toxic to policy this early on. At the beginning, the key is to get the right people around a table and keep them there, communicating candidly without fear of reprisals until initial planning is complete.

Who are the key stakeholders who must be involved from the beginning? An exhaustive list is not possible here, so I will identify the three most important leaders and groups.

In any city, the most important leader is the mayor or city manager. Through their leadership, mayors can ensure that the right people come to the table and that everyone works together. Police and prosecutors will always view violence reduction as an essential element of their mission, but without mayoral leadership, other city agencies may not. Mayors must insist that others outside law enforcement contribute to the cause; otherwise, anti-violence efforts will be enforcement-only, or lacking in coordination between enforcement and prevention activities.

Mayors have obligations that preclude them from taking on day-to-day oversight of these initiatives, but it must be clear that the mayor is committed and involved. The best way to do this is to establish an office headed by an official who reports directly to the mayor to handle this and other public safety initiatives that require collaboration among multiple agencies and constituencies. In fact, a crude but effective means of measuring a mayor's commitment to these issues is to see whether such an office exists, and if it does, to examine the size of its budget and scope of its authority. In Los Angeles, for instance, the deputy mayor for public safety oversees the Gang Reduction Youth Development office, which has an annual budget of over $26 million and dozens of employees.[2]

The next most important leader is the police commissioner, superintendent, or chief. Because the police will be the largest single component of any serious anti-violence effort, it is especially important that they endorse the fundamentals of focus, balance, and fairness. The police must be willing to engage, collaborate, and coordinate with outside stakeholders, particularly those from impacted communities. If police see themselves as the only answer to urban violence, this must be corrected before the effort moves forward.

The third most important group of stakeholders are representatives from the communities where the majority of violence takes place. Any sustainable effort must be seen as legitimate, and legitimacy requires the meaningful participation of those who are most affected by the effort's activities. They can be faith, community, civic, or other leaders,

but whoever they are, they must authentically represent their constituents both in terms of their need for safety and their desire for social
justice. They must also be willing to look at the data and evidence and
not just rely on their own beliefs, knowledge, and experience. In short,
they must be problem-solvers, not just advocates or activists.

Diagnosis

With an agreement in principle among these three constituencies,
the effort can move forward, but before action there must be analysis.
This is a step that many cities rush or overlook, creating problems
down the line. Cities that wish to be sustainably successful in reducing urban violence must take the time and effort to fully understand
the violence in their particular jurisdiction. Only then can they craft
appropriate evidence- and community-informed solutions.

This analysis must answer three basic but specific questions: who is
committing the violence, where they are committing it, and why. The
effort can use social network analysis, group audits, or other tools to
identify the small cohorts of young men most likely to shoot or be shot.
It can also use crime mapping to identify the hot spots where violence
concentrates. Whatever the specific analytic tools may be, they must
combine data and human intelligence to understand the underlying
dynamics of the violence, with an emphasis on proximate, not root,
causes—if the analysis produces a superficial conclusion that violence
happens mostly to poor people and mostly in poor neighborhoods, it
is next to useless.

Treatment

With the diagnosis completed, preparations for treatment can begin.
A plan can be created based on the analysis from the previous step.
That plan should include a set of focused, balanced, and fair strategies
that specifically address the people, places, and behaviors driving violence in the city. Evidence-informed strategies should be identified

and selected based on whether they fit the specific needs and abilities of the jurisdiction. Once selected, they must be adapted to the local context with input from the community, then implemented using a framework that aligns multiple strategies that will operate at the same time. (A sample framework can be found in appendix A.) Finally, the plan should set aside funds for ongoing analysis, performance management, and evaluation.

Whatever the specific strategies may be, they should include efforts to work with would-be shooters, support someday shooters, and put away bona fide shooters. Would-be and someday shooters must be identified, engaged, stabilized, treated, and then offered opportunities to better themselves and their communities. If would-be shooters persist in violence, they must be addressed as bona fide shooters and subject to law enforcement action. The GVRS is the leading strategy in this area. Street outreach can and should be conducted as well. Efforts to intervene with at-risk individuals should also include a robust cognitive behavioral component.

In addition to people-based strategies, the plan should include place-based efforts to reduce violence in crime hot spots, first with policing, then with a combination of place making and community building. The leading strategy here should be partnership-oriented crime prevention done in hot spots, or hot spots policing done in partnership with community members, business and property owners, and others, supplemented by efforts to remove blight and restore city services.

Finally, with hot people in hot spots, behaviors such as illegal gun carrying, gangbanging, and violent drug dealing must be targeted for enforcement. Guns safely and legally stored in the home should not be the focus. Gangs that are not stalking their rivals should be deprioritized. Drugs are an anti-violence priority when only they are the subject of violent disputes, either among rival dealers or because they are being abused by people with a predilection for violence. When drug abuse is the problem, however, the evidence tells us that treatment, not incarceration, works best.

With a plan in place, a task force, working group, or committee should be established to put the plan into practice. The task force should have relatively few members—only those necessary to implement the people-, place-, and behavior-based strategies above. Too many members will make close coordination difficult, if not impossible.

While small in terms of numbers, the group should be strong in terms of stature. Task force members should be elite members of their respective professions, as is often the case with law enforcement task forces. They should be authorized by their superiors to work long hours, cut red tape, and work around bureaucratic barriers in order to get the job done. They should be well equipped and well funded, both for the work itself and in terms of additional compensation to aid recruitment and as compensation for taking on such demanding work.

This task force must be the local A team, roughly balanced between law enforcement and non–law enforcement members. It will need to communicate in real time and be ready to respond to life-threatening situations at a moment's notice. Members must be willing and able to go to most violent areas of the city in order to provide immediate and potentially lifesaving assistance.

This is a relatively straightforward matter for law enforcement. Police are accustomed to being available twenty-four hours a day, responding immediately to a crisis, and intervening in dangerous situations. One often-overlooked reason that so many initiatives rely excessively on law enforcement is that no other group or agency has the authority or capacity to respond in real time the way law enforcement does.

For those working in social services, doing this work involves a major reenvisioning and restructuring of how services and assistance are delivered. I cannot stress this enough. To ensure that the task force is appropriately balanced, it needs a small group of street outreach and social service providers who are just as empowered as the police to prevent violence. Like law enforcement, they must work in shifts in order to be available at all hours, they must have adequate communication and transportation that allow them to respond quickly, and they must have access to resources that can be deployed instantly in order to remedy a dangerous situation.

If, in order to head off a homicide, it becomes necessary to respond to the house of a would-be shooter at 3 a.m., drive that individual to a bus station, and then buy them a ticket to get them temporarily out of town, then that is what task force members must be able to do. Similarly, when working with social service agencies, members must have agreements in place allowing them to skip to the front of the line, getting at-risk individuals priority access to scarce resources. Similarly, when a streetlight overlooking a hot spot goes out, it should not go through routine bureaucratic procedures—it must be prioritized and turned back on immediately.

The treatment plan should also specify what *not* to do. It should be made clear from the outset that low-risk people and places will not be addressed by these efforts. It should be said out loud that anti-violence assistance will go to people and places truly at risk for violence, and not to those needing help more generally. Relatedly, there should be an explicit agreement that anti-violence resources will be devoted only to violence elimination, not general crime reduction. Everyone must be on the same page that they are involved in an anti-violence, not anti-poverty or anti-crime, effort.

THE TREATMENTS OUTLINED in this book operate within the laws already on the books today. They depend on preexisting agencies, institutions, and systems. To make a big difference in the lives of the urban poor, new laws and new structures are not necessary—at least not right away. For now, what is required is money, along with small but vocal constituencies to demand that it be spent the right way.

Effective violence reduction may be expensive on a per capita basis, but when properly focused on only the people, places, and behaviors driving the problem, it is cheap in absolute terms. Devoting an additional $30,000 per homicide per year to reducing violence would work wonders in cities suffering from serious violence, and it would be affordable by any reasonable budgetary standard. For Chicago, based on its 2017 homicide figures, that would mean an extra $19.6 million per year. For Baltimore, it would translate to $10.3 million a year. For both cities, these amounts are less than 0.5 percent of their annual budgets. These sums are not negligible, but policy makers would not need to move mountains to make such funds available.[3]

In 2009, then–education secretary Arne Duncan told Chicagoans concerned about urban violence, "This is not about the money. Money alone will never solve this problem. It's about our values." He was doubly wrong—not only is a certain amount of funding necessary for any serious policy endeavor, but the amount of funding also signals how much an issue matters to decision-makers and the public. Former vice president Joe Biden, Duncan's fellow cabinet member at the time, had it right: "Don't tell me what you value. Show me your budget, and I'll tell you what you value."[4]

To put the strategies in this book into action, it's really all about the money. As Kim Odom told me, "You have to find those funds somewhere, because if you don't pay up front, you're going to pay in the end. We keep going around in circles, we keep saying there's no money—but there's money." If we truly value our fellow citizens who live under constant threat of violence, then we can find the modest sums necessary to keep them safe from harm.

Assuming these funds can be secured, how should they be spent? In short, funds should be allocated with the requirement that they be disbursed for one purpose: reducing killings and shootings. Those spending the funds should be required to provide progress reports showing that monies are being spent on the people, places, and behaviors that had been previously identified as driving the violence—and showing that their efforts are saving lives. Consistent with the fundamental of balance, a requirement should be in place that funds are distributed roughly equally across enforcement and prevention strategies. Those spending the funds should also be required to include impacted communities in their decision-making processes.

Funds should come with a requirement that only strategies with a strong base of evidence may be used. Localities should decide what works for them and their particular circumstances, but they must choose from a set of strategies that have been shown to work. Multiple strategies must be used—no single strategy is strong enough on its own. A good example of an effort that puts all these requirements together is New York State's Gun Involved Violence Elimination (GIVE) initiative, which I played a role in developing and leading. A description of GIVE, along with more concrete guidance on how to connect all the strategies set out in this book, can be found in appendix A.

Prognosis

Properly funded and implemented, the strategies outlined in this book could be transformative in terms of saving lives. In cities with high rates of homicide, these strategies could achieve a 10 percent reduction in homicide every year for the foreseeable future—causing a massive long-term reduction in crime along the lines of what New York City has experienced. An annual reduction of 10 percent is an extremely conservative estimate, given that several of the strategies in this book are capable of producing such a decline on their own, much less in combination with other programs.[5]

Let's assume that Chicago launched such an effort in 2017, the latest year we have federal data for. Assume further that that effort lasted eight years—two mayoral terms—but that no reduction was achieved during the first year because that time was used for planning purposes. Allow the funding ($30,000 per homicide) to follow the number of homicides as they decline. Finally, assume that for each homicide averted, each life saved, the city will be spared approximately $10 million in medical costs, criminal justice costs, lost wages and earnings, reduced quality of life, and other costs. (In chapter 2, the cost of a single homicide was credibly estimated at $10 million, $13.5 million, and $19.2 million per killing—I've used the most conservative of those estimates here.) In total, the anti-violence initiative would cost Chicago approximately $112 million over eight years, including just under $19.6 million the first year.

What would this mean for Chicago? In 2017, the city suffered 653 homicides. A 10 percent annual reduction (skipping the first year) would result in 312 homicides in the year 2025. Over the course of those eight years, *1,505 lives would be saved,* with a net social benefit of $14.9 billion. For every public dollar spent, $135 in costs would be saved. In Baltimore, using the same assumptions, *788 lives would be saved,* with a savings of $7.8 billion and the same return on investment. (A detailed breakdown of the local and national calculations in this chapter can be found in appendix B.)

Now consider the impact of two national initiatives that work the same way—one funding the twenty cities with the most homicides overall, and a partner program focusing on the twenty cities with the highest per capita homicide rates. The first program focuses on the larger jurisdictions where the most lives could be saved, while the second responds to smaller cities in desperate need of relief. The total cost of these efforts, over eight years, would be about $899 million, with the first year costing $158 million and less each year thereafter as homicides gradually decline. The *total number of lives saved would be 12,132* over eight years—a truly stunning figure. The total costs avoided by the country would also be enormous—$120 billion. For every dollar spent, $135 would be saved. Keep in mind, in all these cases, these are just the estimates for homicide alone—they do not capture the enormous benefits gained and costs avoided by reducing nonfatal violent crime at the same time.

The yearly price of the national efforts—$158 million for the first year and less every year thereafter—is a rounding error in a federal budget of almost $4 trillion annually. For this small sum we could be a dramatically safer nation in a very short time. What would such a nation look like?

Imagine the country's most distressed urban neighborhoods—just under seven thousand of them, containing about twenty-four million citizens in total. Now imagine those neighborhoods as poor but safe, or at least as safe as the rest of the country. Visualize entire communities where, though crime and drugs might still be present, lethal violence is largely absent, and then think about how much easier it would be to help such communities. Think of how much easier it would be for kids to concentrate on schoolwork if trauma was not taxing their minds. Think about the parks and playgrounds they might enjoy if there were no threats of gunfire. Think about the shops, restaurants, and other businesses that might thrive if the safety of customers and employees were assured. Think about the jobs, revenues, and other benefits these ventures would bring. Think of the growing tax base and the services and assistance to the poor that cities could now afford.[6]

Think about a nation stained by slavery and seething with racial resentment. Think about that nation's struggle to achieve "a more perfect union" and its painfully slow progress in the pursuit of social and economic justice. Then think about how much easier it would be to address these challenges if poor people of color were not demonized as dangerous and brutal. Finally, think about how much easier it would be for Americans to empathize with one another a bit more if they feared each other a little less.

THE PROGRAMS AND policies described in this book will not, by themselves, solve all the persistent, seemingly intractable problems of America's urban poor. But they are the right places to start. Anti-violence strategies should be properly understood as the tip of the anti-poverty, anti-racism spear. Long-term efforts to address root causes and reform institutions can and should be paired with short-term investments in the people and places that matter most for violence reduction. This book focuses on these short-term investments because they are less well known and understood, and because others are already advocating for longer-term investments in our cities.

Metaphorically speaking, whether the patient is a young man suffering from a gunshot wound, a community riddled with such injuries, or a nation filled with such communities, the treatment is the same: first and foremost, focus on the violence. Dramatically reducing urban homicide is the first thing we should do, and we can do it relatively easily. The fact that we don't is, well, criminal.

Americans have become accustomed to shootings and killings. They happen daily, even hourly. We might muster some outrage when children are executed in their own classrooms or when parishioners are assassinated as they pray in church, but beyond that, little seems sacred. We largely overlook the thousands of black and brown young men who die violently each year, caught up in cycles they do not fully understand and cannot easily escape.

When someone privileged dies violently, we pay attention because it is unusual. We often fail to acknowledge the deaths of the poor and marginalized because they happen so frequently. But we should never numb ourselves to murder, no matter who the victim might be.

This nation is in need of a moral reckoning. Americans on the right and left may disagree on how best to address poverty, but we should all be able to agree that the poor do not deserve to die suddenly and violently at the end of a gun barrel. They do not deserve to see their family and friends pierced and punctured by bullets. No one does. Surely this truth lies above some universal baseline of compassion that we all share.

For most of you reading this book, murder does not happen in your community. That said, it is happening in your city and in your country, and it may be closer than you think—many peaceful, affluent neighborhoods are separated from violent hot spots by only a few city blocks. We should all be outraged when young people die a short walk from our doorsteps. We should all take to the presses, airwaves, and streets, demanding that our leaders bring this unnecessary slaughter to an end. It just doesn't have to be this way.

"Violence is not a Chicago problem any more than it is a black problem, a white problem or a Hispanic problem," then–attorney general Eric Holder said in 2009. "It is something that affects communities big and small and people of all races and all colors. It is an American problem." It is our patriotic duty to help save the lives of our fellow citizens. Will you do your part?[7]

ACKNOWLEDGMENTS

NOBODY ACHIEVES ANYTHING OF SUBSTANCE ENTIRELY ON THEIR own, and I am no exception. In writing this book I relied heavily on a broad array of professional and personal relationships, depending on friends, colleagues, and even a few strangers to share their time, expertise, and experiences with me.

First and foremost, I must thank the men and women who shared their stories of struggle and survival. I hope this book conveys just how searing but ultimately inspiring these stories are. Talking about the most intimate and traumatic aspects of one's life is difficult under any circumstances, but many of those I spoke with were meeting me for the first time or knew me only in passing. They opened up their lives to a stranger in order to make a difference, in hopes that their experiences could educate and inspire others. They spoke so that others might be spared their suffering. I am deeply indebted to Elizabeth Banach, Dante Barksdale, Anthony Blockmon, Eddie Bocanegra, Jessica Cardenas, Byron Conaway, John Curry, Jon Feinman, Marie Gonzalez, Melvyn Hayward Jr., Erik King, Jose Lopez, Mario Maciel, Ronald Noblet, Ruth Rollins, Raymond Solórzano, Phillip Tingirides, and Anthony Williams. I am especially indebted to Kim Odom for speaking with me extensively about the tragic loss of her beloved son Steven. I would also like to thank Paul Carrillo, Maurice Classen, Teny Gross, and Daniel Webster for their assistance in arranging several of these interviews.

Harvard University provided me with a near-perfect setting in which to reflect, engage, and ultimately to produce this book. Since 2014, I have been a senior fellow at the Harvard Kennedy School's Program in Criminal Justice Policy and Management (PCJ), Harvard Law School's Criminal Justice Policy Program (CJPP), and the Kennedy School's Center for International Development (CID). At the PCJ, I thank former executive director Christine Cole and current program administrator Brian Welch. At the CJPP, I thank faculty directors Carol Steiker and Alex Whiting. At CID, I must thank director Ricardo Hausmann, Andrea Carranza, Andrea Hayes, Camila Lobo, Chuck McKenney, and the rest of the CID faculty and staff for their ongoing encouragement and support.

As noted in chapter 1, much of the evidence from this book was originally gathered for a meta-review of anti-violence evaluations performed by my colleague Christopher Winship and myself. I express my gratitude to Chris, with whom I also co-taught two courses on policing, for his work on that project, and for all the insights he has offered me throughout the writing process. I also thank our research assistants, Roberto Patiño and Jason Wilks, for their important contributions. The project was funded by the United States Agency for International Development and stewarded by former Central American Regional Security Initiative (CARSI) coordinators Jeremy Biddle and Enrique Roig. Lastly, I collaborated closely with two colleagues, Enrique Betancourt and Guillermo Cespedes, on related USAID projects, and their insights deeply impressed me and helped inform the substance of this book.

The Joyce Foundation provided early financial assistance for the field research that resulted in the interviews described throughout the book. I thank Nina Vinik, program director for the Gun Violence Prevention Program, not just for her support in securing funding but also for contributing her time, insights, and expertise.

The Harry Frank Guggenheim Foundation hosted a small symposium of scholars and practitioners to review an early draft of the book and offer comments. I thank Guggenheim president Daniel Wilhelm and senior program officer Joel Wallman for their support. I am also extremely grateful to Juan Carter, Walter Katz, David Kennedy, Mark Kleiman, Tracey Meares, Andrew Papachristos, Patrick Sharkey, Nina Vinik, and Daniel Webster, all of whom took time out of their busy schedules to participate in the symposium, review the entire manuscript, and take an entire day to make the book better.

A host of other academics and practitioners provided me with invaluable feedback. I thank Ted Alcorn, Jeff Asher, Christopher Blattman, Anthony Braga, Jeffrey Brown, Phillip Cook, Vaughn Crandall, Nicholas Dawidoff, Scott Decker, Phillip Atiba Goff, Mike Green, Teny Gross, David Hemenway, Christopher Koper, Jill Leovy, Edward Maguire, Lorraine Mazzerolle, Alex Piquero, Jerry Ratcliffe, Robert Sampson, Gary Slutkin, and Justice Tankebe for their input—the book was significantly strengthened as a result of their contributions. I also extend my gratitude and apologies here to anyone I may have neglected to mention.

When I started this endeavor, I was fortunate to already know my subject matter quite well, as I had been deeply involved in both the study and practice of violence reduction for years. I had never written a book, however. First-time authors need sound counsel and warm support, and I received both from my agent, Tina Bennett at William Morris Endeavor. Lara Heimert, Brian Distelberg, Dan Gerstle, and the rest of the team at Basic Books did a fantastic job of bringing the book to market, with Dan expertly guiding me through the writing process and providing crucial edits to help make the book as accessible to a general audience as possible. Samuel Eckersley and Stuart Rogers, two incredible graphic designers who also happen to be good friends, contributed their time and expertise to make the cover of the book as impactful as it is. Two Harvard graduate students, Jasper Frank and Mayu Takeda, performed invaluable background research on several important questions related to the book.

Two old friends, Robert Armstrong and Wiley O'Sullivan, provided early encouragement and advice as I contemplated beginning this project. A newer friend, Tavneet Suri, went above and beyond in supporting this effort. Tavneet, a widely recognized and respected development economist with the MIT Sloan School of Management, took a tremendous amount of time out of her busy schedule to carefully review multiple versions of this book, providing valuable insights and feedback each time. I am especially deeply indebted to Tavneet—the book simply would not be as strong without her.

In 2009, I joined the administration of President Barack Obama, working directly for Laurie Robinson, the assistant attorney general for the Office of Justice Programs at the US Department of Justice. Working for Laurie was a transformative professional experience and I would not be where I am today without her mentorship, support, and wise counsel.

Finally, I must thank my family. My father, Clark Abt, founded and ran Abt Associates, a social science research firm dedicated to improving social and economic well-being worldwide. My mother, Wendy Abt, is an expert on banking and development who spent much of her career advancing financial innovation in sub-Saharan Africa to benefit the poor. My sister, Emily Abt, is an award-winning writer and director who creates films that explore and advance social justice issues. They are my heroes, comrades in arms, and confidants.

APPENDIX A
GETTING CONNECTED

WHEN VIOLENCE THREATENS, IT TEARS COMMUNITIES APART. RESIdents withdraw, afraid to speak up or leave their homes. Businesses depart or fortify themselves in fortresses. Politicians play the blame game, pointing fingers at one another. To break the cycle of violence, there must be a series of moments uniting the community, the state, and everyone in between.

Bringing people together is an important start, but it is not enough. Once assembled, coalitions must be organized into action. Without planning and structure, there is no joint venture, only a chaotic jumble of activity. Individual contributions must be aligned in support of a common purpose: less violence, less death, more peace, more life.

In this book, a number of evidence-informed people-, place-, and behavior-based treatments to reduce urban violence have been introduced. Depending on how you count them, at least a dozen discrete anti-violence strategies have been presented. Each has merit, but even the strongest programs do not work on their own. Even the GVRS, the most directly impactful anti-violence intervention, cannot succeed in isolation. In the world of violence reduction, there are no magic bullets, so to speak.

Because no anti-violence strategy is transformative on its own, multiple strategies must be leveraged to generate game-changing results. What's more, this leveraging must be done thoughtfully, coordinating multiple approaches all operating at the same time to reach the same high-risk people, places, and behaviors. This appendix describes the tools that can help bring the previously described strategies together and organize them into a single integrated response to urban violence.

Networks connect our modern world, loosely aligning stakeholders with similar interests. Frameworks help to organize and align the activities of stakeholders so that they mutually reinforce one another. Plans put networks and frameworks into action, identifying commitments and holding stakeholders accountable. Performance measurement and evaluation adds another layer of accountability, ensuring efforts meet their intended goals.

In this appendix, we will cover the basics of networks, frameworks, plans, and performance measurement in the context of urban violence, followed by two examples of such efforts in action. Let's get started.

Networks

Social network analysis demonstrates that shooters are often connected to one another, loosely organized into competing and collaborating gangs, groups, or crews. Larger gangs like MS-13 often operate via a loose structure of interconnected sets, or *clicas,* often without a single leader or unifying leadership structure. Organized criminal networks are typically fluid, adapting rapidly in response to opportunities that span borders, languages, and cultures. If those who perpetrate crime and violence are networked, those dedicated to preventing such activities should be networked as well. Governmental and nongovernmental stakeholders of all kinds must find ways to leverage resources and align activities in pursuit of public safety.

Contemporary social challenges are complex, sprawling, and constantly evolving, defying easy answers and simple solutions. No single agency or organization is responsible for them, so success is dependent on connecting and collaborating across boundaries, and on quickly adapting from the bottom up rather than managing from the top down. Urban violence is a particularly complicated social phenomenon. Effective responses require an unusually diverse range of stakeholders, including individuals and families; community, business, and faith leaders; social service and public health providers; and law enforcement and criminal justice agencies.

The best way to initially organize these stakeholders is via networks. In today's interconnected and rapidly changing world, the flexibility and adaptability of networks enable them to meet the needs of their members with greater speed and efficiency than more traditional and formal structures. Importantly, networks can operate across the boundaries that normally fragment collective responses to social issues, spanning jurisdictional and bureaucratic boundaries at the federal, state, and local levels. Networks, in my opinion, represent the future of governance, not just for criminal justice but for everything.

Networks are particularly helpful in the context of urban violence. They can distribute and share information, promote collaboration and partnership, spur innovation, and build capacity for action. With the help of networks, successful anti-violence strategies in one jurisdiction can be identified, highlighted, and disseminated to others. Networks can facilitate the formation of multidisciplinary teams and partnerships. They promote the efficient sharing of information and resources. They can also be vehicles for broader institutional and systemic change.

The success of a network depends on the capabilities of its members and on how well those members work together. As John Kania and Mark Kramer outline in their collective impact model, effective networks generally feature a common agenda, shared measurement, mutually reinforcing activities, and regular communication. In addition, many networks perform best when supported by an organization dedicated to advancing the network and its goals.[1]

A common agenda requires a shared understanding of both the problem and the potential solution. Network members must agree, at least in principle, on what researchers call a "theory of change"— that is, how they will achieve their shared goals. Shared measurement requires deciding which inputs, outputs, and outcomes are important and agreeing that this information will be tracked, measured, and shared among network members. Having mutually reinforcing activities means that while network members may not move in lock-step with one another, their conduct should be consistent with the common agenda. Regular communication is necessary to coordinate the ongoing activities of network members. Each element of the network connects to the next: a common agenda is quantified by shared measurement, which helps guide mutually reinforcing activities, all of which are sustained by regular and clear communication.[2]

Finally, networks need dedicated support. Having resources and staff devoted to maintaining the network itself is crucial. "Backbone" organizations manage and support networks through a variety of activities, including meeting facilitation, technology and communications support, data collection and reporting, as well as all the logistical and administrative work necessary for the network to thrive.[3]

With networks, the ultimate goal is not merely to broaden the response to a social challenge but also to create a more considered, effective, and legitimate one. Networks can be measured by their breadth (number of members) and depth (level of coordination among members). As breadth increases, depth becomes more challenging.[4]

When it comes to urban violence networks, the first challenge is ensuring that prospective participants all agree on what the actual problem is. Many may claim to focus on violence but, upon closer inspection, are actually committing to reducing poverty or perhaps crime more generally. They may also be more interested in addressing another form of violence, such as family or school violence. While disagreement on details is allowable, network members must agree on a common definition of the problem. In this case, the problem of urban violence would be defined as serious, potentially lethal violence that occurs in the community, not in the home or school.

Once agreement is reached on the problem, the network can turn to solutions. Again, network members must agree on the broad strokes of a joint strategy. Anti-violence efforts should be informed by both the evidence and affected communities.

This means that network members must agree in advance to be guided not by what feels good but by what the data and evidence tell us works best. This may sound naïve at first, but effective urban violence reduction will inevitably shift resources and focus, creating winners and losers among stakeholders. Agreeing in advance to make those decisions in a transparent and unbiased manner makes such shifts easier and less painful when they occur.

Networks must also include and listen to those whose lives are actually affected by violence. Having members of impacted communities at the policy-making table serves many valuable functions. First, it serves as an essential reality check when applying evidence-informed strategies that often have been developed in other jurisdictions. Those with real-world experience can quickly identify why certain strategies, while effective elsewhere, might not work in the context at hand. Second, they can guide the adaptation of such strategies to make them more appropriate for their particular context. Third, they can provide innovative new ideas that can be piloted, tested, and, if successful, scaled up. Finally, they can help ensure the legitimacy of the effort, both in terms of process and result. They can make sure that impacted communities are not unnecessarily burdened by tough enforcement measures, for instance.

Several years ago, I gave a speech to a large group of community organizers about the Obama administration's evidence-based crime-reduction efforts. The audience listened politely, but as soon as I finished, a hand shot up. "Look, I get what you're saying, but we don't need these professors to tell us what we already know," a man in the audience told me. "We just need the money to solve the problems." I have heard this point made again and again in community meetings across the country. "Respectfully sir, I disagree," I responded. "It's not just a matter of resources. It's also a matter of know-how, and being from the neighborhood doesn't mean you know everything about helping the neighborhood. Neither does working at a university. We need everybody together on this." Moments like these reflect the need for direct, candid conversations about how best to address urban violence. As a colleague at the Justice Department once remarked to me, "It ain't real engagement unless it starts off with some yelling."

Getting everyone on the same page takes time. It involves a lot of listening, airing of differences, addressing those differences, and then slowly, carefully, building consensus. It has to happen in multiple forums: large meetings, small huddles, one-on-one conversations, and more. The most important thing is to fully incorporate into the process the elements of procedural fairness: respect, transparency, and voice. The process should not be rushed, as once the real work begins it is almost impossible to turn back to these fundamental issues.

It's also important not to try to get everyone on board right away. A network can and should start small, with a core group of like-minded individuals and organizations that are truly dedicated to the mission. Additional members can be added later, but unconvinced or unenthusiastic members can kill an effort if they get involved too early.

Once network members agree that reducing urban violence is their mission and that the best way to tackle the problem is by using evidence- and community-informed strategies, you can move on to measurement. It is often during this conversation that a group's commitment to their common agenda is tested. If reducing urban violence is the mission, then the most important measurements must look at violence, most importantly homicides and shootings. Homicide rates are simultaneously the most important and most reliable measures of serious violence. They are also the most politically salient—any police chief will tell you that no matter what happens with rates of other violent or property crime, the media, politicians, and community members will only remember the homicide count and whether it is up, down, or the same as last year.[5]

Some will resist such measures because, deep down, they are unsure whether they can change homicide rates and do not want to be held accountable for something they may not be able to fully control. To my mind, this is simply a test of commitment. If you aren't willing to accept some personal, professional, or reputational risk in the process of trying to save lives, then this work is not for you or your organization.

In urban violence reduction, having mutually reinforcing activities means paying attention to the fundamentals: focusing on the people, places, and behaviors that matter most; balancing enforcement with prevention; and making sure the entire effort is fair and legitimate. Offering services to poor people who are not at risk for violence is not focused. Ramping up police patrols of hot spots without following it up with investment is not balanced. Treating community members brutally, roughly, or rudely is neither legitimate nor fair.

Ideally, networks will have two basic levels of activity coordination, depending on their proximity to the problem. Those dealing directly with violence need to be tightly coordinated, while those who work on the problem from a distance can be more loosely organized. Generally speaking, individuals and organizations whose primary mission is violence reduction will be in the inner circle, and people and groups for whom violence is a secondary interest will be in the outer circle.

There must also be ongoing communication. The closer you are to the violence, the more frequent and structured that communication must be. Police meet daily at the beginning of their shifts. Street outreach workers should be in near-daily contact with the hottest individuals. Police, crime analysts, outreach workers, and key service providers must meet at least weekly to coordinate on the ever-evolving status of disputes, retaliations, and violence. For urgent incidents, like responding to crime scenes, there must be protocols in place, in writing, to govern each group's immediate responsibilities. For less urgent issues and for members of the network not dealing with violence directly, monthly or quarterly meetings will suffice.

Finally, anti-violence networks must be supported. High-performing networks do not happen by accident—they are carefully supported, even curated. There need to be staff and resources dedicated to supporting the network—it is not something that can be done on the side. That said, the scale of network organization should be limited, as networks do their best work through their members, not on their own.

Where this support is centered depends on local circumstances, but there are better and worse options. Government-led networks have several advantages: They leverage the legitimacy of the state and can give a public seal of approval to the work. Importantly, they are also politically accountable. Most importantly, they can leverage the government's massive resources and capacity. On the other hand, government is prone to bureaucratic obstacles and restrictions, political pressure, and, most of all, the disruption of political transitions. Privately led efforts can be politically independent and less vulnerable to changes in administrations. They can also be more flexible, adaptive, and innovative. That said, they will always lack the resources and legitimacy of the state.

Frameworks

Frameworks, in this context, are conceptual tools used to organize collective action. Understanding a complex social phenomenon like urban violence requires a multidisciplinary approach; addressing it demands a multisector response. Frameworks can help coordinate the activities of stakeholders so that they help rather than hinder one another.

In order to be useful, a framework must be theoretically sound but also grounded in the empirical reality of the problem it seeks to address. In addition, it must have practical utility for implementation in the field. In short, an effective framework for responding to urban violence must clearly articulate a reasonably complete, accurate, and useful description of both the problem and its solution.[6]

In order to organize a framework around the problem of urban violence, it must be remembered that violence concentrates among people, in places, and around certain behaviors. Organizing anti-violence responses accordingly makes sense, particularly because the notion of concentrating on clusters of people, places, and behaviors is more easily grasped and readily implemented by practitioners than more abstract and conceptual approaches. Hot spot and problem-oriented policing strategies, for instance, have already been disseminated around the globe, familiarizing many law enforcement agencies with at least a rudimentary understanding of place-, people-, and behavior-based strategies. Organizing responses in this way also reinforces the fundamental concept of focus.

In order to organize around solutions, the framework should account for the types of strategies currently used in the fields of prevention, intervention, enforcement, and reentry. I would simplify this to prevention, intervention, and enforcement, merging reentry with intervention. These terms are familiar to many practitioners in the field, making the framework accessible and easy to use. This organization also reinforces the fundamental concept of balance, ensuring that our collective response includes both carrot and stick, prevention and punishment.[7]

Having provided a means of mapping both the problem and solution to urban violence, we can combine the two, creating a grid (Table 1):

TABLE 1

	Prevention	Intervention	Enforcement
People			
Places			
Behaviors			

Now that we have a framework, we can populate it with the strategies in this book that are proven to work (Table 2). Once we do so, a clearer picture of how these efforts can be coordinated emerges.

TABLE 2

	Prevention	Intervention	Enforcement
People	Cognitive Behavioral Therapy Family-based programming	Cognitive Behavioral Therapy GVRS Street outreach	Homicide clearance improvement GVRS
Places	Community building	Blight and nuisance abatement Service restoration	Hot spots policing
	Partnership-oriented crime prevention		
Behaviors	Cognitive Behavioral Therapy Family-based programming Alcohol restrictions Drug treatment	Cognitive Behavioral Therapy GVRS Street outreach	Hot spots policing GVRS

For those most likely to perpetrate violence, improved homicide clearance rates can take killers off the streets. GVRS initiatives supported by street outreach workers can send a clear message that further shootings will not be tolerated and that alternatives are available. CBT can train young men to control their anger and solve their disputes peaceably. Family-based therapy can assist parents in keeping their children on the right path.

For the hot spots where violence concentrates, hot spots policing can make an immediate difference by chilling violent activity. Blight-and nuisance-abatement strategies, as well as restoring effective city services, can improve transportation, housing, lighting, and vegetation in immediate areas so that reductions in violence are sustained over time. Finally, improving informal social control via police and community partnerships in and around hot spots can build the legitimacy needed for long-term sustainability. These efforts can be united under the umbrella of partnership-oriented crime prevention.

For the most dangerous behaviors, like illegal gun carrying, targeted hot spot patrols can engage repeat offenders and get guns off the street. The GVRS and street outreach programs can reach out to criminal groups, gangs, and dealers to tell them that the violence must stop. Regulations on alcohol can change when, where, and how liquor is sold, making it harder for violent people in hot spots to drink to excess. Drug treatment can help violent offenders get away from the substances that make them most dangerous.

No framework is perfect, but this one has several advantages. First, the framework accounts for both the problem of community violence and potential policy solutions—an advancement over models that describe only one or the other. Second, the framework is informed by the most rigorous evidence currently available, in that it captures the concentrated nature of the phenomenon and synthesizes programmatic evidence of effectiveness. Third, by consolidating and adapting well-recognized theories and models, the framework is relatively readily understood and applied. In short, the proposed framework satisfies the criteria of completeness, accuracy, and usability.

This conceptual framework also has limitations. First, the framework is intended for urban violence only. Violence in homes and schools operates differently than it does in the community, as does organized violence. Second, while the populated framework represents a summary of the best evidence currently available concerning anti-violence programming, the limits of this evidence and of evidence-informed policy generally must be kept in mind. Gaps in evidence remain, and the scientific process is an iterative one, meaning that our understanding of community violence and how best to prevent it must be continually updated and refined. Third, the framework does not address program implementation, another critical component of success.

Finally, and perhaps most importantly, the framework speaks primarily to the identification, selection, and organization of evidence-informed programs, but it must be understood that programs are only one of several components necessary for success in reducing violence. This book, because it focuses on rigorous evidence and immediate change, speaks largely about programmatic innovation, not institutional reform. Programs are embedded within institutions, and institutions are embedded within systems. Programs operating in and among weak institutions and systems can make a temporary difference, but for more sustainable change, there must be deeper and broader change in the institutions themselves.

Improving our institutions—in policing, education, housing, health, and elsewhere—is absolutely essential, but it takes longer. This book is focused on how to stop the bleeding right now—how to make an immediate difference by reducing urban violence. As with many things, the proper course of action is "both-and," not "either-or." We need the concrete strategies described in this book as well as the broader institutional and systematic changes advocated by the criminal justice reform movement, among others.

Even with its limitations, the framework above is a valuable tool for policy action. Using the framework, policy leaders can organize multiple strategies into a single effort that is focused, balanced, and fair.

Plans

Plans put networks and frameworks into action. They push the work forward with concrete commitments and goals. They identify shared metrics to measure stakeholder performance. The number one metric should always remain the number and rate of homicides, but there can be secondary metrics as well. When identifying such metrics, however, care must be taken to spell out exactly how they relate to the primary metric. Here is an example: Measuring the number of jobs or degrees that poor young men in a given jurisdiction maintain or achieve is not an important metric, because many of these men are not and will not get involved in violence. A better metric is the number of jobs or degrees that "hot people," young men who are at demonstrated risk for violence, are able to achieve. Similarly, the number of streetlights repaired is of little significance to an urban violence effort unless it is narrowed to the streetlights in and around violent hot spots.

Plans can articulate the mutually reinforcing activities of networks, as aligned and organized by frameworks. In the case of urban violence, the goal should be to specify concrete activities in each of the nine boxes in the framework: people-, place-, and behavior-based prevention, intervention, and enforcement. It should also specify how these people working on those activities will communicate and coordinate with one another.

An important but often unrecognized element of effective plans is spelling out what activities will not be undertaken—that is, what will not be done. Too many plans, in order to avoid disappointing one constituency or another, avoid the hard but necessary task of spelling out what is beyond the scope of the work. As a result, such efforts lose focus and effectiveness. Trying to do too many things inevitably results in nothing being done well. It is important, when it comes to anti-violence work, to value quality over quantity.

Finally, plans can outline the form and function of the backbone organization that supports and aligns all these activities.

Everything in a plan should be evidence and community informed. It should be true to the data and the research on what works in violence reduction, but it should also be accountable to those most impacted by the issue. Plans should also be practical and actionable, spelling out concrete commitments for every plan participant. These commitments should use SMART (specific, measurable, achievable, relevant, and time-bound) criteria, identifying precisely who will do what, and by when. Finally, plans should be consistently updated and refreshed based upon evaluation and performance. No plan should be set in stone; instead, they must be revisited periodically to ensure that they remain accurate, responsive, and impactful.

Measurement and Evaluation

Performance measurement and program evaluation are essential to keep anti-violence efforts on track. Both help determine whether an effort, in part or as a whole, is achieving its goals, and they can identify areas in need of improvement. They serve different but complementary functions: performance measurement is an ongoing process that monitors progress using shared measures or metrics, while program evaluation uses rigorous research methods to answer specific questions about whether a program is achieving its goals. Performance measures outputs, or whether people are doing what they are supposed to be doing. Evaluation measures outcomes, or whether what they are doing is achieving the intended results.

Evaluation in particular is essential. Without it, one must question an effort's dedication to real results and not just maintaining appearances. The best approach to evaluation is to incorporate it from the beginning. This provides an unanticipated benefit: not only can evaluation tell you whether you are achieving your outcomes, but it can also improve implementation. As criminologist Lawrence Sherman has noted, "Evaluation can provide an early warning to crime prevention leaders that the innovation is not being implemented as planned." Rigorous evaluation, along with adherence to the principles of procedural justice, are two critical but often unappreciated components of effective implementation.[8]

It is important to note that there are many forms of evaluation, including process, design, and impact evaluation. All are important, but it is critical to include a well-designed impact evaluation to examine the causal links among anti-violence activities, outputs, and outcomes.

How can networks, frameworks, plans, performance management, and evaluation all be put into practice? Below I offer two examples based on my experiences in the field.

The National Forum and GIVE

ON SEPTEMBER 24, 2009, Derrion Albert was murdered on Chicago's South Side, near the Christian Fenger Academy High School. Derrion, an honors student at Fenger, was on his way home from school when he was caught in the middle of a fight between students from rival neighborhoods. He was a bystander, but he was brutally beaten nonetheless, knocked unconscious, and then stomped repeatedly as he lay motionless on the street. Derrion died a few hours later at the nearby Advocate Christ Medical Center. The cause of death was blunt head trauma. He was sixteen. "He was in Bible class this Tuesday night, church on Sundays," said Derrion's grandfather, Joseph Walker. "We've lost a really dear friend in my grandson. He was a blessed child."[9]

Derrion's murder was captured on video and was broadcast widely, shocking audiences around the nation. The killing symbolized, for a moment, the brutality of urban violence in Chicago and around the nation. At the White House, the incident hit close to home. President Barack Obama and many of his top advisers were from Chicago, and he quickly dispatched Attorney General Eric Holder and Education Secretary Arne Duncan to the city to talk with government officials, parents, and students about what had happened. While the trip was billed as a listening tour, Holder and Duncan spoke of a stronger federal commitment to addressing the issue of youth violence.

A few days after Holder and Duncan returned from Chicago, I found myself sitting in the White House at a meeting about what would come next. At the time, I served as chief of staff in the Office of Justice Programs, the Department of Justice's primary grant-making agency. My boss, Assistant Attorney General Laurie Robinson, had been summoned to the meeting and she had brought me along.

The meeting was led by Michael Strautmanis, deputy assistant to the president for intergovernmental relations and public engagement, and Mariano-Florentino Cuéllar, special assistant to the president for justice and regulatory policy. Around the large meeting table were senior officials from the Justice, Education, Health and

Human Services, and Housing Departments, among others. Strautmanis informed the group that the White House needed to follow
up on the trip to Chicago with a substantive response on the issue of
youth violence. The specific nature of the response was for the group
to determine, but he told us it should have three elements.

First, the response should respect that youth violence was primarily a local issue and that the federal government should be in a supporting, rather than leading, role. Second, it should be comprehensive,
involving multiple agencies and not just focused on law enforcement.
Third, it had to be cheap—there would be no new funding for the
proposal, at least at first. The agencies would have to scrape together
leftover funds from already-existing budgets in order to make it work.
Cuéllar added a fourth component: that the effort would have to have
demonstrable, measurable results.

A discussion began about what such an effort might look like.
There were some interesting suggestions, but the meeting adjourned
without a clear plan in place. The agencies had their marching orders,
but the question was how we could make a difference given the con-
straints we were facing.

Senior staff in the agencies began to meet regularly to come
up with an appropriate response, but we didn't get far. As weeks
stretched into months, Laurie and I became increasingly concerned
about whether we would deliver the response that the White House
had requested. As the key participating agency at the Department
of Justice, our office was expected to take a leadership role, but so far
we had not been able to bring the agencies together in support of a
common approach.

Then we met Jack Calhoun. A former commissioner of the Administration for Children, Youth and Families, Jack had a long history of
working with and for poor kids and communities. He was visiting
with Laurie to discuss his latest venture, the California City Violence
Prevention Network, which he led on behalf of the National League
of Cities. Jack gave a great presentation about the work of the network: it had real substance, but it led from behind, letting the cities

shine. It offered concrete assistance but did so inexpensively, mostly in the form of training and technical assistance. It also encouraged a comprehensive response to youth violence, blending prevention with intervention, enforcement, and reentry.

Jack left behind the network's handbook, and as I flipped through it that evening, I could see clearly that this was what we had been looking for: a means of uniting the federal agencies under a common banner. I checked in with Laurie and she agreed, so a few colleagues and I set about adapting the California network to our federal context. Once Laurie and Attorney General Holder signed off on it, we pitched it to the other agencies, who bought in. Finally, we went back to Strautmanis and Cuéllar with the idea, and a few weeks later we learned that the president had signed off on it. We were on our way.

We called it the National Forum on Youth Violence Prevention. Through the forum, federal agencies would cooperate with one another, blending funding and resources that were relevant to youth violence, making them easier to access and align. Cities that joined the forum would do the same, creating comprehensive plans to reduce youth violence in their jurisdictions. The network would unite agencies and cities in pursuit of a common goal: saving young lives.

The forum had three goals: raise awareness of youth and gang violence, enhance the capacity of participating cities to address the challenge, and change systems and policy around the issue. To achieve these goals, the forum recommended three approaches: multidisciplinary partnerships, balanced methods, and data-driven strategies.

Participating cities would prepare comprehensive plans organized around the three approaches of the forum. Federal agencies and private partners would support those plans with previously existing funds and with training, technical assistance, and small capacity-building grants. Cities would then put their plans into action, reducing violence and improving outcomes for youth.

We began with six cities and eventually expanded to fifteen. We brought multidisciplinary city teams together in Washington twice a year to celebrate successes as well as to tackle common challenges.

We assigned federal experts to every city who conducted site visits and stayed in touch with local teams via monthly conference calls and frequent emails. And we did all this with minimal funding—the forum was initially established with less than $1 million and was never funded at more than $2 million each year.

For the first few years of the forum, I served as the informal coordinator of the effort, hosting many of the meetings, leading the calls, and updating my bosses at the Justice Department and the White House on our progress. The forum created a palpable sense of hope and optimism among those who participated in it at both the federal and local levels. Many of those who joined had struggled with youth violence in relative isolation, unaware of parallel efforts across the country or even in their own city. The forum created space for a new community to come together across institutional and geographic boundaries.

Did it work? According to an independent assessment performed by the John Jay Research and Evaluation Center, the forum was a modest success. The center surveyed a diverse array of community leaders in forum cities, including those working in criminal justice, social services, and education. While cautioning that these surveys were not a "rigorous evaluation" of the forum, the center was able to successfully measure "the perceptions and attitudes of the individuals most involved in violence prevention efforts in each city participating in the National Forum." The results were encouraging: "The findings from this study suggest that the National Forum provides meaningful assistance to cities. . . . Respondents in all 15 cities exhibit a strong commitment to the Forum and generally believe that their communities are stronger as a result of their participation. These results suggest that National Forum cities benefit by developing greater opportunities for youth, more effective violence prevention approaches, improved perceptions of law enforcement, and a broader engagement of community members."[10]

It wasn't all roses. The attorney general, cabinet secretaries, and senior White House staffers all cheered the forum at its semiannual meetings, but it was never a marquee effort for the administration.

The president never appeared at any forum event, and other federal efforts often seemed to crowd it out for attention and support. Our message to localities—use multidisciplinary partnerships, balanced methods, and evidence-based, data-driven strategies—was sound, but it could have been sharper and more concrete. The forum was a strong advocate for a comprehensive approach to youth violence reduction, but we could have pushed harder for more focused efforts at the local level. In addition, the forum began well before the unrest in Ferguson; at the time we did not fully appreciate the importance of speaking directly to the issues of legitimacy and fairness.

Most importantly, while the forum delivered significant benefits to local jurisdictions with minimal costs to taxpayers, it could have been even more impactful with more robust federal funding. Without significant funds to offer, there were real limits to how much we could expect from participating localities. It is crude but true: the more money you have to give, the more influence you have, absent other levers of influence. The forum was able to make positive changes in every city it engaged, but in many cities those changes happened on the margins or were somewhat superficial.

ONE EVENING IN August 2013, I met Mike Green for dinner at a steakhouse in midtown Manhattan. In a few weeks, I would join Governor Andrew Cuomo's administration as deputy secretary for public safety for New York State. Mike was the commissioner of the Division of Criminal Justice Services, the state's criminal justice grant-making agency. Mike would nominally report to me, as would all the other criminal justice agency heads in the state.

Mike looked like a cop straight out of central casting—crew cut, muscled physique, ramrod-straight posture—but he had actually spent much of his professional life as a prosecutor, ultimately becoming Rochester's district attorney. Mike's gruff exterior also belied a deep sense of empathy—tears would come to his eyes when he spoke of the poor young people in his hometown and the tragic violence that plagued them.

The dinner was just supposed to be a get-to-know-you type of thing, but we quickly got down to business. I expressed my desire to do more on gun violence, noting that the governor was concerned that the rest of the state was not keeping up with New York City. Mike's eyes brightened, and he told me that there was a program—Operation IMPACT—that had been doling out funds to high-crime jurisdictions outside of New York City for years. Over time, the program had lost focus and was now doing little more than giving money away, and Mike was worried the legislature would eventually cut the underperforming effort.

Mike and I decided to revamp the program using the best data and evidence available. We would invite top experts in to help us shape the new effort while keeping our state and local partners in policing, prosecution, and corrections closely involved. We would also create a new network to link law enforcement officials across the state. My hope was to apply the lessons I'd learned from the forum in New York, this time with real money and authority to back them up.

We started right away—looking closely at the violent crime data in each jurisdiction, bringing in top state officials, meeting with local leaders to get their input and buy-in, and engaging the experts. Five nationally recognized leaders in the field—Teny Gross, David Kennedy, John Klofas, Tracey Meares, and Craig Uchida—agreed to work with us in developing the effort. In addition to Mike, Superintendent of State Police Joseph D'Amico, Acting Commissioner of the Department of Corrections and Community Supervision Anthony Annucci, and Director for the New York State Division of Probation and Correctional Alternatives Robert Maccarone, among others, all lent their support and provided valuable input.

Together, we reviewed the evidence on what worked to reduce gun violence. We also conducted an extensive data analysis of all the New York localities with the highest levels of shootings and killings. From this process emerged a relatively simple theory of change: gun violence could be reduced through locally developed, state-supported strategies that used data and evidence to focus on the people and places driving the violence. After an intensive six-month development process, we took the effort to the governor.

We named it Gun Involved Violence Elimination, or GIVE. The initiative was publicly released in conjunction with the governor's State of the State address, and the first round of funding was announced in May 2014. GIVE now supports local law enforcement in their efforts to reduce gun violence, delivering upwards of $13 million each year to the seventeen counties outside New York City with the highest rates of violent crime.

Under GIVE, counties are required to prepare annual plans for their GIVE funding that incorporate three core elements of effectiveness. First, counties must focus their strategies on the people and places driving the gun violence in their jurisdictions. Second, they must align anti-violence operations in their jurisdiction in order to maintain a cohesive, consistent effort. Third, counties must engage relevant stakeholders as well as the community at large in order to ensure that the local efforts have sufficient backing and support.[11]

In addition, annual plans must incorporate at least two strategies from a limited menu of evidence-based strategies that includes focused deterrence, street outreach, hot spots policing, and crime prevention through environmental design (CPTED). Moreover, plans must integrate the principles of procedural fairness into all their efforts in order to ensure that those who encounter law enforcement are being treated fairly and respectfully.

GIVE is a more prescriptive effort than the National Forum on Youth Violence Prevention, but it still allows grantees a good deal of flexibility in how best to select and apply strategies in their jurisdictions. With GIVE, more funding was available, there was a more careful program development process, and, to be candid, as head of the state's public safety agencies, I had far more authority and control over the effort than I did with the forum. For all these reasons, we were able to insist on specific activities and targets.

How does GIVE work in practice? Localities prepare plans using the elements and strategies described above, then use GIVE funding, as well as their own resources, to implement their plans. GIVE also assists jurisdictions in other ways. First, it provides counties with a statewide network that hosts annual meetings, site visits, webinars, and conference calls to allow for cross-jurisdictional information sharing as well as peer-to-peer learning. Second, it offers an array of state-of-the-art training and technical assistance from nationally recognized experts, all offered at no cost. Third, GIVE grantees are supported by the state's award-winning crime analysis centers, which provide jurisdictions with technical support in analyzing gun violence. Fourth, participating state agencies beyond DCJS—such as probation and parole offices—provide support to local GIVE efforts in a variety of ways."

GIVE is the first of its kind—a statewide effort that not only requires its grantees to adopt evidence-informed principles and programs but also insists that they meaningfully integrate them into one cohesive local effort. GIVE's single-minded focus on one key metric— the number of shootings involving injury—also makes it special. As we were developing the effort, I felt strongly that we had to keep a clear focus on a single outcome. As Mike Green has said, "There's no question the target here is shootings and homicides, and our goal here is to drive those down and save lives."[12]

But is it working? GIVE was recognized in 2017 by a national coalition of anti–gun violence organizations as a model that other states should follow to reduce violence and save lives. In their report, the Giffords Law Center to Prevent Gun Violence, PICO National Network, and the Community Justice Reform Coalition cited New York as "one of the nation's leaders when it comes to direct investment in on-the-ground gun violence prevention programming."[13]

A formal evaluation is pending, but in 2018, GIVE jurisdictions reported 705 shooting incidents involving injury, an 8 percent decline from the previous year, a 14 percent decline from the five-year average, and the lowest number of incidents overall in ten years. Like the forum, GIVE succeeds through its local partners, and one of the biggest success stories to date is Newburgh.[14]

In 2010, the *New York Times* chronicled the brutal violence of New York's most dangerous city. "Newburgh is hemorrhaging, and we have to make a change," said a local FBI agent at the time. That year, there were eleven homicides and thirty shootings with injury—remarkably large numbers for a city with approximately twenty-eight thousand residents.[15]

Eight years later, the *Times* went back, this time to document the city's success. "In Newburgh . . . violent crime, especially firearm crime, has plummeted." In 2018, Newburgh had two homicides and eight shootings with injury—a remarkable 82 percent and 73 percent reduction from 2010, respectively.[16]

What was the difference? A new GVRS initiative, launched in 2015 with GIVE funding, has made a significant impact. "It got to the point where community members would come up to us and say, 'We don't feel safe sitting on our porches,'" said one Newburgh police officer. "Routinely, for years, we were number one in the state for violent crime per capita, and we usually made, unfortunately, the top ten in the country." Thankfully, things have changed in Newburgh for the better.[17]

I consider GIVE to be an improvement upon the National Forum on Youth Violence Prevention because it has greater focus on the people, places, and behaviors that matter most and it explicitly accounts for fairness and legitimacy by mandating attention to procedural justice principles. It also has more funding behind it and a greater emphasis on using only programs proven to work with rigorous evidence.

That said, it is not perfect. GIVE is largely a law enforcement effort—it does not support any violence prevention strategies other than CPTED and street outreach. Initially I had hoped to broaden the effort to include more prevention, but it quickly became clear that given the history of Operation IMPACT—a tough-on-crime law enforcement program—it would not be politically possible to change the program's focus so dramatically right away. My hope is that funding will eventually be made available for evidence-informed violence prevention strategies under GIVE or a related effort. Finally, a formal evaluation, currently under way, will give a much better sense of how well GIVE is performing.

NETWORKS ASSEMBLE STAKEHOLDERS. Frameworks organize them. Plans push them to act. Performance measurement and evaluation keep them focused. The National Forum on Youth Violence Prevention and GIVE are concrete examples of anti-violence efforts in practice. Neither is perfect, but they are illustrative of the kind of efforts we need to see in the future.

APPENDIX B
SUPPORTING FIGURES FOR
CHAPTER 11: GETTING STARTED

IN COMPUTING THE BENEFITS AND COSTS OF THE PROPOSED PLANS outlined in chapter 11, as well as their estimated return on investment, a number of steps were taken. These steps are described below for Chicago and for two samples of the nation's most violent cities: the twenty urban jurisdictions with the highest absolute number of homicides, as well as the twenty jurisdictions with the highest homicide rates (excluding any that overlap with the previous sample). The figures supporting the proposed Baltimore plan followed these same steps.[1]

To compute the net benefits, costs, and return on investment of the proposed plans (illustrated using the example of Chicago in Table 3 below), the following steps were completed:

1. Computed the reduction in homicides over an eight-year period, assuming (1) no reduction in the first year and (2) a 10 percent reduction in homicides each year as a result of the anti-violence programs and policies launched by the plan (see column 3 in Table 3).

2. Computed the number of lives saved as the difference between what the homicides would be without the plan (assumed to remain constant at 2017 levels) and the reduced

number of homicides due to the plan programs and policies (column 4).

3. Computed the social savings from the number of lives saved by simply multiplying the number of lives saved by $10 million (column 5).

4. Computed the costs of the plan for each of the eight years. For each year, it is computed as $30,000 times the number of homicides for that year (column 6).

5. Computed the total lives saved over the eight years by summing all the numbers in column 4 (first row, bottom panel).

6. Computed the total social savings over the eight years by adding up all the numbers in column 5 (second row, bottom panel).

7. Computed the total plan costs over the eight years by adding up all the numbers in column 6 (third row, bottom panel).

8. The net benefits of the plan are the total social savings minus the total plan costs, so the number from step 5 was subtracted from the number from step 6 (fourth row, bottom panel).

9. The return on investment was computed as the ratio of the total social savings to the total plan costs, so the total savings was divided by the total costs (fifth row, bottom panel).

TABLE 3: CHICAGO PLAN

Date	Year	Number of Homicides	Number of Lives Saved	Social costs saved due to lives saved ($m)	Plan costs ($m)
2018	1	653	0	0	19.6
2019	2	588 (= 0.9 × 653)	65 (= 653−588)	650	17.6
2020	3	529 (= 0.9 × 588)	124 (= 653−529)	1240	15.9
2021	4	476 (= 0.9 × 529)	177 (= 653−476)	1770	14.3
2022	5	428 (= 0.9 × 476)	225 (= 653−428)	2250	12.9
2023	6	386 (= 0.9 × 428)	267 (= 653−386)	2670	11.6
2024	7	347 (= 0.9 × 386)	306 (= 653−347)	3060	10.4
2025	8	312 (= 0.9 × 347)	341 (= 653−312)	3410	9.4
Total Lives Saved		1,505			
Total Social Costs Saved		$15.1 billion			
Total Plan Costs		$112 million			
Net Benefits		$14.9 billion			
Return on Investment		$135 per dollar spent			

Table 4 shows the results of applying the same methodology to the twenty cities with the highest absolute number of homicides and the twenty cities with the highest homicide rates (excluding any that overlap with the prior list of twenty), based on 2017 Unified Crime Report data.[2]

TABLE 4: NATIONAL PLAN

Total Lives Saved	12,132
Total Social Costs Saved	$121.3 billion
Total Plan Costs	$899 million
Net Benefits	$120.4 billion
Return on Investment	$135 per dollar spent

NOTES

Chapter 1: Bleeding Out

1. "Crime in the United States, 2017," Uniform Crime Reports, Table 1, Federal Bureau of Investigation, https://ucr.fbi.gov/crime-in-the-u.s/2017/crime-in-the-u.s.-2017/topic -pages/tables/table-1; Erin Grinshteyn and David Hemenway, "Violent Death Rates: The US Compared with Other High-Income OECD Countries, 2010," *American Journal of Medicine* 129, no. 3 (2016): 266–273; "Leading Causes of Death Reports, 1981–2016," WISQARS, National Center for Injury Prevention and Control, Centers for Disease Control and Prevention, accessed October 25, 2018, https://webappa.cdc.gov/sasweb/ncipc/leadcause.html.

2. Kathryn E. McCollister, Michael T. French, and Hai Fang, "The Cost of Crime to Society: New Crime-Specific Estimates for Policy and Program Evaluation," *Drug and Alcohol Dependence* 108, no. 1 (2010): 98–109; Mark A. Cohen, Roland T. Rust, Sara Steen, and Simon T. Tidd, "Willingness-to-Pay for Crime Control Programs," *Criminology* 42, no. 1 (2004): 89–110; Matt DeLisi et al., "Murder by Numbers: Monetary Costs Imposed by a Sample of Homicide Offenders," *Journal of Forensic Psychiatry and Psychology* 21, no. 4 (2010): 501–513. These estimates have all been updated to 2017 dollars, multiplied by the number of homicides in 2017, and divided by the US population.

3. "Crime in the United States, 2017," Uniform Crime Reports, Table 12, Federal Bureau of Investigation, https://ucr.fbi.gov/crime-in-the-u.s/2017/crime-in-the-u.s.-2017 /topic-pages/tables/table-12.

4. "Crime in the United States, 2017," Uniform Crime Reports, Expanded Homicide Data Tables 1 and 3, Federal Bureau of Investigation, https://ucr.fbi.gov/crime-in-the -u.s/2017/crime-in-the-u.s.-2017/topic-pages/tables/expanded-homicide-data-table-1 .xls; https://ucr.fbi.gov/crime-in-the-u.s/2017/crime-in-the-u.s.-2017/topic-pages/tables /expanded-homicide-data-table-3.xls.

5. "Crime in the United States, 2017," Uniform Crime Reports, Expanded Homicide Data Table 7, Federal Bureau of Investigation, https://ucr.fbi.gov/crime-in-the-u.s/2017 /crime-in-the-u.s.-2017/topic-pages/tables/expanded-homicide-data-table-7.xls.

6. "Crime in the United States, 2017," Uniform Crime Reports, Expanded Homicide Data Table 10, Federal Bureau of Investigation, https://ucr.fbi.gov/crime-in-the-u.s/2017 /crime-in-the-u.s.-2017/tables/expanded-homicide-data-table-10.xls. This total includes

the following circumstance categories: brawl due to influence of alcohol, brawl due to influence of narcotics, argument over money or property, and other arguments.

7. "Crime in the United States, 2017," Uniform Crime Reports, Expanded Homicide Data Table 2, Federal Bureau of Investigation, https://ucr.fbi.gov/crime-in-the-u.s/2017 /crime-in-the-u.s.-2017/tables/expanded-homicide-data-table-2.xls.

8. Thomas P. Abt, "Towards a Framework for Preventing Community Violence Among Youth," *Psychology, Health and Medicine* 22, suppl. 1 (2017): 266–285. I should also note that while I believe the strategies outlined in this book represent the best chance to significantly reduce urban violence in the US, whether and to what extent these strategies would work to combat urban violence in other countries is the subject of a separate forthcoming article. For now, I will observe that without carefully adapting these strategies to a new and different context, success in reducing violence is less certain.

9. Steven Pinker, *The Better Angels of Our Nature: Why Violence Has Declined* (New York: Viking, 2011), Kindle edition, chap. 8.

10. Bill Keller, "'Ghettoside' Author Jill Leovy on What We Have Learned Since Rodney King," The Marshall Project, March 3, 2016, www.themarshallproject.org/2016/03/03 /what-have-we-learned-since-rodney-king; Gary A. Haugen and Victor Boutros, *The Locust Effect: Why the End of Poverty Requires the End of Violence* (New York: Oxford University Press, 2015), Kindle edition, introduction.

11. Matt DeLisi et al., "Murder by Numbers: Monetary Costs Imposed by a Sample of Homicide Offenders," *Journal of Forensic Psychiatry and Psychology* 21, no. 4 (2010): 501–513. Technically, homicide is the intentional killing of one person by another, while murder is a homicide committed with criminal intent. The distinction is unimportant here so the terms are used interchangeably.

12. Manuel Eisner, "Modernity Strikes Back? A Historical Perspective on the Latest Increase in Interpersonal Violence (1960–1990)," *International Journal of Conflict and Violence* 2, no. 2 (2008): 288–316.

13. University of Maryland Global Terrorism Database, www.start.umd.edu/gtd/; Mark Follman, Gavin Aronsen, and Deanna Pan, "US Mass Shootings, 1982–2018: Data from Mother Jones' Investigation," *Mother Jones,* accessed on November 19, 2018, www.mother jones.com/politics/2012/12/mass-shootings-mother-jones-full-data/; Uniform Crime Reporting Data Tool (database), Federal Bureau of Investigation, accessed October 26, 2018, www.ucrdatatool.gov/index.cfm; "Crime in the United States, 2017," Uniform Crime Reports, Expanded Homicide Data Table 11, Federal Bureau of Investigation, https://ucr.fbi .gov/crime-in-the-u.s/2017/crime-in-the-u.s.-2017/tables/expanded-homicide-data -table-11.xls. For urban homicides, these totals include the following circumstance categories: robbery, burglary, larceny/theft, motor vehicle theft, narcotic drug laws, brawl due to influence of alcohol, brawl due to influence of narcotics, argument over money or property, other arguments, and juvenile gang killings.

14. Uniform Crime Reporting Data Tool (database), Federal Bureau of Investigation, accessed October 26, 2018, www.ucrdatatool.gov/index.cfm; "Crime in the United States, 2017," Uniform Crime Reports, Table 1, Federal Bureau of Investigation, https://ucr.fbi .gov/crime-in-the-u.s/2017/crime-in-the-u.s.-2017/topic-pages/tables/table-1.

15. Despite the tremendous importance of the question, experts have been unable to answer authoritatively why crime and violence rise or fall in the US. In 2007, the National Academy of Sciences convened the nation's top criminologists and statisticians,

commissioned papers, and held meetings to examine crime trends, but what they learned was not encouraging. "Despite its salience in the public arena, very little is known about the factors driving the crime trends," wrote criminologists Alfred Blumstein and Richard Rosenfeld. "The knowledge base is too limited to support intelligent forecasts of the direction in which crime rates are moving." The nation's leading experts basically threw up their hands, observing that without a massive investment in better information systems, it was unlikely that crime trends could be as well understood as trends in health, housing, employment, and economics. Sadly, the state of the science with regard to crime trends has not improved much since then. Alfred Blumstein and Richard Rosenfeld, "Factors Contributing to US Crime Trends," in *Understanding Crime Trends: Workshop Report,* National Research Council (Washington, DC: National Academies Press, 2008), 13–43.

16. The quality of an impact evaluation is determined by many things, but the most important is usually its methodology or design. Impact evaluations can be experimental, quasi-experimental, or nonexperimental. Experiments randomly assign intervention participants to either treatment or control groups, which helps to eliminate bias—these are popularly known as randomized controlled trials, or RCTs. Quasi-experiments do not use randomization when assigning participants to treatment or control groups, and nonexperiments do not have control groups. As one might expect, experiments are generally considered to be the most trustworthy type of impact evaluation, although no evaluation is perfect, because they are best able to identify an if-then, cause-effect relationship between an intervention and its intended impact. Quasi-experiments are generally performed when experiments are not possible, and most researchers have confidence in them when they are well designed. Nonexperiments can be useful in certain circumstances, but because they have no control group, it is hard to be sure that their results are reliable. When researchers have confidence in the results of a study, they say it has internal validity. That said, even the best-designed evaluations can be mistaken, which is why it is important to repeat or replicate evaluations to make sure their results are accurate. Finally, when an evaluation is repeated at different times, in different places, with different people, and the results are the same, one can have more confidence that the results are generalizable across contexts. Researchers call this external validity.

17. This book is about actual efforts to reduce violence that have been tested in the real world. In 2016, sociologist Christopher Winship and I completed a systematic meta-review (a review of systematic reviews) to identify the most effective strategies for reducing urban violence. We searched exhaustively for every single systematic review that dealt directly with crime violence and found more than forty of them. These reviews incorporated the results of more than 1,400 individual impact evaluations. Thomas Abt and Christopher Winship, *What Works in Reducing Community Violence: A Meta-Review and Field Study for the Northern Triangle,* Democracy International (Washington, DC: United States Agency for International Development, February 2016). In 2018, I participated in a related effort, working with economists Christopher Blattman and Santiago Tobón, political scientist Beatriz Magaloni, and the Abdul Latif Jameel Poverty Action Lab (J-PAL) to update and expand the analysis Chris and I had performed, examining over twenty new reviews. Abdul Latif Jameel Poverty Action Lab (J-PAL), *What Works in Preventing Violence Among Youth?,* United States Agency for International Development, September 2018, www .povertyactionlab.org/sites/default/files/documents/White%20Paper%20JPAL_Ingles_ Final.pdf. Lastly, I am a member of the Crime and Justice Coordinating Group for the

Campbell Collaboration, a leading producer of systematic reviews in the social sciences, which has enabled me to stay current on the research in this area. For those interested in the theoretical basis of this work, please consult my article, "Towards a Framework for Preventing Community Violence Among Youth."

Chapter 2: Triage

1. For more information on the National Forum on Youth Violence Prevention, see appendix A.

2. Rolf Rossaint et al., "Management of Bleeding Following Major Trauma: An Updated European Guideline," *Critical Care* 14, no. 2 (2010): R52.

3. Douglas S. Massey and Jonathan Tannen, "A Research Note on Trends in Black Hypersegregation," *Demography* 52, no. 3 (2015): 1025–1034.

4. William Julius Wilson, *The Truly Disadvantaged: The Inner City, the Underclass, and Public Policy* (Chicago: University of Chicago Press, 2012); William Julius Wilson, *When Work Disappears: The World of the New Urban Poor* (New York: Vintage, 2011).

5. Patrick Sharkey, *Stuck in Place: Urban Neighborhoods and the End of Progress Toward Racial Equality* (Chicago: University of Chicago Press, 2013), Kindle edition, chap. 1.

6. Ibid.; Robert J. Sampson and Janet L. Lauritsen, "Racial and Ethnic Disparities in Crime and Criminal Justice in the United States," *Crime and Justice* 21 (1997): 311–374.

7. Sharkey, *Stuck in Place*; Garrett Power, "Apartheid Baltimore Style: The Residential Segregation Ordinances of 1910–1913," *Maryland Law Review* 42, no. 2 (1983): 289; Ben Feldmeyer, "The Effects of Racial/Ethnic Segregation on Latino and Black Homicide," *Sociological Quarterly* 51, no. 4 (2010): 600–623.

8. Feldmeyer, "The Effects of Racial/Ethnic Segregation on Latino and Black Homicide."

9. Jeremy Travis, Bruce Western, and F. Stevens Redburn, eds., *The Growth of Incarceration in the United States: Exploring Causes and Consequences*, National Research Council (Washington, DC: National Academies Press, 2014), 96.

10. Ching-Chi Hsieh and Meredith D. Pugh, "Poverty, Income Inequality, and Violent Crime: A Meta-analysis of Recent Aggregate Data Studies," *Criminal Justice Review* 18, no. 2 (1993): 182–202.

11. Sunghyun Hong and Inger Burnett-Zeigler, "The Frequency of PTSD and Subthreshold PTSD Among African-American Women with Depressive Symptoms in a Disadvantaged Urban Neighborhood: Pilot Study," *Journal of Racial and Ethnic Health Disparities* 4, no. 6 (2017): 1069–1073.

12. Raj Chetty and Nathaniel Hendren, "The Impacts of Neighborhoods on Intergenerational Mobility: Childhood Exposure Effects and County-Level Estimates," *Quarterly Journal of Economics* 133, no. 3 (2018): 1107–1162.

13. Patrick Sharkey and Gerard Torrats-Espinosa, "The Effect of Violent Crime on Economic Mobility," *Journal of Urban Economics* 102 (2017): 22–33; Giffords Law Center, *Protecting the Parkland Generation: Strategies to Keep America's Kids Safe from Gun Violence*, 2018, https://lawcenter.giffords.org/wp-content/uploads/2018/04/Protecting-the-Parkland-Generation_04.05.18.pdf.

14. Yasemin Irvin-Erickson et al., *A Neighborhood-Level Analysis of the Economic Impact of Gun Violence*, Urban Institute, June 2017, www.urban.org/research/publication

/neighborhood-level-analysis-economic-impact-gun-violence; Robert J. Shapiro and Kevin A. Hassett, *The Economic Benefits of Reducing Violent Crime: A Case Study of 8 American Cities*, Center for American Progress, June 2012, www.americanprogress.org/issues /economy/reports/2012/06/19/11755/the-economic-benefits-of-reducing-violent-crime/.

15. Kriston Capps, "The Little-Studied Link Between 'Murder Capitals' and Population Decline," CityLab, July 16, 2014, www.citylab.com/equity/2014/07/the-link-between-so -called-murder-capitals-and-population-decline/374484/. St. Louis, a more recent "murder capital," has been added.

16. Kathryn E. McCollister, Michael T. French, and Hai Fang, "The Cost of Crime to Society: New Crime-Specific Estimates for Policy and Program Evaluation," *Drug and Alcohol Dependence* 108, no. 1 (2010): 98–109; Mark A. Cohen, Roland T. Rust, Sara Steen, and Simon T. Tidd, "Willingness-to-Pay for Crime Control Programs," *Criminology* 42, no. 1 (2004): 89–110; Matt DeLisi et al., "Murder by Numbers: Monetary Costs Imposed by a Sample of Homicide Offenders," *Journal of Forensic Psychiatry & Psychology* 21, no. 4 (2010): 501–513. These estimates have all been updated to 2017 dollars, multiplied by the number of homicides in 2017, divided by the US population.

17. Jennifer Bronson, *Justice Expenditure and Employment Extracts, 2015— Preliminary*, US Department of Justice, Bureau of Justice Statistics, report no. NCJ 251780 (2014), www.bjs.gov/index.cfm?ty=pbdetail&iid=6310.

18. Steven Pinker, *The Better Angels of Our Nature: Why Violence Has Declined* (New York: Viking, 2011), Kindle edition, chap. 10.

19. Aliza Aufrichtig, Lois Beckett, Jan Diehm, and Jamiles Lartey, "Want to Fix Gun Violence in America? Go Local," *The Guardian*, January 9, 2017, www.theguardian.com /us-news/ng-interactive/2017/jan/09/special-report-fixing-gun-violence-in-america.

20. Shapiro and Hassett, *The Economic Benefits of Reducing Violent Crime*.

21. Patrick Sharkey, "Keeping the Peace: Patrick Sharkey on Sustaining the Great Crime Decline," interview by Matthew Watkins, *New Thinking* (podcast), Center for Court Innovation, June 2018, www.courtinnovation.org/publications/patrick-sharkey-podcast.

22. Rolf Pendall, Leah Hendey, Margery Austin Turner, and Erika Poethig, *Revitalizing Neighborhoods: The Federal Role*, Urban Institute, October 2016, www.urban.org/sites /default/files/publication/85236/revitalizing-neighborhoods-the-federal-role_0.pdf.

23. Uniform Crime Reporting Data Tool (database), Federal Bureau of Investigation, accessed October 26, 2018, www.ucrdatatool.gov/index.cfm; "Crime in the United States, 2017," Uniform Crime Reports, Table 6, Federal Bureau of Investigation, https://ucr.fbi .gov/crime-in-the-u.s/2017/crime-in-the-u.s.-2017/tables/table-6.

Chapter 3: Sticky Situations

1. James McKinley, Ashley Southall, and Al Baker, "In the South Bronx, Lives Marred and Erased by Firearms," *New York Times*, April 6, 2017.

2. Lawrence W. Sherman, "The Power Few: Experimental Criminology and the Reduction of Harm," *Journal of Experimental Criminology* 3, no. 4 (2007): 299–321; David Weisburd, "The Law of Crime Concentration and the Criminology of Place," *Criminology* 53, no. 2 (2015): 133–157; Michael G. Vaughn et al., "The Severe 5%: A Latent Class Analysis

of the Externalizing Behavior Spectrum in the United States," *Journal of Criminal Justice* 39, no. 1 (2011): 75–80.

3. Aliza Aufrichtig, Lois Beckett, Jan Diehm, and Jamiles Lartey, "Want to Fix Gun Violence in America? Go Local," *The Guardian*, January 9, 2017, www.theguardian.com /us-news/ng-interactive/2017/jan/09/special-report-fixing-gun-violence-in-america.

4. Ibid.; Nicholas Corsaro and Robin S. Engel, "Most Challenging of Contexts: Assessing the Impact of Focused Deterrence on Serious Violence in New Orleans," *Criminology and Public Policy* 14, no. 3 (2015): 471–505; Andrew V. Papachristos, Christopher Wildeman, and Elizabeth Roberto, "Tragic, but Not Random: The Social Contagion of Nonfatal Gunshot Injuries," *Social Science and Medicine* 125 (2015): 139–150.

5. "Measuring the Extent of Gang Problems: Estimated Number of Gangs," National Youth Gang Survey Analysis, National Gang Center, www.nationalgangcenter.gov/Survey -Analysis/Measuring-the-Extent-of-Gang-Problems#estimatednumbergangs.

6. Anthony A. Braga, Andrew V. Papachristos, and David M. Hureau, "The Concentration and Stability of Gun Violence at Micro Places in Boston, 1980–2008," *Journal of Quantitative Criminology* 26, no. 1 (2010): 33–53; Weisburd, "The Law of Crime Concentration and the Criminology of Place."

7. Chris Baird, *A Question of Evidence, Part Two*, National Council on Crime and Delinquency, January–February 2017, www.nccdglobal.org/blog/nccd-now-question -evidence-pt-2; Adam Neufeld, "In Defense of Risk-Assessment Tools," The Marshall Project, October 22, 2017, www.themarshallproject.org/2017/10/22/in-defense-of-risk -assessment-tools.

8. Similarly, in the world of risk assessment, courts and corrections agencies typically use these tools to identify who should be given leniency, not who should get more punishment. Scoring low on a risk assessment will likely result in being released from court or released early from probation, parole, or prison, with less restrictive conditions. Scoring high means only that the officials are unlikely to depart downward from what the law allows. Baird, *A Question of Evidence, Part Two*.

9. Baird, *A Question of Evidence, Part Two*.

10. Ben Green, Thibaut Horel, and Andrew V. Papachristos, "Modeling Contagion Through Social Networks to Explain and Predict Gunshot Violence in Chicago, 2006 to 2014," *JAMA Internal Medicine* 177, no. 3 (2017): 326–333.

11. Sherman, "The Power Few."

12. Desmond Upton Patton, Robert D. Eschmann, and Dirk A. Butler "Internet Banging: New Trends in Social Media, Gang Violence, Masculinity and Hip Hop." *Computers in Human Behavior* 29, no. 5 (2013): A54-A59.

13. Anthony Braga, "Crime and Policing Revisited," *New Perspectives in Policing*, National Institute of Justice, US Department of Justice, September 2015, NCJ 248888, www .ncjrs.gov/pdffiles1/nij/248888.pdf; Jennifer Wong et al., *Effectiveness of Street Gang Control Strategies: A Systematic Review and Meta-Analysis of Evaluation Studies*, Public Safety Canada, 2012, https://pdfs.semanticscholar.org/5a58/65e8e6d88aceba26522c31bd0b4d 842a8039.pdf; Anthony Petrosino et al., "Cross-sector, Multi-agency Interventions to Address Urban Youth Firearms Violence: A Rapid Evidence Assessment," *Aggression and Violent Behavior* 22 (2015): 87–96; Jennifer L. Matjasko et al., "A Systematic Meta-Review of Evaluations of Youth Violence Prevention Programs: Common and Divergent Findings from 25 Years of Meta-Analyses and Systematic Reviews," *Aggression and Violent*

Behavior 17, no. 6 (2012): 540–552; Clive R. Hollin, "Treatment Programs for Offenders: Meta-Analysis, 'What Works,' and Beyond," *International Journal of Law and Psychiatry* 22, nos. 3–4 (1999): 361–372; Mary Ann Limbos et al., "Effectiveness of Interventions to Prevent Youth Violence: A Systematic Review," *American Journal of Preventive Medicine* 33, no. 1 (2007): 65–74.

14. One systematic review of the research found that "since 1990, there have been five main reviews of empirical studies that report on displacement. . . . All five reviews arrive at the same basic conclusions: there is little evidence that crime prevention strategies lead to displacement." Cody W. Telep et al., "Displacement of Crime and Diffusion of Crime Control Benefits in Large-Scale Geographic Areas: A Systematic Review," *Journal of Experimental Criminology* 10, no. 4 (2014): 515–548. In another review, researchers reported that "over 30 years of research evidence on this topic . . . suggests that crime relocates in only a minority of instances. More commonly, it has been found that the opposite, a diffusion of crime reduction benefits in nearby areas not targeted by interventions, occurs at a rate that is about equal to observations of displacement." Shane D. Johnson, Rob T. Guerette, and Kate Bowers, "Crime Displacement: What We Know, What We Don't Know, and What It Means for Crime Reduction," *Journal of Experimental Criminology* 10, no. 4 (2014): 549–571.

15. Mark A. R. Kleiman, *When Brute Force Fails: How to Have Less Crime and Less Punishment* (Princeton, NJ: Princeton University Press, 2009).

16. Ibid., 4.

17. Ibid., 4.

Chapter 4: Carrot and Stick

1. Patrick Sharkey, *Uneasy Peace: The Great Crime Decline, the Renewal of City Life, and the Next War on Violence* (New York: W. W. Norton & Company, 2018).

2. See generally Terrie E. Moffitt, "Adolescence-Limited and Life-Course-Persistent Antisocial Behavior: A Developmental Taxonomy," *Psychological Review* 100, no. 4 (1993): 674–701.

3. A good example of this is aggressive drug enforcement. See Dan Werb et al., "Effect of Drug Law Enforcement on Drug Market Violence: A Systematic Review," *International Journal of Drug Policy* 22, no. 2 (2011): 87–94.

4. Elizabeth Seigle, Nastassia Walsh, and Josh Weber, *Core Principles for Reducing Recidivism and Improving Other Outcomes for Youth in the Juvenile Justice System* (New York: Council of State Governments Justice Center, 2014); William Meyer, "Ten Science-Based Principles of Changing Behavior Through the Use of Reinforcement and Punishment," *Journal of Drug Issues* 31, no. 1 (2012): 207–232.

5. Stephanie Lee et al., *Return on Investment: Evidence-Based Options to Improve Statewide Outcomes, April 2012* (Olympia, WA: Washington State Institute for Public Policy, 2012); Bruce Western, *Punishment and Inequality in America* (New York: Russell Sage Foundation, 2006).

6. Cody W. Telep and David Weisburd, "Policing," in *What Works in Crime Prevention and Rehabilitation: Lessons from Systematic Reviews,* ed. David Weisburd, David P. Farrington, and Charlotte Gill (New York: Springer, 2016), 137–168.

7. David Weisburd, Elizabeth R. Groff, and Sue-Ming Yang, "Understanding and Controlling Hot Spots of Crime: The Importance of Formal and Informal Social Controls," *Prevention Science* 15, no. 1 (2014): 31–43.

8. Ibid., 40.

Chapter 5: No Justice, No Peace

1. US Department of Justice, *Report Regarding the Criminal Investigation into the Shooting Death of Michael Brown by Ferguson, Missouri Police Officer Darren Wilson*, March 4, 2015, www.justice.gov/sites/default/files/opa/press-releases/attachments/2015/03/04/doj_report_on_shooting_of_michael_brown_1.pdf.

2. US Department of Justice, *Investigation of the Ferguson Police Department*, March 4, 2015, www.justice.gov/sites/default/files/opa/press-releases/attachments/2015/03/04/ferguson_police_department_report.pdf.

3. US Department of Justice, *Investigation of the Ferguson Police Department*, 2.

4. Ibid.

5. Ibid.

6. Ibid., 81, 6.

7. Julie Bosman and Joseph Goldstein, "Timeline for a Body: 4 Hours in the Middle of a Ferguson Street," *New York Times*, August 23, 2014.

8. Josh Voorhees, "Everything That's Going Wrong in Ferguson," Slate, November 25, 2014, https://slate.com/news-and-politics/2014/11/ferguson-police-mistakes-documenting-the-police-response-to-the-latest-round-of-michael-brown-protests.html.

9. US Department of Justice, Office of Community Oriented Policing Services and Institute for Intergovernmental Research, *After-Action Assessment of the Police Response to the August 2014 Demonstrations in Ferguson, Missouri*, 2015, https://ric-zai-inc.com/Publications/cops-p317-pub.pdf; Tim Devaney, "McCaskill: Police Treated Ferguson Protesters Like 'Enemy Combatants,'" The Hill, September 9, 2014, https://thehill.com/regulation/217087-missouri-senator-questions-need-for-militarized-police-forces; Barack Obama, "Statement by the President" (press release), August 14, 2014, https://obamawhitehouse.archives.gov/the-press-office/2014/08/14/statement-president.

10. US Department of Justice, *After-Action Assessment of the Police Response to the August 2014 Demonstrations in Ferguson, Missouri*; "2014 Year in Review: Top Ten Crime Stories," Tyndall Report, n.d., http://tyndallreport.com/yearinreview2014/crime/.

11. "Crime in the United States, 2014," Uniform Crime Reports, Table 6, Federal Bureau of Investigation, https://ucr.fbi.gov/crime-in-the-u.s/2014/crime-in-the-u.s.-2014/tables/table-6; "Crime in the United States, 2015," Uniform Crime Reports, Table 6, Federal Bureau of Investigation, https://ucr.fbi.gov/crime-in-the-u.s/2015/crime-in-the-u.s.-2015/tables/table-6.

12. Jess Bidgood, "The Numbers Behind Baltimore's Record Year in Homicides," *New York Times*, January 15, 2016.

13. Max Kapustin et al., *Gun Violence in Chicago, 2016*, University of Chicago Crime Lab, January 2017.

14. Christine Byers, "Crime Up After Ferguson and More Police Needed, Top St. Louis Area Chiefs Say," *St. Louis Post-Dispatch,* November 15, 2014.

15. Heather Mac Donald, "The New Nationwide Crime Wave," *Wall Street Journal,* May 29, 2015; Caroline May, "Sheriff David Clarke: Law Enforcement Officers 'At a Tipping Point,'" Breitbart, May 19, 2015; Steven Cohen, "The Ferguson Effect Gets the Trump Treatment," *New Republic,* January 15, 2016.

16. Sam Fulwood, "The Myth of Police Reluctance," Center for American Progress, October 28, 2015, www.americanprogress.org/issues/race/news/2015/10/28/124357/the-myth-of-police-reluctance; Ames Grawert and James Cullen, "What the Data Tell Us About Crime and the 'Ferguson Effect,'" Brennan Center for Justice, March 7, 2016, www.brennancenter.org/blog/what-data-tell-us-about-crime-and-'ferguson-effect'; David Graham, "The FBI Director's Troubling Comments on the 'Ferguson Effect,'" *The Atlantic,* October 26, 2015.

17. Thomas Abt, "A Most Violent Year," The Marshall Project, January 11, 2016, www.themarshallproject.org/2016/01/11/a-most-violent-year; Richard Rosenfeld, Shytierra Gaston, Howard Spivak, and Seri Irazola, *Assessing and Responding to the Recent Homicide Rise in the United States,* US Department of Justice, National Institute of Justice, report no. NCJ 251067, November 2017, www.ncjrs.gov/pdffiles1/nij/251067.pdf.

18. Albert Einstein, *Einstein on Peace,* ed. Otto Nathan and Heinz Norden (London: Methuen, 1968); Stephen B. Oates, *Let the Trumpet Sound: A Life of Martin Luther King, Jr.* (Edinburgh: Canongate Books, 1998).

19. Jean-Marc Coicaud, *Legitimacy and Politics: A Contribution to the Study of Political Right and Political Responsibility* (New York: Cambridge University Press, 2002); Justice Tankebe, "Viewing Things Differently: The Dimensions of Public Perceptions of Police Legitimacy," *Criminology* 51, no. 1 (2013): 103–135; David Beetham, *The Legitimation of Power* (New York: Palgrave Macmillan, 2013), 15. My formulation of legitimacy here is also influenced by the work of criminologists Anthony Bottoms and Justice Tankebe, who argued that the main components of police legitimacy are effectiveness, distributive fairness, procedural fairness, and lawfulness. "Beyond Procedural Justice: A Dialogic Approach to Legitimacy in Criminal Justice," *Journal of Criminal Law and Criminology* 102, no. 1 (2012): 119–170.

20. Ibid., 19–20.

21. Matthew Desmond, Andrew V. Papachristos, and David S. Kirk, "Police Violence and Citizen Crime Reporting in the Black Community," *American Sociological Review* 81, no. 5 (2016): 857–876; Robert J. Sampson and Dawn Jeglum Bartusch, "Legal Cynicism and (Subcultural?) Tolerance of Deviance: The Neighborhood Context of Racial Differences," *Law and Society Review* 32 (1998): 777–804.

22. Desmond, Papachristos, and Kirk, "Police Violence and Citizen Crime Reporting in the Black Community."

23. Quoctrung Bui, "Calls to 911 from Black Neighborhoods Fell After a Case of Police Violence," *New York Times,* September 29, 2016.

24. Ibid.; Tom R. Tyler, Jeffrey Fagan, and Amanda Geller, "Street Stops and Police Legitimacy: Teachable Moments in Young Urban Men's Legal Socialization," *Journal of Empirical Legal Studies* 11, no. 4 (2014): 751–785.

25. Elijah Anderson, *Code of the Street: Decency, Violence, and the Moral Life of the Inner City* (New York: W. W. Norton & Company, 2000); David S. Kirk and Andrew V. Papachristos, "Cultural Mechanisms and the Persistence of Neighborhood Violence," *American Journal of Sociology* 116, no. 4 (2011): 1190–1233.

26. Andrew V. Papachristos, Tracey L. Meares, and Jeffrey Fagan, "Why Do Criminals Obey the Law? The Influence of Legitimacy and Social Networks on Active Gun Offenders," *Journal of Criminal Law and Criminology* (2012): 397–440.

27. Tyler, Fagan, and Geller, "Street Stops and Police Legitimacy"; Robert J. Sampson, *Great American City: Chicago and the Enduring Neighborhood Effect* (Chicago: University of Chicago Press, 2012); Gary LaFree, *Losing Legitimacy: Street Crime and the Decline of Social Institutions in America* (New York: Routledge, 2018); Randolph Roth, *American Homicide* (Cambridge, MA: Harvard University Press, 2012); Manuel Eisner and Amy Nivette, "Does Low Legitimacy Cause Crime? A Review of the Evidence" (working paper, Violence Research Centre, University of Cambridge, 2013); Devon Johnson, Edward R. Maguire, and Joseph B. Kuhns, "Public Perceptions of the Legitimacy of the Law and Legal Authorities: Evidence from the Caribbean," *Law and Society Review* 48, no. 4 (2014): 947–978.

28. Anthony Braga and Rodney Brunson, "The Police and Public Discourse on 'Black-on-Black' Violence," *New Perspectives in Policing,* National Institute of Justice, US Department of Justice, May 2015, NCJ 248588, www.ncjrs.gov/pdffiles1/nij/248588.pdf; Michelle Alexander, *The New Jim Crow: Mass Incarceration in the Age of Colorblindness* (New York: New Press, 2012), Kindle edition, chap. 5.

29. "Crime in the United States, 2017," Uniform Crime Reports, Table 25, Federal Bureau of Investigation, and https://ucr.fbi.gov/crime-in-the-u.s/2017/crime-in-the-u.s.-2017/tables/table-25.

30. Charles Wellford and James Cronin, "Clearing Up Homicide Clearance Rates," *National Institute of Justice Journal* 243 (2000): 1–7.

31. US Department of Justice and US Attorney's Office, Northern District of Illinois, *Investigation of the Chicago Police Department,* January 13, 2017, www.justice.gov/opa/file/925846/download.

32. Rich Morin, Kim Parker, Renee Stepler, and Andrew Mercer, "Behind the Badge: Amid Protests and Calls for Reform, How Police View Their Jobs, Key Issues and Recent Fatal Encounters Between Blacks and Police," Pew Research Center, January 11, 2017, www.pewsocialtrends.org/2017/01/11/behind-the-badge/.

33. Jane Jacobs, *The Death and Life of Great American Cities* (New York: Vintage, 1961).

34. Tom R. Tyler, *Why People Obey the Law* (Princeton, NJ: Princeton University Press, 2006).

35. Cesare Beccaria, *On Crime and Punishments* (Indianapolis, IN: Hackett, 1985).

36. "Crime in the United States, 2014," Uniform Crime Reports, Tables 1 and 6, Federal Bureau of Investigation, https://ucr.fbi.gov/crime-in-the-u.s/2014/crime-in-the-u.s.-2014/tables/table-1 and https://ucr.fbi.gov/crime-in-the-u.s/2014/crime-in-the-u.s.-2014/tables/table-6; "Crime in the United States, 2016," Uniform Crime Reports, Tables 1 and 4, Federal Bureau of Investigation, https://ucr.fbi.gov/crime-in-the-u.s/2016/crime-in-the-u.s.-2016/topic-pages/tables/table-1 and https://ucr.fbi.gov/crime-in-the-u.s/2016/crime-in-the-u.s.-2016/tables/table-4.

37. Richard Rosenfeld and Joel Wallman, "Did De-policing Cause the Homicide Rise?," *Criminology and Public Policy* 18, no. 1 (forthcoming 2019).

38. Richard Rosenfeld, *Documenting and Explaining the 2015 Homicide Rise: Research Directions,* US Department of Justice, National Institute of Justice, report no. NCJ 249895, June 2016, www.ncjrs.gov/pdffiles1/nij/249895.pdf.

39. Tom R. Tyler, "Procedural Justice, Legitimacy, and the Effective Rule of Law," *Crime and Justice* 30 (2003): 283–357; Tom R. Tyler, Jeffrey Fagan, and Amanda Geller, "Street Stops and Police Legitimacy: Teachable Moments in Young Urban Men's Legal Socialization," *Journal of Empirical Legal Studies* 11, no. 4 (2014): 751–785.

40. Tracey L. Meares and Peter Neyroud, "Rightful Policing," *New Perspectives in Policing,* National Institute of Justice, US Department of Justice, February 2015, report no. NCJ 248411, www.ncjrs.gov/pdffiles1/nij/248411.pdf.

41. Lorraine Mazerolle et al., "Procedural Justice and Police Legitimacy: A Systematic Review of the Research Evidence," *Journal of Experimental Criminology* 9, no. 3 (2013): 245–274; Christopher Donner, Jon Maskaly, Lorie Fridell, and Wesley G. Jennings, "Policing and Procedural Justice: A State-of-the-Art Review," *Policing: An International Journal of Police Strategies and Management* 38, no. 1 (2015): 153–172. For a broader discussion of the weaknesses and strengths of the evidence supporting procedural fairness, see Daniel S. Nagin and Cody W. Telep, "Procedural Justice and Legal Compliance," *Annual Review of Law and Social Science* 13 (2017): 5–28, and Tom Tyler, "Procedural Justice and Policing: A Rush to Judgment?," *Annual Review of Law and Social Science* 13 (2017): 29–53.

42. Donner, Maskaly, Fridell, and Jennings, "Policing and Procedural Justice"; Emily Owens, David Weisburd, Karen L. Amendola, and Geoffrey P. Alpert, "Can You Build a Better Cop? Experimental Evidence on Supervision, Training, and Policing in the Community," *Criminology and Public Policy* 17, no. 1 (2018): 41–87.

43. Megan Quattlebaum, Tracey Meares, and Tom Tyler, *Principles of Procedurally Just Policing,* Justice Collaboratory at Yale Law School, January 2018, https://law.yale.edu /system/files/area/center/justice/principles_of_procedurally_just_policing_report.pdf; Stephen J. Schulhofer, Tom R. Tyler, and Aziz Z. Huq, "American Policing at a Crossroads: Unsustainable Policies and the Procedural Justice Alternative," *Journal of Criminal Law and Criminology* 101, no. 2 (2011): 335–374.

Procedural fairness can also play a critical role in adapting evidence-informed strategies to local circumstances. Too often, policy makers choose new strategies "off the shelf" without making sure they meet the specific needs of their jurisdiction. This is problematic because what works in one area may not work in another. By making anti-violence strategies community as well as evidence informed, procedural fairness provides an important means of ensuring that they are appropriately tailored to local needs and circumstances.

44. Charles Ramsey, "Challenges to Democracy: The Future of Policing" (Harvard Kennedy School Institute of Politics Forum, Cambridge, Massachusetts, February 5, 2015), https://iop.harvard.edu/forum/challenges-democracy-future-policing.

Chapter 6: Pacifying Shooters

1. Thomas Abt and Christopher Winship, *What Works in Reducing Community Violence: A Meta-Review and Field Study for the Northern Triangle,* Democracy International (Washington, DC: United States Agency for International Development, February 2016); National Academies of Sciences, Engineering, and Medicine, *Proactive Policing: Effects on Crime and Communities* (Washington, DC: National Academies Press, 2018). These results were driven by two systematic reviews performed by Anthony Braga and his colleagues. Published in 2012, the first review found that focused deterrence substantially reduced crime in nine out of the ten studies included, with especially significant reductions in gun violence and homicide. The second review, published in 2018, updated the first with new evidence and even stronger results. In nineteen of twenty-four studies, focused deterrence was successful, and it succeeded a stunning twelve out of twelve times when focused specifically on reducing group violence. In the six years since the original review, the top performer in violence reduction had only gotten better. Anthony A. Braga and David L. Weisburd, "The Effects of Focused Deterrence Strategies on Crime: A Systematic Review and Meta-Analysis of the Empirical Evidence," *Journal of Research in Crime and Delinquency* 49, no. 3 (2012): 323–358; Anthony A. Braga, David Weisburd, and Brandon Turchan, "Focused Deterrence Strategies and Crime Control: An Updated Systematic Review and Meta-Analysis of the Empirical Evidence," *Criminology and Public Policy* 17, no. 1 (2018): 205–250.

2. Anthony Braga, Gregory Zimmerman, Rod Brunson, and Andrew Papachristos, *Oakland Ceasefire Impact Evaluation: Key Findings,* August 10, 2018, https://p.eastbayexpress .com/media/pdf/oakland_ceasefire_impact_evaluation_key_findings.pdf; Lauren Hernandez, "With Gun Killings Down in Oakland, Police Credit Ceasefire Program," *San Francisco Chronicle,* August 24, 2018.

3. Here I am describing the GVRS model as it has been developed and implemented in Oakland. In other cities, the GVRS works in similar but not necessarily identical ways.

4. Another means of identifying individuals and groups is audits that gather intelligence on the various gangs, sets, cliques, or crews that associate with one another and are involved in violent crime. In addition, incident reviews work through past cases in order to identify underlying dynamics that will be useful in preventing such cases in the future. Vaughn Crandall, Stewart Wakeling, and Daniela Gilbert, *Outreach and Support: An Evidence-Based Approach to Services That Reduces Violence in the Near Term,* California Partnership for Safe Communities, September 2016, http://thecapartnership.org/cms/assets /uploads/2016/09/CPSC_OutreachandSupport.pdf; Brian Freskos, "Chicago Criminals Are 'Handshakes' Away from Illegal Guns, Study Finds," The Trace, May 24, 2018, www .thetrace.org/rounds/chicago-illegal-gun-study-network-analysis/.

5. Stewart Wakeling, Daniela Gilbert, and Vaughn Crandall, *Strengthening Police-Community Relationships Goes Hand-in-Hand with Reducing Violence: An Update on Oakland Ceasefire,* California Partnership for Safe Communities, April 2016, http://the capartnership.org/cms/assets/uploads/2016/05/Oakland-Ceasefire-Update-Brief-April -2016-FINAL.pdf.

6. Crandall, Wakeling, and Gilbert, *Outreach and Support.*

7. Ibid.

8. Max Rivlin-Nadler, "How a Group Policing Model Is Criminalizing Whole Communities," *The Nation,* January 12, 2018.

9. Martin Gold and Hans W. Mattick, *Experiment in the Streets: The Chicago Youth Development Project. Final Report,* Ford Foundation and US Department of Labor, report no. DLMA-91-24-68-41, 1974; Malcolm W. Klein, "Gang Cohesiveness, Delinquency, and a Street-Work Program," *Journal of Research in Crime and Delinquency* 6, no. 2 (1969): 135–166; Malcolm W. Klein, *Street Gangs and Street Workers* (Englewood Cliffs, NJ: Prentice-Hall, 1971); Walter B. Miller, "The Impact of a 'Total-Community' Delinquency Control Project," *Social Problems* 10, no. 2 (1962): 168–191.

10. Sheyla A. Delgado et al., *The Effects of Cure Violence in the South Bronx and East New York, Brooklyn,* Denormalizing Violence (series), John Jay College of Criminal Justice Research and Evaluation Center, October 2017, https://johnjayrec.nyc/wp-content/uploads/2017/10/CVinSoBronxEastNY.pdf; Wesley G. Skogan, *Brief Summary: An Evaluation of CeaseFire-Chicago,* Institute for Policy Research, Northwestern University, 2008, www.ipr.northwestern.edu/publications/papers/urban-policy-and-community-development/docs/ceasefire-pdfs/summary.pdf; Jennifer M. Whitehill, Daniel W. Webster, and Jon S. Vernick, "Street Conflict Mediation to Prevent Youth Violence: Conflict, Characteristics and Outcomes," *Injury Prevention* 19, no. 3 (2013): 204–209; Douglas J. Boyle, Jennifer L. Lanterman, Joseph E. Pascarella, and Chia-Cherng Cheng, "The Impact of Newark's Operation Ceasefire on Trauma Center Gunshot Wound Admissions," *Justice Research and Policy* 12, no. 2 (2010): 105–123; Jeremy M. Wilson and Steven Chermak, "Community-Driven Violence Reduction Programs: Examining Pittsburgh's One Vision One Life," *Criminology and Public Policy* 10, no. 4 (2011): 993–1027; David M. Hureau, Anthony A. Braga, Tracey Lloyd, and Christopher Winship, *Evaluating StreetSafe Boston: A Report to the Boston Foundation,* 2014.

11. Jeffrey Butts and Sheyla Delgado, "Repairing Trust: Young Men in Neighborhoods with Cure Violence Programs Report Growing Confidence in Police," Research Brief, John Jay Research and Evaluation Center, 2017, https://johnjayrec.nyc/wp-content/uploads/2017/10/Repairing2017.pdf.

12. Wilson and Chermak, "Community-Driven Violence Reduction Programs."

13. Jeffrey Brantingham, Nick Sundback, Baichuan Yan, and Kristine Chan, *GRYD Intervention Incident Response & Gang Crime 2017 Evaluation Report,* City of Los Angeles Mayor's Office of Gang Reduction and Youth Development, 2017, www.lagryd.org/sites/default/files/reports/GRYD%20IR%20and%20Gang%20Crime%20Report_2017_FINALv2_0.pdf.

14. Jonathan Purtle et al., "Hospital-Based Violence Prevention: Progress and Opportunities," *Annals of Internal Medicine* 163, no. 9 (2015): 715–717; Communities Partnering 4 Peace website, Metropolitan Family Services, www.metrofamily.org/cp4p/.

15. Mark W. Lipsey, Nana A. Landenberger, and Sandra J. Wilson, "Effects of Cognitive-Behavioral Programs for Criminal Offenders," *Campbell Systematic Reviews* 3 (2007), https://campbellcollaboration.org/media/k2/attachments/1028_R.pdf. See also J. C. Hockenhull, Richard Whittington, Maria Leitner, W. Barr, J. McGuire, M. G. Cherry, R. Flentje, B. Quinn, Y. Dundar, and R. Dickson. "A Systematic Review of Prevention and Intervention Strategies for Populations at High Risk of Engaging in Violent Behaviour: Update 2002-8," *Health Technology Assessment* (Winchester, England) 16, no. 3 (2012): 1.

16. Lipsey, Landenberger, and Wilson, "Effects of Cognitive-Behavioral Programs for Criminal Offenders."

17. More than forty published meta-analyses demonstrate that when reentry programs follow the well-known risk/needs/responsivity framework (RNR), they tend to be successful, and a "cornerstone of the RNR model is an emphasis on programs based on the cognitive-behavioral model." In short, the effectiveness of most reentry efforts depends on the successful deployment of CBT. David Wilson, "Correctional Programs," in *What Works in Crime Prevention and Rehabilitation: Lessons from Systematic Reviews,* ed. David Weisburd, David P. Farrington, and Charlotte Gill (New York: Springer, 2016), 442.

18. Nico Pitney, "Nothing Stops a Bullet Like a Job," Huffington Post, September 30, 2015, www.huffingtonpost.com/entry/greg-boyle-homeboy-industries-life-lessons_us_56030036e4b00310edf9c7a4; L. Duran, Martha Plotkin, Phoebe Potter, and Henry Rosen, *Integrated Reentry and Employment Strategies: Reducing Recidivism and Promoting Job Readiness,* Council of State Governments Justice Center, September 2013, http://csg justicecenter.org/wp-content/uploads/2013/09/Final.Reentry-and-Employment.pp_.pdf; Thomas Abt and Christopher Winship, *What Works in Reducing Community Violence: A Meta-Review and Field Study for the Northern Triangle,* Democracy International (Washington, DC: United States Agency for International Development, February 2016).

19. Sara B. Heller et al., "Thinking, Fast and Slow? Some Field Experiments to Reduce Crime and Dropout in Chicago," *Quarterly Journal of Economics* 132, no. 1 (2017): 1–54. It is important to note that BAM was not explicitly designed to be a violence-reduction program. It is a school-based effort that does not engage youths at the highest risk for violence, many of whom are not in school.

20. Sachiko Donley, Leah Habib, Tanja Jovanovic, Ms Asante Kamkwalala, Mark Evces, Glenn Egan, Bekh Bradley, and Kerry J. Ressler, "Civilian PTSD Symptoms and Risk for Involvement in the Criminal Justice System," *The Journal of the American Academy of Psychiatry and the Law* 40, no. 4 (2012): 522; Lois Beckett, "Living in a Violent Neighborhood Is as Likely to Give You PTSD as Going to War," *Mother Jones,* February 4, 2014, https://www.motherjones.com/politics/2014/02/ptsd-among-wounded-americans-in-violent-neighborhoods/; Bruce Western, "Lifetimes of Violence in a Sample of Released Prisoners" (working paper, Department of Sociology, Harvard University, January 2015), https://scholar.harvard.edu/files/brucewestern/files/lifetimes_of_violence_in_a_sample_of_released_prisoners.pdf.

21. The impact of violent trauma on pregnant women: Martin Foureaux Koppensteiner and Marco Manacorda, "Violence and Birth Outcomes: Evidence from Homicides in Brazil," *Journal of Development Economics* 119 (2016): 16–33. On children: James C. Spilsbury, "Sleep as a Mediator in the Pathway from Violence-Induced Traumatic Stress to Poorer Health and Functioning: A Review of the Literature and Proposed Conceptual Model," *Behavioral Sleep Medicine* 7, no. 4 (2009): 223–244; Patrick T. Sharkey, Nicole Tirado-Strayer, Andrew V. Papachristos, and C. Cybele Raver, "The Effect of Local Violence on Children's Attention and Impulse Control," *American Journal of Public Health* 102, no. 12 (2012): 2287–2293; Patrick Sharkey, "The Acute Effect of Local Homicides on Children's Cognitive Performance," *Proceedings of the National Academy of Sciences* 107, no. 26 (2010): 11733–11738. On adults: See generally Vincent J. Felitti et al., "Relationship of Childhood Abuse and Household Dysfunction to Many of the Leading Causes of Death in Adults: The Adverse Childhood Experiences (ACE) Study," *American Journal of Preventive Medicine* 14, no. 4 (1998): 245–258.

22. Felitti et al., "Relationship of Childhood Abuse and Household Dysfunction to Many of the Leading Causes of Death in Adults."

23. James A. Reavis, Jan Looman, Kristina A. Franco, and Briana Rojas, "Adverse Childhood Experiences and Adult Criminality: How Long Must We Live Before We Possess Our Own Lives?," *Permanente Journal* 17, no. 2 (2013): 44–48; Richard Spano, Craig Rivera, and John M. Bolland, "Are Chronic Exposure to Violence and Chronic Violent Behavior Closely Related to Developmental Processes During Adolescence?," *Criminal Justice and Behavior* 37, no. 10 (2010): 1160–1179.

24. Penelope J. Baughman, Tara A. Hartley, Cecil M. Burchfiel, and John M. Violanti, "Stress and Health in Law Enforcement," NIOSH Science Blog, CDC, August 13, 2012, https://blogs.cdc.gov/niosh-science-blog/2012/08/13/policestress/; Hong Li, Bin Cheng, and Xiao Ping Zhu, "Quantification of Burnout in Emergency Nurses: A Systematic Review and Meta-Analysis," *International Emergency Nursing* (2018).

25. Michael A. Ramirez de Arellano et al., "Trauma-Focused Cognitive-Behavioral Therapy for Children and Adolescents: Assessing the Evidence," *Psychiatric Services* 65, no. 5 (2014): 591–602.

26. Mark A. Cohen and Alex R. Piquero, "New Evidence on the Monetary Value of Saving a High-Risk Youth," *Journal of Quantitative Criminology* 25, no. 1 (2009): 25–49.

27. Alex R. Piquero et al., "Effects of Early Family/Parent Training Programs on Antisocial Behavior and Delinquency," *Journal of Experimental Criminology* 5, no. 2 (2009): 83–120. In this review, criminologist Alex Piquero and his colleagues analyzed fifty-five high-quality studies and found that parenting programs had moderately positive impacts on childhood behavior problems, delinquency, and crime. These results reinforced the conclusions of two previous systematic reviews, which had found similarly favorable results. In 2016, the review was updated, adding twenty-three new studies for a total of seventy-eight, sixty-seven of which had positive impacts, with the overall results even stronger than before.

28. Like home visiting and parent training programs, FFT is also associated with other positive outcomes, including fewer risky behaviors and improved life skills. Donald A. Gordon, Jack Arbuthnot, Kathryn E. Gustafson, and Peter McGreen, "Home-Based Behavioral-Systems Family Therapy with Disadvantaged Juvenile Delinquents," *American Journal of Family Therapy* 16, no. 3 (1988): 243–255; Thomas Sexton and Charles W. Turner, "The Effectiveness of Functional Family Therapy for Youth with Behavioral Problems in a Community Practice Setting," *Journal of Family Psychology* 24, no. 3 (2010): 339–348.

29. Emily Morgan, Nina Salomon, Martha Plotkin, and Rebecca Cohen, "The School Discipline Consensus Report: Strategies from the Field to Keep Students Engaged in School and Out of the Juvenile Justice System," *The Council of State Governments Justice Center,* 2014, http://csgjusticecenter.org/wp-content/uploads/2014/06/The_School _Discipline_Consensus_Report.pdf.

30. George Sugai and Brandi Simonsen, "Positive Behavioral Interventions and Supports: History, Defining Features, and Misconceptions," *Center for PBIS & Center for Positive Behavioral Interventions and Supports,* University of Connecticut 14 (2012).

31. Delisi et al., "Murder by Numbers."

32. Jill Leovy, *Ghettoside: A True Story of Murder in America* (New York: Spiegel & Grau, 2015), Kindle edition, chap. 1.

33. David Simon, "President Obama Interviews the Creator of 'The Wire' David Simon," interview by Barack Obama, *What's Happening* (blog), the White House, March 27, 2015, https://obamawhitehouse.archives.gov/blog/2016/08/18/president-obama-interviews-creator-wiredavid-simon.

34. "America's Declining Homicide Clearance Rates 1965–2017," Murder Accountability Project, www.murderdata.org/p/reported-homicide-clearance-rate-1980.html.

35. Wesley Lowery, Kimbriell Kelly, and Steven Rich, "An Unequal Justice," *Washington Post*, July 25, 2018, www.washingtonpost.com/graphics/2018/investigations/black-homicides-arrests.

36. Phillip Cook and Jens Ludwig, "Policing Guns: Why Gun Violence Is Not (Just) a Public Health Problem," Items, November 6, 2018, https://items.ssrc.org/policing-guns-why-gun-violence-is-not-just-a-public-health-problem/.

37. Anthony A. Braga and Desiree Dusseault, "Can Homicide Detectives Improve Homicide Clearance Rates?," *Crime & Delinquency* 64, no. 3 (2018): 283–315. The figure cited refers to adjusted homicide clearance rates—unadjusted rates increased by 10 percent.

38. Timothy Keel, *Detecting Clues in Homicide Management: A Homicide 'Best Practices' Research Project*, Federal Bureau of Investigation, National Center for the Analysis of Violent Crime, May 2011, www.nationalpublicsafetypartnership.org/clearinghouse/Content/ResourceDocuments/Detecting%20Clues%20in%20Homicide%20Management.pdf; Philip J. Cook, Anthony A. Braga, Brandon S. Turchan, and Lisa M. Barao, "Why Do Gun Murders Have a Higher Clearance Rate Than Gunshot Assaults?," *Criminology and Public Policy* 18 no. 3 (forthcoming 2019); Kimbriell Kelly, Wesley Lowery, and Steven Rich, "Buried Under Bodies: Even with Murder Rates Falling, Big-City Detectives Face Daunting Caseloads," *Washington Post*, September 13, 2018, www.washingtonpost.com/news/national/wp/2018/09/13/feature/even-with-murder-rates-falling-big-city-detectives-face-daunting-caseloads.

Chapter 7: Cooling Hot Spots

1. Cynthia Lum and Christopher Koper, "Place-Based Approaches and Hot Spots Policing," in *Evidence-Based Policing: Translating Research into Practice*, ed. Cynthia Lum and Christopher Koper (Oxford, UK: Oxford University Press, 2017), 60.

2. David Weisburd, "Bringing Social Context Back into the Equation: The Importance of Social Characteristics of Places in the Prevention of Crime," *Criminology & Public Policy* 11, no. 2 (2012): 317–326.

3. Anthony A. Braga, Andrew V. Papachristos, and David M. Hureau, "The Concentration and Stability of Gun Violence at Micro Places in Boston, 1980–2008," *Journal of Quantitative Criminology* 26, no. 1 (2010): 33–53.

4. National Research Council, *Fairness and Effectiveness in Policing: The Evidence* (Washington, DC: National Academies Press, 2004); National Academies of Sciences, Engineering, and Medicine, *Proactive Policing: Effects on Crime and Communities* (Washington, DC: National Academies Press, 2018).

5. Jerry H. Ratcliffe, Travis Taniguchi, Elizabeth R. Groff, and Jennifer D. Wood, "The Philadelphia Foot Patrol Experiment: A Randomized Controlled Trial of Police Patrol

Effectiveness in Violent Crime Hotspots," *Criminology* 49, no. 3 (2011): 795–831; Elizabeth R. Groff et al., "Does What Police Do at Hot Spots Matter? The Philadelphia Policing Tactics Experiment," *Criminology* 53, no. 1 (2015): 23–53.

6. Samantha Melamed, "Study: High Rates of Stop-and-Frisk Even in Philly's Lowest-Crime Black Areas," Philly.com, October 2, 2017, www.philly.com/philly/news/crime/stop-frisk-policing-philadelphia-racial-bias-lance-hannon-villanova-20171002.html; Phillip Jackson, "City Expert Says ACLU's Numbers on Stop and Frisk Are 'Inflated,'" *Philadelphia Tribune*, January 22, 2018.

7. *Time* magazine, January 15, 1996; James Q. Wilson and George L. Kelling, "Broken Windows," *Atlantic Monthly* 249, no. 3 (1982): 29–38.

8. German Lopez, "A Conservative Columnist Admits It: 'We Were Wrong About Stop-and-Frisk,'" Vox, January 8, 2018, www.vox.com/policy-and-politics/2018/1/8/1686 5730/national-review-stop-and-frisk-police.

9. David Weisburd, Cody W. Telep, and Brian A. Lawton, "Could Innovations in Policing Have Contributed to the New York City Crime Drop Even in a Period of Declining Police Strength? The Case of Stop, Question and Frisk as a Hot Spots Policing Strategy," *Justice Quarterly* 31, no. 1 (2014): 129–153; Franklin E. Zimring, *The City That Became Safe: New York's Lessons for Urban Crime and Its Control* (New York: Oxford University Press, 2011).

10. Anthony A. Braga, Brandon C. Welsh, and Cory Schnell, "Can Policing Disorder Reduce Crime? A Systematic Review and Meta-Analysis," *Journal of Research in Crime and Delinquency* 52, no. 4 (2015): 567–588.

11. Andrew Wheeler, Jasmine Silver, Robert Worden, and Sarah McLean, "Mapping Attitudes Towards the Police at Micro Places," November 29, 2017, https://ssrn.com/abstract=3079674; Anthony A. Braga, "The Science and Practice of Hot-Spots Policing," in *Advancing Criminology and Criminal Justice Policy*, ed. Thomas G. Blomberg, Julie Mestre Brancale, Kevin M. Beaver, and William B. Dales (New York: Routledge, 2016), 139–149.

12. Charles C. Branas et al., "Urban Blight Remediation as a Cost-Beneficial Solution to Firearm Violence," *American Journal of Public Health* 106, no. 12 (2016): 2158–2164; Michelle C. Kondo et al., "Neighborhood Interventions to Reduce Violence," *Annual Review of Public Health* 39 (2018): 253–271; Sandra Bogar and Kirsten M. Beyer, "Green Space, Violence, and Crime: A Systematic Review," *Trauma, Violence, & Abuse* 17, no. 2 (2016): 160–171.

13. Brandon C. Welsh and David P. Farrington, "Effects of Improved Street Lighting on Crime," *Campbell Systematic Reviews* 13 (2008): 1–51.

14. Brandon C. Welsh, Mark E. Mudge, and David P. Farrington, "Reconceptualizing Public Area Surveillance and Crime Prevention: Security Guards, Place Managers and Defensible Space," *Security Journal* 23, no. 4 (2010): 299–319.

15. Branas et al., "Urban Blight Remediation as a Cost-Beneficial Solution to Firearm Violence."

16. In chapter 4, we reviewed Patrick Sharkey's groundbreaking finding that "community nonprofits" were important contributors to the nation's crime decline. According to Sharkey, these are "local nonprofits . . . with the specific goal of building stronger communities and confronting the problems of crime and violence." Sharkey offers Chicago's BAM program as an example, but BAM is clearly a school-based, people-based CBT program that is not connected to a "community" in any significant sense. Sharkey's community

nonprofits are perhaps better understood as alternatives to law enforcement, some of which may be grounded in the community, some of which may not be.

17. David Kennedy, "Community Crime Prevention," in *Advancing Criminology and Criminal Justice Policy,* ed. Thomas G. Blomberg, Julie Mestre Brancale, Kevin M. Beaver, and William B. Dales (New York: Routledge, 2016), Kindle edition, chap. 7.

18. Charlotte Gill et al., "Community-Oriented Policing to Reduce Crime, Disorder and Fear and Increase Satisfaction and Legitimacy Among Citizens: A Systematic Review," *Journal of Experimental Criminology* 10, no. 4 (2014): 399–428; National Research Council, *Fairness and Effectiveness in Policing*; National Academies of Sciences, Engineering, and Medicine, *Proactive Policing.*

19. "Mayor Eric Garcetti Announces New Expansion of Community Safety Partnership," Mayor Eric Garcetti official website, March 3, 2017, www.lamayor.org/mayor-garcetti-announces-new-expansion-community-safety-partnership.

20. US Government Accountability Office, *Community Policing Grants: COPS Grants Were a Modest Contributor to Declines in Crime in the 1990s,* GAO-06-104, October 2005, www.gao.gov/new.items/d06104.pdf.

21. Trevor Bennett, Katy Holloway, and David P. Farrington, "Does Neighborhood Watch Reduce Crime? A Systematic Review and Meta-Analysis," *Journal of Experimental Criminology* 2, no. 4 (2006): 437–458; Welsh, Mudge, and Farrington, "Reconceptualizing Public Area Surveillance and Crime Prevention."

22. See generally Robert J. Sampson, Stephen W. Raudenbush, and Felton Earls, "Neighborhoods and Violent Crime: A Multilevel Study of Collective Efficacy," *Science* 277, no. 5328 (August 1997): 918–924.

23. Weisburd, "Bringing Social Context Back into the Equation."

24. Tammy Rinehart Kochel and David Weisburd, "The Impact of Hot Spots Policing on Collective Efficacy: Findings from a Randomized Field Trial," *Justice Quarterly* (2018): 1–29; Elise Sargeant, "Policing and Collective Efficacy: The Relative Importance of Police Effectiveness, Procedural Justice and the Obligation to Obey Police," *Policing and Society* 27, no. 8 (2017).

25. See generally Lorraine Mazerolle and Janet Ransley, *Third Party Policing* (Cambridge University Press, 2006).

26. Gisela Bichler, Karin Schmerler, and Janet Enriquez, "Curbing Nuisance Motels: An Evaluation of Police as Place Regulators," *Policing: An International Journal of Police Strategies and Management* 36, no. 2 (2013): 437–462; Daniel F. Higgins and James R. Coldren, *Evaluating Gang and Drug House Abatement in Chicago,* Illinois Criminal Justice Information Authority, April 2000, www.icjia.org/assets/pdf/ResearchReports/CAPSAbatement.pdf; National Academies of Sciences, Engineering, and Medicine, *Proactive Policing.*

27. Lorraine Mazerolle, "The Power of Policing Partnerships: Sustaining the Gains," *Journal of Experimental Criminology* 10, no. 3 (2014): 341–365.

Chapter 8: Guns, Gangs, and Drugs

1. David Hemenway, *Private Guns, Public Health* (Ann Arbor, MI: University of Michigan Press, 2017); Franklin E. Zimring and Gordon Hawkins, *Crime Is Not the Problem: Lethal Violence in America* (New York: Oxford University Press, 1999); Erin Grinshteyn and

David Hemenway, "Violent Death Rates: The US Compared with Other High-Income OECD Countries, 2010," *American Journal of Medicine* 129, no. 3 (2016): 266–273.

2. Deborah Azrael, Lisa Hepburn, David Hemenway, and Matthew Miller, "The Stock and Flow of US Firearms: Results from the 2015 National Firearms Survey," *RSF* 3, no. 5 (October 2017): 38–57; Small Arms Survey, *Small Arms Survey 2007: Guns and the City*, Graduate Institute of International Studies, Geneva, Switzerland, 2007, www.smallarms survey.org/publications/by-type/yearbook/small-arms-survey-2007.html; German Lopez, "Guns Killed More People Than Car Crashes in 2017," Vox, December 11, 2018, www.vox .com/future-perfect/2018/12/11/18135976/gun-deaths-us-2017-suicide.

3. Planty and Truman, *Firearm Violence, 1993–2011*; Christopher S. Koper and Evan Mayo-Wilson, "Police Strategies to Reduce Illegal Possession and Carrying of Firearms: Effects," *Campbell Systematic Reviews* 8 (2012), www.campbellcollaboration.org/media /k2/attachments/Koper_Firearms_Review.pdf; Melinda Moyer, "More Guns Do Not Stop More Crimes, Evidence Shows," *Scientific American*, October 1, 2017, www.scientific american.com/article/more-guns-do-not-stop-more-crimes-evidence-shows/.

4. Lopez, "Guns Killed More People Than Car Crashes in 2017."

5. Anthony A. Braga, "Guns and Crime," in *The Oxford Handbook of Law and Economics*, ed. Francesco Parisi, vol. 3, *Public Law and Legal Institutions* (Oxford, UK: Oxford University Publishing, 2017), 344–369.

6. Daniel W. Webster and Garen J. Wintemute, "Effects of Policies Designed to Keep Firearms from High-Risk Individuals," *Annual Review of Public Health* 36 (2015): 21–37.

7. Koper and Mayo-Wilson, "Police Strategies to Reduce Illegal Possession and Carrying of Firearms"; National Academies of Sciences, Engineering, and Medicine, *Proactive Policing: Effects on Crime and Communities* (Washington, DC: National Academies Press, 2018).

8. Lawrence W. Sherman and Dennis P. Rogan, "Effects of Gun Seizures on Gun Violence: 'Hot Spots' Patrol in Kansas City," *Justice Quarterly* 12, no. 4 (1995): 673–693; Koper and Mayo-Wilson, "Police Strategies to Reduce Illegal Possession and Carrying of Firearms."

9. Koper and Mayo-Wilson, "Police Strategies to Reduce Illegal Possession and Carrying of Firearms," 36.

10. Ibid.

11. Braga, "Guns and Crime."

12. Braga, "Guns and Crime"; Webster and Wintemute, "Effects of Policies Designed to Keep Firearms from High-Risk Individuals"; Christopher S. Koper, Daniel J. Woods, and Bruce E. Kubu, "Gun Violence Prevention Practices Among Local Police in the United States," *Policing: An International Journal of Police Strategies and Management* 36, no. 3 (2013): 577–603.

13. Lawrence W. Sherman et al., *Preventing Crime: What Works, What Doesn't, What's Promising*, National Institute of Justice, US Department of Justice, July 1998, report no. NCJ 171676, https://www.ncjrs.gov/pdffiles/171676.pdf; Matthew D. Makarios and Travis C. Pratt, "The Effectiveness of Policies and Programs That Attempt to Reduce Firearm Violence: A Meta-Analysis," *Crime and Delinquency* 58, no. 2 (2012): 222–244.

14. Philip J. Cook and John J. Donohue, "Saving Lives by Regulating Guns: Evidence for Policy," *Science* 358, no. 6368 (2017): 1259–1261; Christopher S. Koper et al., "Criminal Use of Assault Weapons and High-Capacity Semiautomatic Firearms: An Updated

Examination of Local and National Sources," *Journal of Urban Health* (2017): 1–9; Ali Rowhani-Rahbar, Joseph A. Simonetti, and Frederick P. Rivara, "Effectiveness of Interventions to Promote Safe Firearm Storage," *Epidemiologic Reviews* 38, no. 1 (2016): 111–124.

15. Kara E. Rudolph, Elizabeth A. Stuart, Jon S. Vernick, and Daniel W. Webster, "Association Between Connecticut's Permit-to-Purchase Handgun Law and Homicides," *American Journal of Public Health* 105, no. 8 (2015): e49–e54; Daniel Webster, Cassandra Kercher Crifasi, and Jon S. Vernick, "Effects of the Repeal of Missouri's Handgun Purchaser Licensing Law on Homicides," *Journal of Urban Health* 91, no. 2 (2014): 293–302; Cassandra K. Crifasi et al., "Association Between Firearm Laws and Homicide in Urban Counties," *Journal of Urban Health* 95, no. 3 (2018): 383–390.

16. David Hemenway, "Reducing Firearm Violence," *Crime and Justice* 46, no. 1 (2017): 201–230.

17. Mark Follman, Gavin Aronsen, and Deanna Pan, "A Guide to Mass Shootings in America," *Mother Jones,* accessed on September 25, 2018, www.motherjones.com/politics /2012/07/mass-shootings-map/; UCR historical data at www.ucrdatatool.gov/.

18. Follman, Aronsen, and Pan, "A Guide to Mass Shootings in America."

19. Lois Beckett, "America's Response to School Massacres? A Booming Classroom Security Industry," *The Guardian,* November 18, 2017; Micere Keels, "The False Comfort of Securing Schools," *New York Times,* September 6, 2018; Lois Beckett et al., "America's Gun Problem Is So Much Bigger Than Mass Shootings," *The Guardian,* June 21, 2016.

20. David E. Stark and Nigam H. Shah, "Funding and Publication of Research on Gun Violence and Other Leading Causes of Death," *JAMA* 317, no. 1 (2017): 84–85.

21. Nathan Rott, "California Launches First State-Funded Gun Violence Research Center," *Morning Edition,* NPR, March 26, 2018, www.npr.org/2018/03/26/596942384 /california-launches-first-state-funded-gun-violence-research-center; Laura and John Arnold Foundation, "Research Collaborative Formed to Study Gun Violence" (press release), May 31, 2018, www.arnoldfoundation.org/research-collaborative-formed-to -study-gun-violence/.

22. Hayley Miller, "Parkland Survivors Call Out Media for Ignoring Gun Violence in Black Communities," Huffington Post, March 19, 2018, www.huffingtonpost.com/entry /parkland-gun-violence-black-communities_us_5ab00986e4b0e862383a68f9. My favorite journalists on these issues include Lois Beckett from *The Guardian,* German Lopez from *Vox,* and Tina Rosenberg from the *New York Times,* along with a number of journalists doing good work at *The Trace,* a nonpartisan news organization dedicated to covering gun violence.

23. Dana Peterson, Terrance J. Taylor, and Finn-Aage Esbensen, "Gang Membership and Violent Victimization," *Justice Quarterly* 21, no. 4 (2004): 793–815; Terrance J. Taylor, Dana Peterson, Finn-Aage Esbensen, and Adrienne Freng, "Gang Membership as a Risk Factor for Adolescent Violent Victimization," *Journal of Research in Crime and Delinquency* 44, no. 4 (2007): 351–380; Scott H. Decker, Charles M. Katz, and Vincent J. Webb, "Understanding the Black Box of Gang Organization: Implications for Involvement in Violent Crime, Drug Sales, and Violent Victimization," *Crime and Delinquency* 54, no. 1 (2008): 153–172.

24. David C. Pyrooz, Andrew M. Fox, and Scott H. Decker, "Racial and Ethnic Heterogeneity, Economic Disadvantage, and Gangs: A Macro-Level Study of Gang Membership in Urban America," *Justice Quarterly* 27, no. 6 (2010): 867–892; Scott H. Decker, Chris Melde,

and David C. Pyrooz, "What Do We Know About Gangs and Gang Members and Where Do We Go from Here?," *Justice Quarterly* 30, no. 3 (2013): 369–402; Anthony A. Braga, David M. Hureau, and Andrew V. Papachristos, "Deterring Gang-Involved Gun Violence: Measuring the Impact of Boston's Operation Ceasefire on Street Gang Behavior," *Journal of Quantitative Criminology* 30, no. 1 (2014): 113–139; Andrew V. Papachristos and David S. Kirk, "Changing the Street Dynamic: Evaluating Chicago's Group Violence Reduction Strategy," *Criminology and Public Policy* 14, no. 3 (2015): 525–558; George Tita and Allan F. Abrahamse, *Homicide in California, 1981–2008: Measuring the Impact of Los Angeles and Gangs on Overall Homicide Patterns,* Governor's Office of Gang and Youth Violence Policy, 2010.

25. Connie Rice, keynote speech (Los Angeles Gang Prevention and Intervention Conference, Los Angeles, CA, May 1, 2017).

26. Scott H. Decker and G. David Curry, "Gangs, Gang Homicides, and Gang Loyalty: Organized Crimes or Disorganized Criminals," *Journal of Criminal Justice* 30, no. 4 (2002): 343–352.

27. Jeff Asher, "Gang Stats Aren't Remotely Reliable, but Voters Keep Hearing About Them Anyway," FiveThirtyEight, November 3, 2017, https://fivethirtyeight.com/features /gang-stats-arent-remotely-reliable-but-voters-keep-hearing-about-them-anyway/.

28. Arlen Egley Jr., James C. Howell, and Meena Harris, "Highlights of the 2012 National Youth Gang Survey," *Juvenile Justice Fact Sheet,* Office of Juvenile Justice and Delinquency Prevention, US Department of Justice, December 2014, https://www.ojjdp.gov /pubs/248025.pdf; David C. Pyrooz and Gary Sweeten, "Gang Membership Between Ages 5 and 17 Years in the United States," *Journal of Adolescent Health* 56, no. 4 (2015): 414–419.

29. Asher, "Gang Stats Aren't Remotely Reliable."

30. Asher, "Gang Stats Aren't Remotely Reliable"; Decker and Curry, "Gangs, Gang Homicides, and Gang Loyalty."

31. Decker, Melde, and Pyrooz, "What Do We Know About Gangs and Gang Members and Where Do We Go from Here?"

32. One hopeful exception is work that began in Los Angeles that now is also being implemented in Central America. Los Angeles's Gang Reduction Youth Development (GRYD) program is the nation's largest, most comprehensive anti-gang, anti-violence effort. Among other things, it delivers evidence-informed services to families with youths at elevated risk for violence and joining gangs. The Youth Services Eligibility Tool (YSET) is a tool used by GRYD and now elsewhere to diagnose not just whether a youth is at risk for joining a gang but also whether that risk is sufficiently high to merit intervention.

33. Herrick Fisher, Frances Gardner, and Paul Montgomery, "Cognitive-Behavioural Interventions for Preventing Youth Gang Involvement for Children and Young People (7–16)," *Cochrane Database of Systematic Reviews* 2 (2008); Herrick Fisher, Paul Montgomery, and Frances Gardner, "Opportunities Provision for Preventing Youth Gang Involvement for Children and Young People (7–16)," *Cochrane Database of Systematic Reviews* 2 (2008); Angela Higginson et al., "Preventive Interventions to Reduce Youth Involvement in Gangs and Gang Crime in Low- and Middle-Income Countries: A Systematic Review," *Campbell Systematic Reviews* 11, no. 18 (2015); Scott Decker, "Responding to Gangs," *Freedom from Fear,* July 19, 2017; Jason Gravel et al., "Keeping Promises: A Systematic Review and a New Classification of Gang Control Strategies," *Journal of Criminal Justice* 41, no. 4 (2013): 228–242. According to Angela Higginson and her colleagues, "Many documents make reference to preventive interventions and their 'known' effectiveness, but frequently

this knowledge is theoretically derived, the product of author opinion, or only supported by pre-post analyses of outcomes with no control group."

34. Finn-Aage Esbensen et al., "Short- and Long-Term Outcome Results from a Multisite Evaluation of the G.R.E.A.T. Program," *Criminology and Public Policy* 12, no. 3 (2013): 375–411; Cheryl L. Maxson, "Do Not Shoot the Messenger: The Utility of Gang Risk Research in Program Targeting and Content," *Criminology and Public Policy* 12, no. 3 (2013): 421–426.

35. Father Greg Boyle, "I Thought I Could 'Save' Gang Members. I Was Wrong," *America: The Jesuit Review*, March 28, 2017, www.americamagazine.org/faith/2017/03/28/father -greg-boyle-i-thought-i-could-save-gang-members-i-was-wrong.

36. David M. Kennedy, *Don't Shoot: One Man, a Street Fellowship, and the End of Violence in Inner-City America* (New York: Bloomsbury USA, 2011), Kindle edition, chap. 5.

37. Gravel et al., "Keeping Promises"; T. P. Thornberry et al., "Reducing Crime Among Youth at Risk for Gang Involvement," *Criminology and Public Policy* 17 (2018): 984.

38. "Overdose Death Rates," National Institute on Drug Abuse, rev. August 2018, accessed October 24, 2018, www.drugabuse.gov/related-topics/trends-statistics/overdose-death-rates.

39. Alfred Blumstein and Joel Wallman, eds., *The Crime Drop in America* (New York: Cambridge University Press, 2006).

40. Katy R. Holloway, Trevor H. Bennett, and David P. Farrington, "The Effectiveness of Drug Treatment Programs in Reducing Criminal Behavior: A Meta-Analysis," *Psicothema* 18, no. 3 (2006): 620–629; Ojmarrh Mitchell, David B. Wilson, Amy Eggers, and Doris L. MacKenzie, "Assessing the Effectiveness of Drug Courts on Recidivism: A Meta-Analytic Review of Traditional and Non-traditional Drug Courts," *Journal of Criminal Justice* 40, no. 1 (2012): 60–71; Ojmarrh Mitchell, David B. Wilson, and Doris L. MacKenzie, "Does Incarceration-Based Drug Treatment Reduce Recidivism? A Meta-Analytic Synthesis of the Research," *Journal of Experimental Criminology* 3, no. 4 (2007): 353–375; Lorraine Mazerolle, David W. Soole, and Sacha Rombouts, "Street-Level Drug Law Enforcement: A Meta-Analytical Review," *Journal of Experimental Criminology* 2, no. 4 (2006): 409–435; Dan Werb et al., "Effect of Drug Law Enforcement on Drug Market Violence: A Systematic Review," *International Journal of Drug Policy* 22, no. 2 (2011): 87–94; Thomas Kerr, Will Small, and Evan Wood, "The Public Health and Social Impacts of Drug Market Enforcement: A Review of the Evidence," *International Journal of Drug Policy* 16, no. 4 (2005): 210–220; Anthony A. Braga, David Weisburd, and Brandon Turchan, "Focused Deterrence Strategies and Crime Control: An Updated Systematic Review and Meta-Analysis of the Empirical Evidence," *Criminology and Public Policy* 17, no. 1 (2018): 205–250.

41. Mark A. R. Kleiman, *When Brute Force Fails: How to Have Less Crime and Less Punishment* (Princeton, NJ: Princeton University Press, 2009); Dylan Matthews, "Mark Kleiman on Why We Need to Solve Our Alcohol Problem to Solve Our Crime Problem," *Washington Post*, March 28, 2013.

42. Claire Wilkinson, Michael Livingston, and Robin Room, "Impacts of Changes to Trading Hours of Liquor Licenses on Alcohol-Related Harm: A Systematic Review 2005–2015," *Public Health Research and Practice* 26, no. 4 (2016); World Health Organization, *Preventing Violence by Reducing the Availability and Harmful Use of Alcohol*, Violence Prevention: The Evidence (series), 2009, www.who.int/violence_injury_prevention /violence/alcohol.pdf.

Chapter 9: How Talk Informs Action

1. Rudy Giuliani, interview by Sean Hannity, *Hannity,* Fox News, December 8, 2014, http://insider.foxnews.com/2014/12/08/rudy-giuliani-i-saved-more-black-lives-any-mayor -history-new-york-city.

2. Bill O'Reilly, "How Black Lives Matter Is Killing Americans," *The O'Reilly Factor,* May 25, 2016, www.foxnews.com/transcript/bill-oreilly-how-black-lives-matter-is -killing-americans.

3. Al Baker, David Goodman, and Benjamin Mueller, "Beyond the Chokehold: The Path to Eric Garner's Death," *New York Times,* June 13, 2015.

4. Alexia Cooper and Erica L. Smith, *Homicide Trends in the United States, 1980–2008,* US Department of Justice, Bureau of Justice Statistics, report no. NCJ 236018, November 2011, www.bjs.gov/content/pub/pdf/htus8008.pdf.

5. Ibid.

6. There is little hard data on the subject, but one recent study estimates that 24 percent of African Americans and 6 percent of the total American population have been convicted of a felony, with violent and financial offenses constituting fractions of these totals. Sarah K. S. Shannon et al., "The Growth, Scope, and Spatial Distribution of People with Felony Records in the United States, 1948–2010," *Demography* 54, no. 5 (2017): 1795–1818. It should also be noted that there is good reason to believe that white people are overrepresented in financial and white-collar criminal activity, but that most criminal justice data relates to personal and property-related offenses, so it is likely for this and other reasons that the overall criminal offending rates of white people are underrepresented. Robert J. Sampson and Janet L. Lauritsen, "Racial and Ethnic Disparities in Crime and Criminal Justice in the United States," *Crime and Justice* 21 (1997): 311–374.

7. Anthony Allan Braga and Rodney Brunson, "The Police and Public Discourse on 'Black-on-Black' Violence," *New Perspectives in Policing,* National Institute of Justice, US Department of Justice, May 2015, report no. NCJ 248588, www.ncjrs.gov/pdffiles1 /nij/248588.pdf; David S. Kirk and Andrew V. Papachristos, "Cultural Mechanisms and the Persistence of Neighborhood Violence," *American Journal of Sociology* 116, no. 4 (2011): 1190–1233.

8. Todd Lighty, Morgan Greene, and Patrick M. O'Connell, "Police Arrest Antiviolence Protesters Trying to March on Kennedy Expressway Near O'Hare," *Chicago Tribune,* September 3, 2008, www.chicagotribune.com/news/ct-met-kennedy-expressway -protest-chicago-20180904-story.html.

9. Khalil Gibran Muhammad, *The Condemnation of Blackness* (Cambridge, MA: Harvard University Press, 2011).

10. Donald Trump, presidential announcement speech (New York City, June 16, 2015), http://time.com/3923128/donald-trump-announcement-speech/; Aaron Blake, "The First Trump-Clinton Presidential Debate Transcript, Annotated," *Washington Post,* September 26, 2016, www.washingtonpost.com/news/the-fix/wp/2016/09/26/the-first-trump-clinton -presidential-debate-transcript-annotated; Donald Trump, "Inaugural Address" (speech, Washington, DC, January 20, 2017), White House website, www.whitehouse.gov/briefings -statements/the-inaugural-address/; Donald J. Trump (@realDonaldTrump), "If Chicago doesn't fix the horrible 'carnage' going on, 228 shootings in 2017 with 42 killings (up 24% from 2016), I will send in the Feds!" Twitter, January 24, 2017, 6:25 p.m., https://twitter

.com/realdonaldtrump/status/824080766288228352; Donald J. Trump, (@realDonald Trump), "When we have an 'infestation' of MS-13 GANGS in certain parts of our country, who do we send to get them out? ICE!" Twitter, July 3, 2018, 3:49 a.m., https://twitter.com /realdonaldtrump/status/1014098721460686849.

11. Graham C. Ousey and Charis E. Kubrin, "Immigration and Crime: Assessing a Contentious Issue," *Annual Review of Criminology* 1 (2018): 63–84; Michael T. Light and Ty Miller, "Does Undocumented Immigration Increase Violent Crime?," *Criminology* 56, no. 2 (2018): 370–401; Lorraine Bailey, "Chicago Accuses Sessions of Flouting Sanctuary-City Ruling," Courthouse News Service, October 12, 2018, www.courthousenews.com /chicago-accuses-sessions-of-flouting-sanctuary-city-ruling/.

12. Stephen Raphael and Jens Ludwig, "Prison Sentence Enhancements: The Case of Project Exile," in *Evaluating Gun Policy: Effects on Crime and Violence,* ed. Jens Ludwig and Philip J. Cook (Washington, DC: Brookings Institution Press, 2003), 251–286; Richard Rosenfeld, Robert Fornango, and Eric Baumer, "Did Ceasefire, Compstat, and Exile Reduce Homicide?," *Criminology and Public Policy* 4, no. 3 (2005): 419–449.

13. Michelle Alexander, *The New Jim Crow: Mass Incarceration in the Age of Colorblindness* (New York: The New Press, 2012), introduction, Kindle.

14. Paul Butler, *Chokehold: Policing Black Men* (New York: The New Press, 2017), introduction, Kindle.

15. Muhammad, *The Condemnation of Blackness,* introduction, Kindle.

16. Michael R. Smith, Jeff J. Rojek, Matthew Petrocelli, and Brian Withrow, "Measuring Disparities in Police Activities: A State of the Art Review," *Policing: An International Journal of Police Strategies and Management* 40, no. 2 (2017): 166–183; Bureau of Justice Statistics, Arrest Data Analysis Tool, accessed on December 16, 2018, www.bjs.gov /index.cfm?ty=datool&surl=/arrests/index.cfm; Fatal Force Database, *Washington Post,* accessed on December 16, 2018, www.washingtonpost.com/graphics/national/police -shootings-2017; Todd D. Minton and Zhen Zeng, *Jail Inmates in 2015,* US Department of Justice, Bureau of Justice Statistics, report no. NCJ 250394, December 2016, www.bjs.gov /content/pub/pdf/ji15.pdf; E. Ann Carson and Elizabeth Anderson, *Prisoners in 2015,* US Department of Justice, Bureau of Justice Statistics, report no. NCJ 250229, December 2016, www.bjs.gov/content/pub/pdf/p15.pdf; Danielle Kaeble, Laura M. Maruschak, and Thomas P. Bonczar, *Probation and Parole in the United States, 2015,* US Department of Justice, Bureau of Justice Statistics, report no. NCJ 250230, December 2016 (rev. February 2, 2017), www.bjs.gov/content/pub/pdf/ppus15.pdf.

17. Jennifer H. Peck, "Minority Perceptions of the Police: A State-of-the-Art Review," *Policing: An International Journal of Police Strategies and Management* 38, no. 1 (2015): 173–203.

18. Smith, Rojek, Petrocelli, and Withrow, "Measuring Disparities in Police Activities"; Meghan E. Hollis, "Measurement Issues in Police Use of Force: A State-of-the-Art Review," *Policing: An International Journal of Police Strategies and Management* 41, no. 6 (2018): 844–858; Ojmarrh Mitchell, "A Meta-Analysis of Race and Sentencing Research: Explaining the Inconsistencies," *Journal of Quantitative Criminology* 21, no. 4 (2005): 439–466; Cassia Spohn, "Race, Crime, and Punishment in the Twentieth and Twenty-First Centuries," *Crime and Justice* 44, no. 1 (2015): 49–97.

19. Colleen Walsh, "The Costs of Inequality: A Goal of Justice, a Reality of Unfairness," *Harvard Gazette,* February 29, 2016, https://news.harvard.edu/gazette/story/2016/02 /the-costs-of-inequality-a-goal-of-justice-a-reality-of-unfairness/.

20. Shira Angert, *The Intersection of Gun Violence, Policing and Mass Incarceration in Communities of Color: Research Results,* Benenson Strategy Group, April 28, 2016, www .joycefdn.org/assets/images/Memo_on_Communities_of_Color_Survey_Results _FIN.pdf.

21. Malcolm Gladwell, "Million-Dollar Murray," *The New Yorker,* February 13, 2006.

22. Glenn Jeffers, "'A Mass Shooting, Only in Slow Motion,'" *Nieman Reports,* June 26, 2017, https://niemanreports.org/articles/a-mass-shooting-only-in-slow-motion/.

23. Chris Mills Rodrigo, "Trump Signs Criminal Justice Overhaul," The Hill, December 21, 2018, https://thehill.com/homenews/administration/422517-trump-signs -criminal-justice-reform-bill.

24. Rick Perlstein, "Exclusive: Lee Atwater's Infamous 1981 Interview on the Southern Strategy," *The Nation,* November 13, 2012.

25. "Statement of Principles," Right on Crime, accessed October 24, 2018, http://righton crime.com/the-conservative-case-for-reform/statement-of-principles/; "Our Beliefs," Prison Fellowship, accessed October 24, 2018, www.prisonfellowship.org/about/beliefs.

26. US Census Bureau, "Census Bureau Reports There Are 89,004 Local Governments in the United States" (press release), August 30, 2012, www.census.gov/newsroom/releases /archives/governments/cb12-161.html.

27. Ta-Nehisi Coates, "The Case for Reparations," *The Atlantic,* June 2014, 54–71.

28. Trevor Noah, "Trevor Noah: Let's Not Be Divided. Divided People Are Easier to Rule," *New York Times,* December 5, 2016.

Chapter 10: Redemption and Recovery

1. "About Us," Victory Outreach North Hollywood, accessed October 25, 2018, www.vonorthhollywood.org/about.

2. Christopher Winship, Jenny Berrien, and Gary S. Katzmann, "An Umbrella of Legitimacy: Boston's Police Department–Ten Point Coalition Collaboration," in *Securing Our Children's Future,* ed. Gary S. Katzmann (Washington, DC: Brookings Institution Press, 2002), 200–228.

3. Ryan King and Brian Elderbroom, *Improving Recidivism as a Performance Measure,* Urban Institute, October 2014, www.urban.org/sites/default/files/publication/23031 /413247-Improving-Recidivism-as-a-Performance-Measure.PDF; William Rhodes et al., "Following Incarceration, Most Released Offenders Never Return to Prison," *Crime and Delinquency* 62, no. 8 (2016): 1003–1025.

4. See http://unitedplayaz.org/.

5. Alfred Blumstein and Kiminori Nakamura, *Extension of Current Estimates of Redemption Times: Robustness Testing, Out-of-State Arrests, and Racial Differences,* document no. 240100, November 2012, www.ncjrs.gov/pdffiles1/nij/grants/240100.pdf.

6. National Inventory of Collateral Consequences of Conviction (database), Justice Center, Council of State Governments, accessed October 25, 2018, https://niccc.csgjustice center.org/database/results/.

Chapter 11: Getting Started

1. See appendix A for an explanation of why shootings with injury is an appropriate measure of urban violence.

2. "2018–2019 Adopted Budget," Office of the Los Angeles Controller, www.lacity.org /your-government/government-information/city-finance-budget.

3. The estimate of $30,000 per homicide is an admittedly rough figure based on my own past professional experiences in funding such programs, but even if the estimate were doubled, costing $60,000 per homicide, the net social savings and rate of return would still be extremely high. "Your City, Your Budget," Baltimore City Bureau of the Budget and Management Research, accessed October 25, 2018, http://openbudget.baltimorecity.gov/#!/year /default; City of Chicago, *City of Chicago 2018 Budget Overview,* n.d., www.cityofchicago .org/content/dam/city/depts/obm/supp_info/2018Budget/2018_Budget_Overview.pdf.

4. US Department of Education, "Attorney General and Education Secretary Call for National Conversation on Values and Student Violence" (press release), October 7, 2009, www.ed.gov/news/press-releases/attorney-general-and-education-secretary-call-national -conversation-values-and-student-violence; Joseph Biden, "Biden's Remarks on McCain's Policies," *New York Times,* September 15, 2008, www.nytimes.com/2008/09/15/us/politics /15text-biden.html.

5. Analyzing the results of systematic reviews for focused deterrence, hot spots policing, and cognitive behavioral therapy yields the following: of the nine focused deterrence evaluations that reported homicide outcomes, homicides were reduced in seven of them by 37 percent on average. For the twelve hot spot evaluations reporting violent crime outcomes, violent crime was reduced by 17.5 percent. Cognitive behavioral therapy reduced criminal recidivism by 25 percent. Therefore, the estimate of an annual homicide reduction of 10 percent, for an effort that would likely employ several of these strategies and more in combination each year, is a conservative one. Anthony A. Braga, David Weisburd, and Brandon Turchan, "Focused Deterrence Strategies and Crime Control: An Updated Systematic Review and Meta-Analysis of the Empirical Evidence," *Criminology and Public Policy* 17, no. 1 (2018): 205–250; Anthony A. Braga, Andrew V. Papachristos, and David M. Hureau, "The Effects of Hot Spots Policing on Crime: An Updated Systematic Review and Meta-Analysis," *Justice Quarterly* 31, no. 4 (2014): 633–663; Mark W. Lipsey, Nana A. Landenberger, and Sandra J. Wilson, "Effects of Cognitive-Behavioral Programs for Criminal Offenders," *Campbell Systematic Reviews* 3 (2007), https://campbellcollaboration .org/media/k2/attachments/1028_R.pdf.

6. Rolf Pendall, Leah Hendey, Margery Austin Turner, and Erika Poethig, *Revitalizing Neighborhoods: The Federal Role,* Urban Institute, October 2016, http://www.urban.org /sites/default/files/publication/85236/revitalizing-neighborhoods-the-federal-role_0.pdf.

7. Susan Saulny, "Attorney General, in Chicago, Pledges Youth Violence Effort," *New York Times,* October 7, 2009.

Appendix A

1. John Kania and Mark Kramer, "Collective Impact," *Stanford Social Innovation Review* 9, no. 1 (Winter 2011), https://ssir.org/articles/entry/collective_impact.

2. Ibid.

3. Ibid.

4. Mark H. Moore, "Creating Networks of Capacity: The Challenge of Managing Society's Response to Youth Violence," in *Securing Our Children's Future,* ed. Gary S. Katzmann (Washington, DC: Brookings Institution Press, 2002), 338–385.

5. Another helpful measure is tracking shootings that result in injury. Shootings generally are an unreliable measure, as shootings without injury are not reliably reported, but shootings with injury provide another important measure for urban violence, especially in smaller jurisdictions where the number of homicides in absolute terms may be small.

6. Thomas P. Abt, "Towards a Framework for Preventing Community Violence Among Youth," *Psychology, Health and Medicine* 22, suppl. 1 (2017): 266–285.

7. Fairness is the final fundamental, but it is not included here because the framework describes what to do, not how to do it. It should be understood that principles of procedural fairness apply to the entire endeavor.

8. Lawrence W. Sherman, *Developing and Evaluating Citizen Security Programs in Latin America: A Protocol for Evidence-Based Crime Prevention,* Inter-American Development Bank, July 2012, https://publications.iadb.org/handle/11319/5504.

9. "Teen Beaten to Death in Roseland Mob Fight," ABC7 News, October 26, 2009, https://abc7chicago.com/archive/7032313/.

10. Kathleen Tomberg and Jeffrey Butts, *Durable Collaborations: The National Forum on Youth Violence Prevention,* John Jay College of Criminal Justice Research and Evaluation Center, City University of New York, June 2016, www.ncjrs.gov/pdffiles1/ojjdp/grants/249995.pdf.

11. New York Division of Criminal Justice Services, *Gun Involved Violence Elimination (GIVE) Initiative: 2016 Annual Report,* September 2016, www.criminaljustice.ny.gov/crimnet/ojsa/GIVE-2016-Annual-Report.pdf.

12. Giffords Law Center, *Investing in Intervention: The Critical Role of State-Level Support in Breaking the Cycle of Urban Gun Violence,* December 18, 2017, https://lawcenter.giffords.org/wp-content/uploads/2018/02/Investing-in-Intervention-02.14.18.pdf.

13. Ibid.

14. New York State Division of Criminal Justice Services, Firearm Activity Reports.

15. Ray Rivera, "In Newburgh, Gangs and Violence Reign," *New York Times,* May 11, 2010; New York State Division of Criminal Justice Services, Firearm Activity Reports.

16. Tina Rosenberg, "Taking Aim at Gun Violence, with Personal Deterrence," *New York Times,* April 3, 2018; New York State Division of Criminal Justice Services, Firearm Activity Reports.

17. Matt Hunter, "Give Program Continues to Target Gun Violence in Most Violent Communities," Spectrum News Hudson Valley, December 14, 2017, http://spectrumlocalnews.com/nys/hudson-valley/news/2017/12/14/state-s-give-program-continues-to-target-gun-violence-in-upstate-s-most-violent-communities.

Appendix B

1. Cities are defined here as having a population of fifty thousand or more.

2. "Crime in the United States, 2017," Uniform Crime Reports, Table 6, Federal Bureau of Investigation, https://ucr.fbi.gov/crime-in-the-u.s/2017/crime-in-the-u.s.-2017/tables /table-6.

INDEX

© MARK OSTOW

Thomas Abt is a senior research fellow at the Harvard Kennedy School of Government. Previously, he served as a policy maker in President Barack Obama's Justice Department and worked for New York governor Andrew Cuomo, overseeing all criminal justice and homeland security agencies in the state. Abt lives in Cambridge, Massachusetts.